Japan before Perry

JAPAN before PERRY
A Short History

CONRAD TOTMAN

UNIVERSITY OF CALIFORNIA PRESS
Berkeley · Los Angeles · London

University of California Press
Berkeley and Los Angeles, California
University of California Press, Ltd.
London England
© 1981 by
The Regents of the University of California
Printed in the United States of America

89

Library of Congress Cataloging in Publication Data

Totman, Conrad D
        Japan before Perry.
        Includes bibliographical references and index.
        1. Japan — History — To 1868. I. Title.
DS835.T58   952   80-14708
ISBN 0-520-04134-8

For Aunt Ruth

Contents

Maps

Preface

This book examines the complex process by which the scattered and small groups of illiterate people who occupied the islands of Japan thousands of years ago developed into the densely populated, elaborately organized, and highly sophisticated society of early-nineteenth-century Japan.

The process involved both evolution and revolution, both developmental and transformational patterns. Accordingly, part of the narrative traces long-term growth of many sorts: of territory, population, economic complexity, social intricacy, political elaborateness, cultural sophistication, intellectual diversity and depth, and overall social capability. Inextricably bound to these developmental patterns were transformational ones that replaced one age with another, giving Japanese history a sort of "cyclical" phasing. These included the rise and decline of particular political systems, the emergence and displacement of dominant groups, and the flourishing and passing of particular configurations of higher culture.

That pattern of "cyclical" phasing has determined the book's organization. Japanese history as thus formulated was characterized by a small number of major epochs. In each of these, patterns of economy, politics, society, and culture were interconnected aspects of a single distinctive historic whole. After a brief introductory reference to prehistoric cultures, three epochs will receive our attention: those of classical, medieval, and early modern Japan. The first began in the seventh century of the Christian era; the second, in the twelfth century; and the third, in the sixteenth.

On the basis of their political character, these three epochs may be labeled, respectively, an age of aristocratic bureaucracy, an age of political fluidity, and an age of integral bureaucracy. In the first, aristocrats living in the imperial capital preserved peace in the hinterland through maintenance of bureaucratic and landholding arrangements that kept patrician and pleb well separated politically, socially, and culturally. In the second epoch, samurai rulers situated at defensible places throughout the country attempted to keep the peace through patterns of bureaucratic appointment, vassalage, and enfeoffment that were of limited success. At the same time, there were created alternate power structures under local samurai, clerics, merchants, and communal leaders, which were only minimally integrated with the larger order. In the third epoch, samurai leaders, working with merchant collaborators, developed a body of integrated political institutions that reached from palace to paddy and applied to all levels of society procedures and principles that had a high degree of internal consistency.

In every epoch, unceasing processes of growth and change led to important alterations in internal characteristics of the social order. Nevertheless the distinctive character of each "cycle" persisted until fundamental changes finally undermined it and gave rise to forces capable of establishing a new historic epoch.

Not all important dimensions of the Japanese experience can be encompassed by these "cyclical" epochs. Two longer-term trends merit particular attention. One of these pertains to relationships within society; the other, to humanity's relationship to its environment. Concerning relationships within society, in classical Japan the ruling elite was sharply separated from the masses. As the centuries progressed, however, the distance separating the two was gradually reduced, and in the process Japan took on more and more of the characteristics of a "nation." This book attempts to suggest how and why that trend developed.

CHRONOLOGY

Date	Era	Major Figure	Cultural Phenomena	Social Phenomena
A.D. 650	Classical — Nara (710–794)	Shōtoku Taishi		Taika Reform
			Kojiki	
			Buddhist sculpture	
750			Man'yōshū	Monastic power
		Emperor Kanmu	Tendai-Shingon	
850	Heian (794–1185)		Poem tales	Shōen system
950		Fujiwara Michinaga		
1050			Tale of Genji	
			Yamato-e	Bushi rise
1150	Medieval — Kamakura (1185–1333)	Minamoto Yoritomo	Amidism and Zen	
			Unkei	
1250			War tales	
			Lotus sect	Rival imperial thrones
1350		Ashikaga Takauji	Essays in idleness	
	Muromachi (1333–1600)		Kan'ami	China trade
1450			Tea ceremony	Proliferation of towns
				Gekokujō
1550			Momoyama	
	Early-Modern — Tokugawa (1600–1867)	Tokugawa Ieyasu	Confucian thought	Growth of cities
1650			Ukiyo	Chōnin
			Saikaku Chikamatsu	
1750			Motoori Norinaga	Rural change
1850			Dutch learning	

As for humanity's relationship to its environment, during most of Japanese history society's leaders paid little attention to what we would today call objective ecological considerations. It is true that even in the classical age there existed restrictive and self-regulative measures that worked to diminish human damage to the environment, but their historic impact was modest and thoroughly outweighed by measures that stimulated social growth even at the expense of the environment. Growth proceeded without significant conscious control, and the environment was exploited as vigorously as possible. From the seventeenth century on, however, that situation changed appreciably, and Japan entered an age characterized by pervasive regulation and restraint, the regulations applying not only to human relationships but also to the relationship of people to their environment.

The emergence of key elements of "nationhood" and even more the development of ecological regulation are thus themes that emerge rather late in our story. They add complexity to later chapters, and they exemplify the more basic perception of history as a story of growth, elaboration, and fundamental change.

I wish to thank the following for their valuable criticisms of earlier drafts of this work: George Dalton, Betty Monroe, James Sheridan, Clarence Ver Steeg, and Robert Wiebe, all of Northwestern University, and James Sheehan, formerly my colleague and now of Stanford. Thanks are due also to Karen Brazell of Cornell, Byron Marshall of Minnesota, Jeffrey Mass of Stanford, Irwin Scheiner of Berkeley, and those candid but anonymous press reviewers whose insightful comments helped me vitalize portions of the original text. For the preparation of the maps I am indebted to Bernard Meltzer, friend and neighbor. For the illustration of Yayoi village life I am indebted to Richard Pearson.

Mr. Eiji Yutani of the East Asiatic Library, University of California, Berkeley, annotated the illustrations in Chapter 4, which were selected from *Edo Meisho Zue* [An illustrated guidebook of noted places in Edo and its surrounding areas], by Saitō Chōshū (1737–1799?). Illustrated by Hasegawa Settan (1778–1843). Edo: 1834–1836. Twenty volumes (double leaves) in two cases, the guidebook is a description of the City of Edo during 1789–1800, based on a survey conducted by the author, Headman of Kanda Ward, and continued by his son and grandson.

In addition, I wish to acknowledge the support of The Japan Foundation of Tokyo, which provided a subsidy toward the publication of this book. The Foundation, through its Publication Assistance Program, promotes the publication of works, in languages other than Japanese, that will contribute to a deeper understanding of Japan and its culture.

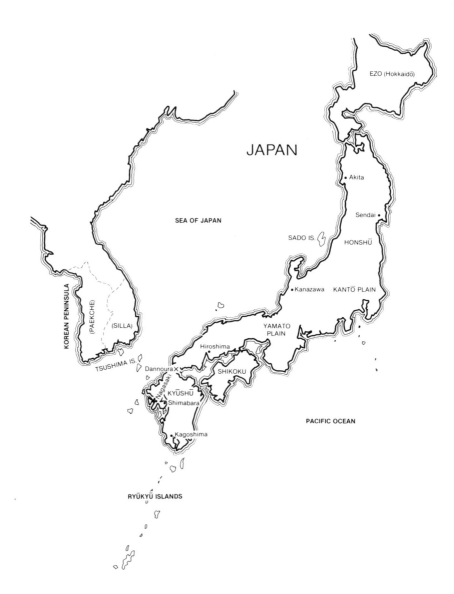

JAPAN

EZO (Hokkaidō)

SEA OF JAPAN

• Akita

Sendai •

SADO IS.

HONSHŪ

KOREAN PENINSULA

(PAEKCHE)

(SILLA)

• Kanazawa

KANTŌ PLAIN

YAMATO
PLAIN

TSUSHIMA IS.

Dannoura✕

Hiroshima

SHIKOKU

Nagasaki

KYŪSHŪ

Shimabara

PACIFIC OCEAN

• Kagoshima

RYŪKYŪ ISLANDS

1

The Beginnings

Riding a sleek train, a present-day visitor to Japan looks with delight at verdant hills soaring skyward and carefully formed rice paddies stretching away mile after mile. As his train approaches the great cities, he is impressed by the closely settled suburbs and car-laden highways that also extend as far as the eye can see.

Under the impact of those impressions, it is difficult to remember that this land is but a small strip of rumpled earthly crust, pressed between the immense and unyielding continent of Asia to the west and the equally immense and relentlessly advancing Pacific plate to the southeast. From time to time, however, the visitor is reminded of the geological foundation of Japan. It is evidenced in periodic earthquakes, smoking volcanoes, and the mountain ridges that tower above one in jagged, inhospitable beauty. It is revealed, too, in the rushing streams that for millennia have tumbled out of those mountains, joining forces with the volcanoes to deposit fertile soil on the deltas below, gradually creating the flatlands for paddies and suburbs alike.

The seasons, too, have helped shape the civilization of these islands. Japan's islands lie in a long arc from the subarctic tip of Hokkaidō south through the elongated main island of Honshū to the subtropical tip of Kyūshū and the Ryūkyū Islands. Despite its length, however, the country is essentially temperate in its annual cycle of warm and cold. Winter winds out of continental Asia blanket the Japan Sea side of the main island with great depths of snow. As the winds flow over the high mountain ridges, they lose their moisture and spread a layer of cold dry air over the heavily populated coastal plains on the Pacific side of the archipelago. Spring ushers in a stimulating season of unpredictable days, some rainy, others cold and gusty, yet others warm and sunny, their passing marked by the successive flowering of plum, peach, and cherry trees. By June, early-summer winds out of the south carry monsoon rains up across all the islands save Hokkaidō, conveniently soaking the earth and nourishing the rice crop. Then drier winds spread across the islands a layer of muggy summer heat that lasts until the crops are grown and ready for harvesting. In the autumn, as chrysanthemums begin their flowering, climatic changes over the Pacific Ocean spawn typhoons that sporadically crash across Japan. Sometimes the winds and water ruin crops and wreck settlements, but they also can provide just enough water to sprout a winter crop, assure its growth, and start another fertile year on its course.

One must not be deceived by this picture of a benign nature. Basically Japan's islands constitute an inhospitable physical setting for a dense population. The precipitous mountains and torrential seasonal rainfall are the stuff of devastating floods, landslides, leached hillsides, and ravaged flatlands. Why, one wonders, did history and geology not conspire to make this a barren, eroded, exhausted land peopled by subsistence peasants and urban slum dwellers? How did Japanese society organize its affairs over the ages so that the habits of earth and rhythms of time were turned to advantage, making the history of Japan a history of growth and achievement rather than a history of deepening poverty, exploitation, and disorder?

PREHISTORIC CULTURES

These habits of earth and rhythms of time existed in Japan long before humans arrived. The story of early human occupation has yet to be fully told, and probably never will be.[1] It is known, however, that some humans were in the area more than thirty thousand years ago, and the first may have arrived long before that. The movement to Japan of these people—and of other creatures such as woolly mammoths—was made possible by land connections to continental Asia. The size of the connections varied with the ebb and flow of the last ice age, and by about fifteen thousand to ten thousand years ago the land was completely cut off from the continent.

Thereafter migration to Japan became more difficult, yet some continued, mostly by way of the Korean peninsula. From about ten thousand to seven thousand years ago, Japan was supporting a population of hunting and fishing peoples who lived in partially sunken, pole-and-thatch dwellings in small and scattered arboreal communities. Most of these settlements were near the seashore, and their residents were dependent upon fish, shellfish, and other seafood for sustenance. These they obtained by netting, diving, digging, and fishing from shore and by maneuvering small dugout boats about the inlets and bays, with an occasional foray offshore on calm days. They supplemented this fare with forest fruit and game, including deer and wild boar.

The arboreal character of this first identifiable Japanese culture persisted until about the third century B.C. However, remnants, notably pottery that bears cord-markings (Jōmon), reflect a gradual cultural enrichment. Improvements and variety were introduced in domestic architecture. The single-room house was enlarged, and its framing was reorganized so that a center pole was no longer needed to support the roof. Drier stone flooring replaced bare earth. House-heating and techniques of enclosure were improved so that houses would retain some warmth even when built on the ground surface rather than in excavations. Improvements in pottery-firing provided more serviceable utensils. An increasing variety of pots and tools of daily use facilitated the handling of

---

1. Richard Pearson, "The Contribution of Archeology to Japanese Studies," *The Journal of Japanese Studies* 2, no. 2 (summer, 1976), pp. 305–27, is a lucid statement of recent thinking on prehistoric Japan.

routine cooking, washing, mending, hunting, fishing, and cutting tasks.

By late Jōmon times some land may have been cleared for garden plots and dry field grain as well as for settlement areas. Most of Japan, however, remained a verdant forest-covered chain of islands, its soil held in place by undisturbed root systems and the ubiquitous *sasa*, a miniature-bamboo ground cover that gave the hillsides exceptional stability. Beneath the leafy cover of these sturdy forests walked generation after generation of families, accompanied by their dogs, leaving no mark upon the land save for mounds of refuse, pieces of skeleton in burial sites, and remnants of buildings, stone tools, and small decorative paraphernalia.

Beginning about the third century B.C., a new and dramatically different culture system, called Yayoi after an early archeological discovery site, made its appearance in southwest Japan. Its most notable elements were probably brought to the islands by migrants fleeing political turmoil on the continent. These elements offered Yayoi people distinct advantages of life style and equipped them with the power to overwhelm, if necessary, the less densely populated, less well-organized, and less well-armed Jōmon folk.

Most important, Yayoi people were basically agricultural, growing paddy rice as well as dry-field grains and storing the harvest in their villages in elevated granary buildings modeled on simpler Jōmon precedents. This food supply, being expandable and more subject to human control than were fish and game, enabled the people to live in much larger villages, some including perhaps as many as five to six hundred houses.[2] Yayoi culture thus sustained a much larger and probably a more healthy population. The development of a cultivated food supply freed more people for tasks other than food-gathering. This is suggested by the evidence of larger, more comfortable, and more sophisticated dwellings and outbuildings, more elaborate religious rituals, specialized metal and pottery production, limited trading activities, and a

---

2. Takeo Yazaki, *Social Change and the City in Japan* (Tokyo: Japan Publications, Inc., 1968), p. 7.

wealthy and powerful community leadership. This larger, more elaborately organized, and more productive population, whatever its origin or ethnic composition, was able to absorb the Jōmon peoples. How that was done, whether by peaceful conversion, integration, forcible subjugation, or a combination of processes, is unknown, but within some four centuries Yayoi customs had spread eastward and displaced older Jōmon practices throughout the archipelago.

Like the Jōmon people before them, Yayoi people enriched their culture as the centuries passed. However, whereas Jōmon enrichment was extremely slow and seems mostly to have been a product of indigenous evolution, that of Yayoi was much more rapid, indigenous creative impulses being enriched by an accelerating cultural inflow from the continent and the subsequent modification of newly acquired elements. As generations passed, Yayoi people employed more elaborate burial procedures. They acquired the potter's wheel and improved their kiln techniques. They refined and improved their tools of cultivation, replacing stone implements with metal ones, and they kept more domestic animals. They developed a spinning and weaving technology. They acquired and accumulated treasures from China, Korea, and other continental sources, including coins, mirrors, bracelets, and beads. After initially importing their metalware, they eventually acquired a bronze and iron technology of their own, which in turn made possible superior craftsmanship for functional, decorative, and religious purposes.

By the second century of the Christian Era, a substantial population, the ancestral core of today's Japanese, extended from Kyūshū to northeastern Honshū. These people lived in a large number of agricultural villages that were linked, locally at least, by primitive trade, social interchange, and political organization. They were sustained by an irrigated rice culture whose basic character was to remain unchanged until the modern age. Despite temporal and regional variations, they shared much material culture and many social practices, for example in their manner of tillage and their burial customs. In its spread to the east, Yayoi culture had changed profoundly the character of human life in Japan. It had also

Artist's Conception of Yayoi Villagers at Work

Courtesy of the Museum of Anthropology, University of British Columbia set in motion a visual metamorphosis, turning more and more of the forested lowlands into open, sunlit fields of paddy rice that even our modern visitor would find strikingly familiar.

THE YAMATO AGE

The ecological transformation that Yayoi people set in motion during the third century B.C. laid the foundation for social changes that would, by the sixth century of the Christian Era, alter the face of Japanese society as profoundly as the spread of rice culture was changing the face of the land. Although the course of the social transformation is not sharply delineated, its general character is evident. Most strikingly a new technology of warfare made its appearance, and those who employed it were able to impose on Japan a radically new phenomenon: political consolidation. The new social element was fighting men mounted on horses, protected by slat armor and helmets, and armed with swords and bows. It is not clear whether these fighting men were large numbers of invaders from the continent or mostly, as seems more probable, natives of the islands who acquired continental weaponry and then reproduced it in quantity for their own use. What is clear is that by the fourth century this new military technology was enabling some people to impose their will over larger and larger numbers of others and thereby wrest from them the resources necessary to live more elegantly and extend their sway further than had ever before been possible in Japan.

Little is known about the common people whose exertions sustained this ruling elite, because so few records mention them. The most useful written source is a Chinese report of ca. A.D. 297. It speaks of the Japanese, called "the people of Wa," in this way:

> The land of Wa is warm and mild. In winter as in summer the people live on raw vegetables and go about barefooted. They have [or live in] houses; father and mother, elder and younger, sleep separately.

The Chinese visitor reported of Japanese religious practices that

> Whenever they undertake an enterprise or a journey and discussion arises, they bake bones and divine in order to tell whether fortune will be good or bad. First they announce the object of divination, using the same manner of speech as in tortoise-shell divination; then they examine the cracks made by the fire and tell what is to come to pass.

Japanese family relations also caught the Chinese eye:

> In their meetings and in their deportment, there is no distinction between father and son or between men and women. . . . Ordinarily, men of importance have four or five wives; the lesser ones, two or three. Women are not loose in morals or jealous.

Concerning crimes and their adjudication the visitor reported,

> There is no theft, and litigation is infrequent. In case of violation of law, the light offender loses his wife and children by confiscation; as for the grave offender, the members of his household and also his kinsmen are exterminated.

Even the social and political order did not escape notice:

> There are class distinctions among the people, and some men are vassals of others. Taxes are collected. There are granaries as well as markets in each province, where necessaries are exchanged under the supervision of the Wa officials.

The "men of importance" who enjoyed the company of "four or five wives" also enjoyed the deference of their inferiors.

> When the lowly meet men of importance on the road, they stop and withdraw to the roadside. In conveying

messages to them or addressing them, they either squat or kneel, with both hands on the ground. This is the way they show respect. When responding, they say "ah," which corresponds to the affirmative "yes."[3]

Most other surviving records date from later centuries and really describe the world of the rulers, the "men of importance," not that of the tillers and haulers. One can form a general picture of the religious lives of these early Japanese, however, by combining the evidence of these later records with the recorded folk practices of recent centuries. The picture that emerges is one of villagers who made their way through life as have people in other societies, in the face of various evil spirits and with the support of many helpful deities (*kami*) of place and moment. *Kami* of children, the harvest, the hearth, and of travel and awesome places were accessible by prayer at a multitude of tutelary shrines. And throughout the year, village festivals provided moments to pacify fickle or fearsome deities and thank the gods for their benevolence or restraint.

Of the rulers much more is known because this new aristocratic leadership used its resources to assure its eternal glory. The splendor of those early rulers is still visible, immortalized in huge hillock-sized burial mounds, some of them surrounded by wide moats, the largest of which embrace oblong areas as much as a half-mile in length. The great size of these tombs shows the immense work forces that rulers were able to employ year after year. The tombs also contain artifacts that disclose many aspects of the age. Buried with a dead ruler were the implements of his life: helmet, armor, swords, bows, arrows, knives, beads, pottery, and other possessions. Decorative designs and wall drawings illustrative of his glories also recorded the taste and events of the day. And around the tomb were placed clay figurines (*haniwa*) of warriors, other people, houses of many sorts, furnishings, saddled horses, and other paraphernalia of life. These remains demonstrate the military character of

3. Ryusaku Tsunoda et al., comp., *Sources of Japanese Tradition* (New York: Columbia University Press, 1958), pp. 6–7. From the *Wei Chih*.

this ruling elite. However, an enduring supremacy cannot be maintained by might alone, and the more subtle aspects of this aristocracy's governance are reflected in the oldest surviving domestic written records of Japan. These include fragmentary local records called *Fudoki* [Topographical records] and, more important, two works entitled *Kojiki* [Records of ancient matters] and *Nihongi* [Chronicles of Japan], which were written in the years 712 and 720 respectively. These records yield much information on both the structure and process of the new governing system. They suggest that the new elite arose by gradually forging local and then regional polities dominated by hereditary aristocratic familial groups (*uji*). By about A.D. 300 several major *uji* in the Yamato plain near present-day Osaka and Kyoto had been subordinated to one of their number, an *uji* commonly called the Yamato *uji* and putatively ancestral to the later imperial family of Japan. With the Yamato *uji*'s assertion of a preeminent role in a populous part of Japan, the first identifiable Japanese state had come into being.

The *Kojiki* and *Nihongi* record these initial successes of the Yamato *uji* because they are written versions of its orally transmitted traditions. They were set down at a time when Yamato rulers were seeking to strengthen their position by claiming an imperial authority in Japan analogous to that of the triumphant emperors of the contemporary T'ang dynasty in China. They asserted the unique character of the Yamato *uji*, and hence the propriety of its sovereign claims, by showing the direct descent of its chieftains from the Sun Goddess Amaterasu and through her from the original godly founders of the universe. The *Kojiki* and *Nihongi* also record the subsequent growth of Yamato power, showing that the process involved not only conquest but also complex political maneuver. Yamato leaders, who could be either male or female, frequently formed alliances with heads of other *uji*, most often through the kinship mechanisms of marriage and adoption. These ties they solidified by guaranteeing allied *uji* their lands and by awarding their chiefs appropriately gratifying titles and honors. The treatment of deities, whose genealogical relationships were carefully elaborated in the written record, suggests too that Yamato leaders consistently tried to conciliate the vanquished, or at least clarify their new political status, by incorporating their gods into the Yamato pantheon at prudently subordinate levels. From about A.D. 300 to 550, Yamato leaders used political techniques of this sort to extend their sway within the islands. After consolidating a base position in the Osaka-Kyoto district, they spread outward. Gradually most of Japan west of the Kantō plain (surrounding Tokyo) came under their influence. They established and maintained diplomatic contact with rulers in both Korea and China. And they assisted allied rulers in Korea by dispatching military expeditions involving hundreds of vessels and tens of thousands of men.[4]

By about A.D. 500, Yamato rulers were imposing a substantial degree of order on their aristocratic subordinates. They were developing a rather standardized set of hereditary ranks and titles, often assigning them, however, in accordance with the real power of the aristocratic recipients. They tried to limit the land-holding authority of subordinate *uji* chiefs by claiming that such chiefs were permitted to administer their lands and people only by direct appointment of the Yamato ruler and in accordance with Yamato regulations. Of necessity as much as choice, no doubt, Yamato rulers utilized the leaders of some powerful *uji* as regular governmental councillors. However, they tried to offset their influence by assigning governmental functions to others who did not command large *uji*. These latter, some of whom were recent immigrants, served as scribes, religious functionaries, supervisory experts on such matters as metal or textile production, military commanders, and territorial administrators in the Yamato *uji*'s own lands.

Certain aspects of the polity, notably the character of governing authority and the central importance of kinship and heredity, deserve fuller attention because they were to remain key aspects of Japanese governance until recent times. The value attached to kinship and heredity was re-

4. John W. Hall, *Japan: From Prehistory to Modern Times* (New York: Dell Publishing Co. Inc., 1970), p. 38.

flected in the central role in social organization of the patrilineal principle—the belief that leadership of a group properly descended generation by generation to that man (or in certain ages man or woman) who is the designated heir, either by birth or adoption, of the current chief.[5] Thus in the Yamato age the apex of the polity was the Yamato ruler, the hereditary chief (*uji no kami*) of the Yamato *uji*, and most of his major subordinates were hereditary chiefs of lesser *uji*.

The character of governing authority was apparent in the functions claimed by these hereditary Yamato rulers. The chief, whether male or female, claimed authority in both secular and religious spheres. These embraced the secular tasks of military and political command, settlement of disputes, and reward and punishment and the religious task of assuring the benevolence of the gods. The importance of the secular functions seems self-evident to us, but clearly Yamato rulers also regarded the handling of the religious task as central to their temporal authority. Rituals that would sustain the links between ruler and deity were carefully performed at Yamato *uji* shrines, most notably that at Ise, south of modern Nagoya. And great care was taken to preserve memories of the ruler's ancestry, as shown by the tortuous genealogies of gods and rulers in the *Kojiki*. Later, in the seventh century, the Yamato *uji*'s body of religious tradition was given lexical identity as Shintō, "the way of the gods," and apologists for the regime asserted that Shintō was the indigenous religion of the entire society over which Yamato chiefs ruled. Having

5. John Whitney Hall, *Government and Local Power in Japan* (Princeton: Princeton University Press, 1966), has used this principle of patrilineage in organizing his study of long-term evolution of the Japanese polity. As Hall points out, from the days of Yamato to the nineteenth century patrilineages were perceived as the basic building blocks of most Japanese politics, whether in the form of *uji*, classical aristocratic lineages, or later *bushi* families. Repeatedly attempts were made to organize land and human resources according to patrilineal principles. Indeed, one can argue that the root determinant of the periodic crises of the Japanese polity was the natural biological limitation of patrilineal governance, meaning the proliferation of progeny until the emotional bonds of kinship were stretched so far over social, spatial, and chronological distance that they lost their persuasiveness. This statement could apply to the crises of the Yamato state, the Taika state, the *shōen* system, the Hōjō regency, medieval *bushi* lineages, and finally the Tokugawa bureaucratic order.

made this claim, they could then try to rebuff challengers by insisting that because of the Yamato ruler's special genealogical link to Amaterasu and the founding gods, only the ruler or properly designated experts could communicate effectively with the gods and so bring peace and order to the realm.

Chiefs of other *uji* held assigned hereditary titles, but they also were identified by the Yamato chief in terms of kinship ties. These ties might stem from a marriage or adoption arrangement, or they might be traced back to the gods if a more immediate relationship could not be claimed. The Yamato ruler asserted that the duties expected of a subordinate chief were a function of that hereditary familial linkage, and not a function of individual appointment. Hence it was the ascribed duty of all members of subordinate *uji*, as putative relatives of the Yamato, to serve the successive heads of the Yamato family line, no matter how independent in actuality the subordinate group might be.

Some functions that required special skills were entrusted to nonrelatives, often craftsmen from Korea, but in those cases too the functions were regarded as hereditary tasks. It was up to the person entrusted with the task to perform it faithfully for his master's lineage and to train his descendants to take his place. These expectations made that relationship quasi-kin in nature, hereditary, and identified with a specific function. The Yamato ruler's position was thus buttressed not only by military power, civil alliance, and material reward, but also by principles of religious authority, kin obligation, and hereditary privilege.

It would be misleading to think of the Yamato state as a stabilized political system. It was not. It was a system in constant flux and marked by severe tensions and sharply contradictory tendencies. It was shaken by periodic power struggles at the center and by military and diplomatic reverses in the field. One reason for this situation was that the centuries of Yamato power were centuries of political turmoil on the continent. China was ravaged by a long era of civil strife that ended with reunification under the Sui (590–618) and T'ang (618–906) dynasties. The Korean peninsula was torn by war among competing Korean states. The latter turmoil involved Japan because Japanese military forces that had been deployed to Korea were defeated during the mid-sixth century, to the detriment of Yamato prestige. Moreover the continental disorder produced a flow of refugees to Japan, and with them came ideas and equipment from the mainland.

During the sixth century the most influential of these mainland ideas were associated with Buddhism, which appealed to Japanese in several ways. The Yamato ruler's authority was rooted in the Shintō myth of special origin that gave him unique access to the god-ancestors and hence a unique capacity to obtain godly intercession that could bring good fortune and avert catastrophe. Buddhism, with its basic canon (sutras) and extensive theological commentaries, presented alternative statements about the path to godly power. Through knowledge of the sutras, the ceremonies, and the secrets of Buddhism one could invoke godly powers independently of Yamato wishes, and the prospect of political advantage made Buddhism attractive to the ambitious. The introduction of Buddhism to Japan was also facilitated by its congenial similarity to Shintō.[6] It encompassed a large number of benevolent deities and religious practices and offered them freely to a people accustomed to thinking of *kami* as a variegated collection of forces to be dealt with through an equally varied set of rituals and activities. Furthermore, as thoughtful Japanese probed the deeper philosophical levels of Buddhism, they discovered a transcendent religious vision quite unlike anything present in Shintō. That vision opened up a conceptual universe of breathtaking proportions and impelled people to investigate other facets of continental learning as well, most notably Confucianism, with its elaborate body of secular political wisdom.

Perhaps the most notable new equipment from the continent was the supply of horses and mounted fighting paraphernalia, which kept growing in quantity. Rivals of Yamato, some of whom were situated in western Japan and nearer to

6. Kyoko Motomachi Nakamura, trans., *Miraculous Stories from the Japanese Buddhist Tradition* (Cambridge, Mass.: Harvard University Press, 1973), pp. 45ff., discusses Shintō-Buddhist similarities thoughtfully.

Korea than the Yamato themselves, had access to it. Thus Yamato leaders found themselves facing ever more powerful domestic challenges, which compelled them to increase their own power and rely on ever more powerful—and hence ever less docile—supporters. In short, the regime was engaged in an arms race.

Continental influences also played a broader historic role by helping make these centuries of Yamato rule ones in which the economy of Japan expanded rapidly. Increased use of draft animals, notably horses and oxen, and better hoes, spades, and sickles increased per-capita productivity. The spreading use of millet and barley and diffusion of sericulture permitted tillage of drier areas and better utilization of work time. The use of green fertilizer and night soil, the careful arranging of rice fields, more extensive irrigation systems, and the use of wooden pipes and more sturdy dikes increased per-hectare crop yields. These factors, together with the opening of more and more land to tillage, were linked to population as an ecological "cybernetic loop." Thanks to increasing amounts of available food, more and more people lived into the productive and reproductive years of adulthood, and that in turn allowed yet more land to be opened to production. In consequence the population of the islands continued growing, reaching perhaps two to three million by ca. A.D. 550.[7]

Most of these people lived in peasant families, but some were artisans engaged in industrial activities, often, no doubt, as by-employments. Enriched by mainland techniques, Yamato-era Japanese used better carpenter tools, including saws, clamps, and nails. They mastered gold, silver, and copper casting and gilding. More varieties of silk and hemp weaving and dyeing became established. A highway system facilitated movement of people and goods, and a sub-

---

7. The figure of two to three million is an arbitrary compromise. Michiko Y. Aoki, *Ancient Myths and Early History of Japan* (New York: Exposition Press, 1974), p. 71, reports that 7,053 households constituted 3 percent "of the total taxable population in Japan at that time" (ca. A.D. 550). At five persons per household this gives a taxable population of about 1,175,000 people. Untaxable numbers are not given. According to Irene B. Taeuber, *The Population of Japan* (Princeton: Princeton University Press, 1958), the tradi-

stantial coastal fleet developed, vessels being used for entrepreneurial trade within Japan and between Japan and the continent. A few ports such as Naniwa, in the vicinity of modern Osaka, became established as regular transfer points supervised by government officials.

More food, fodder, equipment and able-bodied manpower meant bigger armies, more chiefs, and greater need for governing organization and control. Yamato leaders therefore could not stand still. Either their power would keep growing as society grew, or others would displace them. They chose to expand, but that very expansion, no matter how delicately handled, contributed to a high level of political disorder as other *uji* leaders maneuvered, plotted, and fought to protect their interests and enhance their positions.

By ca. A.D. 550 the Yamato *uji* seemed to be in a precarious position. It had pressed its dominion further than could be sustained, given the considerable delegation of power and authority to aristocratic landholders that characterized the Yamato political system. Yamato leaders had lost the capacity to sustain an expeditionary force in Korea. They were having difficulty collecting from subordinate *uji* the tribute they called for, which suggests that those *uji* (and their subordinates in turn) were successfully retaining considerable organizational independence even as they increased their total power. The most influential aristocratic advisors of Yamato chiefs were becoming bitter enemies, and some were

---

tional figure of 4,998,842 is given (p. 9) for a census of A.D. 610; while recent scholarship (referred to on pp. 14, 20, and 22) offers these population estimates:

A.D.	Pop. (estd.)
823	3,694,331
859–922	3,762,000
990–1080	4,416,650
1185–1333	9,750,000
1572–1591	18,000,000
1726	26,548,998
1852	27,201,400

In Susan B. Hanley and Kozo Yamamura, *Economic and Demographic Change in Preindustrial Japan, 1600–1868* (Princeton: Princeton University Press, 1977), Hanley, the demographer, mentions alternate figures of "5 to 6 million during the eighth century" (p. 45), 12,273,000 in 1600 (p. 44), "28.7 to 29.2 million for 1852" (p. 46), and 33,110,796 for 1872 (p. 46).

even plotting to usurp the ruler's prerogatives. Such plotting was made easier by those Buddhist doctrines that mocked the sacred pretensions of the Yamato *uji* and its religious servitors and that were starting to function as an ideological weapon in a rapidly escalating power struggle.

In effect what had happened in Japan was that the influx from the mainland of new technology—military, economic, and intellectual—had led to more growth and change than the existing political system could handle. The ingredients of rice culture, mounted warfare, and aristocratic familial organization had transformed both the land and society of Japan. Politically they had fostered consolidation in the fourth and fifth centuries, but by the sixth they had begun to do more to exacerbate than to overcome the decentralizing forces operating in the larger society of that day. Although Yamato leaders attempted to cope with the problem by rationalizing their system of *uji* control, their efforts were not succeeding. Such political cohesion as the Yamato *uji* had established during three centuries of political effort seemed in danger of being lost.

2

Classical Japan: An Age of Aristocratic Bureaucracy

Members of the Yamato elite solved the political crisis of their day and in so doing gave rise to the classical age of Japan, which spanned the centuries from about A.D. 650 to 1150. It was an age in which a group of established aristocratic lineages endeavored to preserve their interests by sharing power and privilege among themselves and with powerful Buddhist monasteries that were established in the seventh century. The supreme lineage was that of the imperial family, which claimed direct descent from the Yamato *uji*. The whole structure of power and privilege was rooted in the legitimacy of that family and its complex bureaucratic governing arrangements.

These governing arrangements gave enough stability to the classical age so that what most impresses one about it is the slowness of social change and the continuity in character and composition of the ruling elite. Long-term processes of growth and change did occur, of course, and they led to important modifications in the ways by which that elite sustained itself. Those modifications occurred so gradually, however, that the basic continuity of aristocratic membership was maintained. As a corollary, the life style of the aristocracy experienced only gradual incremental and adaptive changes.

The observer is more conscious, therefore, of the enduring themes and tone of classical higher culture than of any dramatic breaks or radical departures during this long period of five centuries.

Similarly one is struck by the persistence of a profound gulf between the world of metropolitan patrician and that of hinterland pleb. The gulf first formed, no doubt, when mounted warriors imposed their rule on ever larger numbers of people during the second and third centuries. It was widened by the process of Yamato consolidation, and widened even further by the particular way in which aristocrats turned continental learning to advantage in solving their political problems during the seventh century. Subsequently the cleavage was perpetuated by modifications in the ruling system, and it began to close only from about the eleventh century, as the classical age started to wane.

The stability of the classical age was maintained not by thwarting social growth but by accommodating it. And such growth did occur. By the twelfth century, Japan was a far bigger, far more complex society than it had been in the seventh. Although the aristocratic bureaucratic order had enabled an important part of the Yamato elite to realign, revitalize, and thereby sustain itself and give Japan an age of cultural brilliance, that order ultimately became obsolete. During the twelfth century, society was again plunged into social and political turmoil and the classical age came to a close.

THE ORIGINS OF ARISTOCRATIC BUREAUCRACY

The aspect of classical Japan that most sharply distinguished it from the Yamato age was the beginning of literacy. Although it was literacy for only the aristocratic few, its ramifications were profound. In any society the development of literacy by even a small segment of the populace is only part of a much more complex change, because it requires prior or parallel development of a host of ancillary social skills and enough time and other resources to develop those skills. As it becomes established, literacy in turn makes possible yet more changes because it extends and solidifies society's capacity to

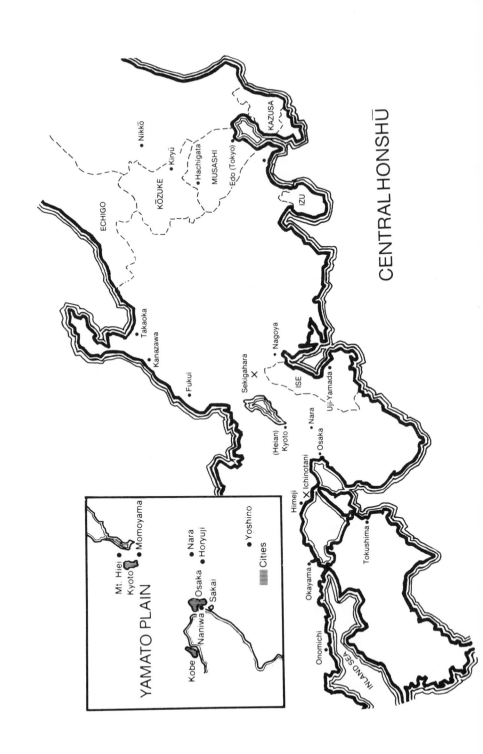

CENTRAL HONSHŪ

Nikkō

KŌZUKE
Kiryū
Hachigata
MUSASHI
Edo (Tokyo)

KAZUSA

IZU

ECHIGO

Takaoka
Kanazawa

Fukui

Sekigahara
X

Nagoya

ISE

Uji-Yamada

(Heian)
Kyoto •
• Nara

Osaka

Himeji
X Ichinotani

Okayama

Tokushima

Onomichi

INLAND SEA

YAMATO PLAIN

Mt. Hiei •
Kyoto • • Momoyama

• Nara
Osaka • • Horyuji
Kobe • Naniwa Sakai

• Yoshino

▦ Cities

communicate through both time and space. The cumulative effect of such a trend may in any instance be transformational; certainly it was in Japan.

The profound changes that literacy wrought were shaped by both the intellectual content of the written word and the particular context in which it came to the islands. Prior to the sixth century the leaders of Yamato society were themselves illiterate, but they knew of writing because they employed as scribes immigrants who wrote Chinese. The immigrants gradually brought to Japan not only Chinese script but also much of contemporary continental higher culture, notably Buddhist theology and Confucian concepts of governance. This meant that when literacy came to Japan, it came not as crude symbols that were slowly developed and refined to give halting expression to indigenous ideas but as a sophisticated, internally coherent writing system that arrived in conjunction with an equally sophisticated conceptual system. The writing was not fully separable from its content, and so it was impossible, when Japanese used Chinese writing, not to introduce a great many Chinese concepts into Japan.

Moreover, as noted earlier, the Yamato elite of the sixth century was in disarray, beset by political tension and mutual distrust. Within that context, continental wisdom, notably Confucian ideas of political organization and practice, and the writing system that could communicate that wisdom and make it function, proved especially attractive. From both choice and necessity, then, the introduction of literacy to Japan entailed the introduction of far more than a medium of expression. Both content and context shaped the transformation that eventuated in the classical age.

The story of how Yamato leaders turned continental ideas to their own advantage can be followed from about A.D. 550 when a family named Soga acquired considerable influence in the Yamato government's tax-collecting offices and established close marriage ties to the Yamato chief's immediate family. Soga leaders supported Yamato attempts to expand their lands and authority at the expense of other *uji*. The Soga, moreover, were involved in the Yamato ruler's military ventures in Korea and thereby gained some knowledge of Buddhism and continental civilization. Not surprisingly, as the upstart Soga gained more and more influence, they came into collision with other more aristocratic lineages. One of these was the Nakatomi family, which had hereditary duties handling the Yamato *uji*'s customary Shintō religious rituals. The Nakatomi found Soga advocacy of Buddhism particularly galling. When in 584 the Soga erected a temple for the worship of a Buddhist image, recruited nuns for it, and initiated regular services, the Nakatomi and other opponents retaliated. In the ensuing political and military struggle the Soga triumphed, and for the next five decades they and their allies shaped Yamato policy.

Soga leaders continued to promote interest in continental civilization and encouraged the study of Buddhism. They maintained their marriage ties to the Yamato lineage, strengthened the Yamato *uji*'s (and their own) position, and encroached on the private interests of other magnates. During the first two decades of the seventh century they received the vigorous cooperation of Shōtoku Taishi, regent to the Yamato ruler and a man well-versed in the Buddhist sutras. Under the leadership of Soga and Shōtoku, study missions were sent to China and vigorous support was given Buddhism at home. By the time of Shōtoku's death in 622 there were nearly fifty monasteries and nunneries in Japan, supported by assigned lands and sustaining over a thousand monks and nuns. The most famous survivor of the fifty is the Hōryūji near the ancient city of Nara. In these monasteries the sutras were studied, Buddhism was propagated, and education of the aristocracy was advanced.

It was also during the era of Shōtoku that Yamato rulers began referring to themselves as emperors comparable to Chinese emperors. They were aware that contemporary Sui and T'ang leaders, who had succeeded in reunifying China, claimed to govern on the basis of transcendent Confucian principles. The crucial principle asserted that a single hereditary sovereign, who was sanctioned by Heaven, was charged with administrative, judicial, and fiscal control of the realm. He exercised that control through an officialdom that was elaborately organized and centrally controlled and through an army that was directly subject to himself. Yamato leaders doubtlessly recognized that many of their own longer-term techniques for consolidating control of the country were quite in line with these arrangements, and they concluded that Confucian ideas and practices would be as useful for themselves as for Chinese leaders. They began to assert that the realm could have only one ruler and that he must follow the will of Heaven in governing all the people. The argument may have been designed merely to reinforce an authority already based on the unique Yamato link to the Sun Goddess, but it embodied a fundamental redefinition of the relationship between ruler and people that denied completely the residual autonomous authority of other *uji* leaders.

By way of giving institutional expression to this new authority, during Shōtoku's time the old hereditary aristocratic titles were supplemented by a new set of imperially assigned ranks. An official calendar for annual observances was adopted, and rules of court etiquette were spelled out. The cumulative tendency of these moves was to assert an unprecedented degree of imperial authority in the daily affairs of the great aristocratic families. The effectiveness of this initial imperial assertion is unclear, but unquestionably the Soga benefited from their direction of affairs. By the 640s they were even accused, perhaps rightly, of hungering after the imperial title itself.

In 645, complicated succession disputes culminated in a bloody palace coup and the utter destruction of Soga power. The coup was engineered by members of the Nakatomi family and their supporters. They were led by Nakatomi no Kamatari, who acted together with the cooperative imperial prince Naka no Ōe. As soon as the Soga were destroyed, the new leaders moved to shore up their position. Their basic strategy was the one earlier employed by the Soga: to use imperial authority to undermine their rivals' private power and to entrench themselves in the upper reaches of the imperial bureaucracy. Acting quickly, they dispatched officials to investigate the countryside and disarm dissidents. They required officials to take oaths of loyalty, and they granted themselves new Chinese-style ministerial titles.

Once their immediate position was strengthened, the new leaders moved to implement longer-range changes that would establish a more enduring political order. These longer-range changes are known as the Taika Reform. On New Year's Day of 646 the imperial government issued an edict whose four clauses foreshadowed fundamental changes in governmental organization and landholding. The edict called upon all aristocrats to surrender certain of their hereditary lands and accept in return lands assigned by the court in accord with their official ranks. It proposed the establishment of a permanent imperial city and a bureaucratic administrative order of provinces and districts in the surrounding region. It called for new regulations to register population, assign farm lands, regularize taxation, and establish a systematic and unified militia.

It was one thing to propose such radical changes, but quite another to implement them. The process of the Taika Reform went on for decades, proceeding in fits and starts, its progress often impeded by the surviving power of regional leaders. In 671, however, the death of Emperor Tenchi, the former Naka no Ōe, led to the Jinshin disturbance, a succession war between armies supporting his brother and his son. After months of civil strife the brother won, and as the Emperor Tenmu he used his powerful military position to ram through such crucial centralizing measures as the surrender of much hereditary land. By the year 700 the Taika Reform had worked a radical change in Japanese government and society. It had given a structural foundation to the new principle of imperial governance that had been foreshadowed by Shōtoku Taishi nearly a century earlier. And in doing so it assured that he would be enshrined in the hearts of future generations as the extraordinarily gifted and far-sighted founder of a glorious new era.

In the reform a new imperial-government organization was set up. A hierarchy of civil offices modeled directly on that of China was formed to handle secular affairs. As a reflection of the imperial family's Shintō legacy and the Nakatomi family's historic religious function, a parallel hierarchy was established to administer religious affairs of the imperial family and major Shintō shrines. Subject to these central offices an elaborate territorial administrative structure was created to govern the sixty-six provinces and nearly six hundred subordinate districts into which the whole country was newly divided. A new system of landholding and taxation was put into operation in much of central Japan. It gave the imperial government detailed cadastral records containing population data, land-holding titles, and information on agricultural production and tax arrangements. The new order was codified in sets of statutory laws and regulations, most notably the Taihō Code of 702. And the new order was given a fixed geographical center in Nara, a permanent capital city built on a geometric Chinese model during the years 708–12.

In 669, Nakatomi no Kamatari had been given the new family name Fujiwara, and he, his son, and grandsons played key roles in the implementation of the Taika Reform. Not surprisingly, they were able to enhance their own family's interests while solidifying the position of the imperial family. They did so by maintaining close marriage ties to the latter and by linking office to family status: only high-ranking families such as their own were to be permitted access to high office. They also protected their interests by handling the land-reorganization process so as to retain legitimate Fujiwara title to substantial estates. These techniques helped perpetuate the old politics of kinship and hereditary standing and assured that favored aristocratic families were not injured by the reform.

By the time the imperial family was ensconced in its elegant new palace in Nara, the reformers had resolved the political crisis that had faced the Yamato elite for over a century. It was a solution that brought power more securely than ever before into the hands of those leading families that were active in the reform, most notably the Fujiwara. It did so, however, by giving the imperial institution a structural and philosophical foundation of unprecedented strength. By both design and later accommodation it was a solution that used the elaboration of imperial bureaucracy to secure aristocratic privilege while aristocratic interest worked to assure imperial primacy.

This solution, the formation of what may be termed aristocratic bureaucracy, had been possible only because important people in the old illiterate Yamato elite had been transformed into literate and sophisticated political leaders. They had learned how to prepare, issue, and implement written edicts, and how to read and understand those works of religious and political theory that explained the principles of Buddhist theology and Confucian governance. Knowing those principles, they were able to systematize the structure and practices of Shintō and preserve it as a vital element in the ideological foundation of a regime whose structure and procedures were sharply changed from those of the old Yamato order.

EVOLUTION OF THE POLITICAL ORDER, A.D. 700–1100

The construction of a permanent capital at Nara was not the final step in forming the aristocratic bureaucratic order. Rather, the process of extending imperial power into the hinterland continued. In each of the provinces a capital town (*kokufu*) was laid out and office buildings, storehouses, garrison barracks, a school, a monastery, and a nunnery were erected. A governor and his assistants were dispatched from Nara to supervise provincial affairs through administrative, finance, real estate, police, and military offices. These centrally appointed officials kept local notables under control, and the central government, in turn, controlled its appointees by maintaining an extensive system of highways and waterways, by enforcing regular reporting and auditing procedures, and by transferring its provincial administrators at regular intervals. Through these bureaucratic instruments the peace was kept and tax income flowed into the imperial treasury.[1]

It appears, however, that from the outset trends subversive of the new order were able to manifest themselves even as the territorial administrative structure was filling out. A major contributor to this development was institutional Buddhism. To elaborate, back in the sixth century one element in

1. Hall, *Government and Local Power*, pp. 66ff.

the Soga-Nakatomi rivalry had been Soga's espousal of Buddhism. By the time Nakatomi no Kamatari had dislodged the Soga in 645, however, the position of Buddhism had become well entrenched within the Yamato elite. Several major monasteries already existed. Moreover, the monastic orders were linked to the state through regulations and appointment procedures, and the Taika reformers did not attempt to eliminate Buddhist influence among the aristocrats. Rather, they reached a truce of sorts in which the influence of both Shintō and Buddhist ideas and interests were represented in the new order. Both Buddhist monasteries and Shintō shrines received grants of land; both Buddhist monks and Shintō priests participated in religious rituals of state; both monasteries and shrines were objects of imperial pilgrimages and ceremonial messages.

During the eighth century and especially during the reign of the pious Emperor Shōmu (r. 724–49) Buddhist monasteries gained great power in and around Nara. Exploiting the new land regulations, which allowed them to gain title to and receive income from any fields they opened to tillage, monasteries acquired vast estates and great wealth, mostly in the form of produce from their lands and gold from mining operations. By mid-century their combination of wealth and sacred authority enabled them to exercise great influence in imperial politics, complicating the existing rivalries among Fujiwara and other aristocratic families. Shortly before the end of the century the Emperor Kanmu (r. 781–806) and his Fujiwara allies resolved to move the imperial capital to a new site away from the monasteries. After some abortive attempts the move was made in 794 to a newly erected palace at a spot some forty kilometers north of Nara, within the boundary of present-day Kyoto. The site was chosen because Chinese geomantic principles, which divined the prospects of a location by examining the arrangement of surrounding hills and streams, indicated it to be an auspicious choice. The new city was designated Heian-kyō (capital of peace and tranquility).

By then, Fujiwara and other aristocratic families had begun to use the same legal devices as the monasteries to acquire and enlarge estates of their own. The aristocrats succeeded, moreover, in gradually altering the land-holding regulations so as to give themselves tax advantages and eventually total tax immunity. They also acquired administrative authority over their estates, which came to be known as *shōen,* and managed them through family offices called *mandokoro.*

Shōen must not be confused with "estates" as known in other societies. Most *shōen* were tracts of agricultural land within which were found some paddies, dry fields, or forest land that belonged to others. Holders of *shōen* were not rural gentry living in manor houses but aristocrats, most of whom lived in Heian, or monasteries or shrines whose headquarters were in the vicinity of Nara-Heian. Commonly a large-scale holder possessed several *shōen* scattered about central Japan. *Shōen* were not "owned" in the sense of an owner holding title free and clear with unrestricted rights of purchase and sale. Rather, a *shōen* holder held an imperial-government charter identifying the boundaries of his lands and the limits of his tax liability and administrative authority in those lands. A *shōen* holder, whether aristocratic family, monastery, or shrine, thus was in effect a chartered corporate body empowered to administer the affairs of its own estates, subject only to the limitations written into its charter.[2]

As the Heian period progressed, sporadic social disorder prompted tillers and holders of small estates to seek the protection of more powerful figures. As a result, *shōen* holders acquired lands by commendation. In the process they developed the practice of negotiating officially sanctioned estate rights (*shiki*) with the subordinate people who participated in operation of the estate. By the eleventh century, cultivators, local managers, and such other administrative or guardian figures as might be involved all received legally binding *shiki* that specified their duties and emoluments in the *shōen.* The manager's *shiki,* for example, would specify the scope of his authority, his income, and his rent-collecting obligations.

2. I am indebted to Cornelius J. Kiley, "Estate and Property in the Late Heian Period," in John W. Hall and Jeffrey P. Mass, eds., *Medieval Japan: Essays in Institutional History* (New Haven: Yale University Press, 1974), pp. 109–24, for this general interpretation of the *shōen* system.

These *shiki* "were alienable and divisible" and "could change hands through sale, inheritance, or donation without disturbing the function of the *shōen* as an economic unit."[3] The use of *shiki* thus rooted the *shōen* system in the authority and legal enforcement powers of the imperial government while enabling it to accommodate changing power relations in society at large. It was a land-holding system that prompted *shōen* holders to sustain the imperial authority that guaranteed their holdings while paying only modest attention to the lands themselves so long as subordinate *shiki* holders delivered the stipulated rents.

Exercising on their *shōen* a limited authority derived from specific imperial decrees, aristocratic families, monasteries, and shrines gradually assumed the real functions of government. During the ninth and tenth centuries, *mandokoro* and associated organs in the family mansions in Heian took over functions that formerly had been vested in central-provincial-district offices of the imperial government: administering the populace, collecting taxes as estate rents, and keeping the peace by use of mercenary forces. They were becoming de facto governmental bodies themselves.

This *shōen* system supplanted much of the old Taika system in function, but it only supplemented it in form and depended on it for legitimate authority. Aristocrats in Heian continued to be appointed to the various posts of the Taika political hierarchy, but many of them also held separate posts in the *shōen* governments of their own families. Out in the provinces some men continued to bear provincial and district office titles while they or others held other posts such as local managers of *shōen*, whose duties overlapped those of the government offices. This multiplication of titles and nominal functions together with the system of flexible *shiki* rights gave rise to jurisdictional quarrels. They in turn led to litigation and the issuance of an endless stream of imperial decrees and official judgments designed to resolve disputes and keep the peace. This process of administrative adjudication produced

3. Elizabeth Sato, "The Early Development of the *Shōen*," in Hall and Mass, p. 107. Italics added.

a massive quantity of documents concerned with landholding and administration, and these accumulated documents constituted a body of precedents that gave order and comprehensibility to the whole system of landholding. Hence a long-term process of case-by-case legislation led not to chaos but to the emergence of a system of corporate government that was rooted in imperial authority.

The emergence of the *shōen* system did not constitute a direct decentralization of power. The same elite that had ruled through the Taika imperial arrangements was more and more ruling through its own corporate institutions, even while retaining its place in the city of Heian. There the greatest of these corporate bodies, the Fujiwara family, entrenched itself by merging its own power with imperial authority. During the ninth and tenth centuries, Fujiwara daughters habitually married imperial princes and begat future emperors. Fujiwara leaders also acquired the customary right to staff the office of regent to a child emperor (*sesshō*), which they supplemented in 880 with the new post of regent to an adult emperor (*kanpaku*). During the ninth century, other offices in the imperial government were also reorganized, giving the head of the Fujiwara family (called *uji no chōja*) ever greater and more effective control of the imperial government.

As time went on, the Fujiwara position came to have a dual base. One was its *shōen* scattered about the country, the source of its income and manpower. The other was its ties to the imperial court in Heian, which assured that its requests would be officially legitimized. The *quid pro quo* for imperial sanction was that the Fujiwara helped sustain the imperial institution by carrying out many government functions in the countryside, by staffing the capital bureaucracy, and by assuring continuity of the imperial line itself through judicious marital arrangements. The Fujiwara governing style of political maneuver and structural manipulation perpetuated at least the form of aristocratic bureaucracy itself. In the process the Fujiwara also strengthened the idea that the title and person of the emperor were sacrosanct even when he was impotent and demonstrated that such sanctity did not prevent the successful pursuit of power by the ambitious. They thus helped give the imperial institution a suprapolitical form that could last indefinitely because it was potentially of use to so many and threatening to so few.

The Fujiwara hegemony reached its zenith about A.D 1000 with the astute regent Michinaga (966–1027), whose generous and calculated attention to the imperial family was matched only by his lavish support of Buddhist monasteries and Shintō shrines. Predictably, however, Fujiwara rule was as dissatisfying to others as Nara monastic power had been to the Fujiwara. By that date, moreover, the Fujiwara had so proliferated that family branches had become rivals of one another, and it was the Hokke or northern branch of the Fujiwara that really dominated affairs, to the chagrin of other branches. The position of the northern Fujiwara was sufficiently strong, however, that no effective military challenges were presented to them. The few plots and revolts that were attempted were foiled or crushed almost at the outset. Rivals at court were maneuvered into obscure posts, as when the high-ranking and erudite Sugawara Michizane was effectively banished in 901 to a post in Kyushu and when the stubborn young Emperor Kazan was tricked in 986 into taking the tonsure. Unable to mount effective challenges either at court or in the field, the discontented usually chose to pursue their interests as best they could by building up estates just as the Fujiwara had done.

This choice of strategies avoided most overt confrontations for another century, but from about 1150 on, political strife intensified and the classical age shortly came to an end. By then, however, the great aristocratic families in Heian had maintained their preeminence for five centuries. Because they had chosen to pursue their interests, in effect, by plundering the imperial domain and primeval forests rather than one another's *shōen*, the history of the centuries from 700 to 1100 had been one not of warfare but of gradual change in the distribution of power and privilege within a stable elite.

HIGHER CULTURE

The higher culture of classical Japan—meaning religious thought, arts, and letters as distinct from "culture" in the all-inclusive anthropological sense—is fascinating for its intrinsic aesthetic worth.[4] One can speak of classical higher culture passing from a phase of fascination with continental wisdom to a phase articulating domestic themes. The former accompanied the Taika Reform and lasted through the move to Heian in 794. As the Taika administrative system gave way to the *shōen* system, however, the aristocrats turned away from continental higher culture and developed a rich indigenous tradition that bequeathed to humankind aesthetic monuments of the highest quality.

For the purpose of our inquiry, classical higher culture commands attention primarily because it was an inseparable part of the larger social experience of the day. Classical Buddhism, for example, moved through an era of intellectual exploration and diversity to an era of religious consolidation that sanctioned and sustained aristocratic bureaucracy. In arts and letters, as well, the accumulation and refinement of elegant accomplishments by the literate few served increasingly to validate their feelings of rightful superiority.

Aristocratic Buddhism

Continental higher culture first flourished in Japan in the Buddhist monasteries of the seventh and eighth centuries. Their immigrant and indigenous scholars, their libraries, and their commitment to philosophical inquiry opened new vistas of thought and action to the intellectually curious. We are told in the *Nihongi* that the leaders of the Taika Reform, Nakatomi no Kamatari and Prince Naka no Ōe, first met when playing kickball in the grounds of the monastery, Hōjōki. After that they became friends and "both took in their hands yellow rolls [Chinese books], and studied personally the doctrines of Chou and Confucius with the learned [scholar-diplomat] Minabuchi."[5] Subsequently they developed and executed their plans for political reform.

4. For a felicitous introduction to Japanese higher culture *qua* higher culture, readers may turn to G. B. Sansom, *Japan, A Short Cultural History* (New York: Appleton-Century Crofts, Inc., 1943), or to H. Paul Varley, *Japanese Culture: A Short History* (New York: Praeger Publishers, 1973).

5. Tsunoda, p. 71. From the *Nihongi*. The Duke of Chou was an ancient Chinese statesman.

Buddhist thought, like Confucian, originally appealed to members of the Yamato elite because of its practical utility, but its philosophical richness could only excite the inquiring mind, and the doctrinal teachings of the Taika reform decades became scholarly and sophisticated, grappling with philosophical questions about the nature of reality and Buddhahood. By their character, these questions—whether, for example, the elements of corporeal reality actually existed in their particularity or whether the only reality was consciousness itself—were most accessible to students of sharp mind and intuitive insight, regardless of their social origins. During the decades when social and political position was in relatively rapid flux, this intellectual diversity evidently was acceptable to the rulers, who permitted various schools of thought to flourish, who encouraged the construction of monasteries for families and even for commoners, and who allowed unlicensed as well as licensed monks to teach.[6] Some monks even pursued their teachings and good works among the people at large. Most notable, perhaps, was the monk Gyōgi (670?–749), who propagated Buddhism

> through easily understandable teachings and public services done in the Buddhist spirit. The last included the founding of charity hospitals, orphanages, and old people's homes; excavation of canals for navigation and irrigation; the building of irrigation ponds; bridge construction; harbor construction in the Inland Sea near [the later] Osaka and Kobe; free clinics; free lodging houses.[7]

As the eighth century progressed, efforts to channel and restrict Buddhist thought and practice became more pronounced. The teachings of the Hossō sect, which held that Buddhist enlightenment was accessible only to the gifted, and the Ritsu sect, which attempted to regularize all priestly study and ordination, attracted more support among the aristocrats. And during the 740s Emperor Shōmu, the great ben-

6. Nakamura, pp. 18ff.

7. Ichiro Hori, *Folk Religion in Japan: Continuity and Change* (Tokyo: University of Tokyo Press, 1968), p. 87, note 6.

efactor of Buddhism, actively promoted the *Kegon* (*Avatam-saka* or *Flower Wreath*) sutra, one of the most elegant and intellectually awesome of Buddhist texts. He fostered construction of state-controlled provincial monasteries and nunneries in which religion was to be studied systematically and lavished great wealth on the construction in Nara of a gigantic bronze Buddha image cast in the spirit of the Kegon teachings. The image (which still exists, much repaired, in the Tōdaiji) was to serve as the central expression of a unified religious order.

Despite these measures, Buddhism continued to flourish beyond state control, with unlicensed monks proliferating and monasteries acquiring more and more land. The imperial court repeatedly tried to control the numbers of monks and the number and activities of family and village monasteries.[8] Finally, as earlier noted, court leaders tried to solve their problem by moving the capital away from the monastic headquarters, going from Nara to Heian, hoping to weaken the entrenched monasteries by cutting their links to the regime.

It was in this context that two monks, Saichō and Kūkai, introduced new teachings to Japan. Both presented their doctrines as beneficial to the state and both proposed to organize them in ways that would assure state control of monastic activity. Their arguments did not fall on deaf ears. The attractiveness of the teachings, the institutional weakness of their proponents, and their obvious readiness to cooperate with the court made them useful to a ruling elite that wished to reduce the pretensions and power of the established sects at Nara. In consequence the two monks quickly won support and their teachings flourished, becoming the dominant forms of Buddhism in Heian Japan.

Saichō enjoyed the personal support of Emperor Kanmu, who sent him to China in 804 to master and bring back to Japan a new teaching that would overshadow the obstreperous sects at Nara. Saichō went as instructed and brought back the Tendai doctrine of Buddhism. His teachings received court approval, and his headquarters monastery on Mt. Hiei

8. Yoshito S. Hakeda, *Kūkai: Major Works* (New York: Columbia University Press, 1972), pp. 21–22.

near Heian became the most powerful religious establishment in classical Japan, the chief training ground for the priesthood, and the birthplace of most later sectarian movements. Hiei's strength derived in part from characteristics of Tendai teachings themselves and in part from Saichō's success in linking it to the Heian court.

Saichō based his teachings on the *Lotus* sutra (*Saddharma-pundarika* or *Hokke-kyō*), which Tendai proponents considered the final revelation of the Buddha Sakyamuni and hence superior to—but not exclusive of—the "lesser" teachings of other Buddhist texts, such as those espoused by the monks at Nara. As introduced to Japan by Saichō, Tendai offered a rich theological vision and wide latitude in religious practice. It held that all three forms of religious action—good works, meditation, faith—helped one attain enlightenment. Tendai thereby accommodated the practices of the established sects while still presenting itself as a further, higher stage of religious endeavor that all persons eventually should seek to master. It thus established for itself a theological superiority that justified court support without necessarily antagonizing people who preferred the religious practices of older sects.

The care with which Saichō cultivated his link to the court is reflected in the set of six regulations he issued for students attending his monastery on Mt. Hiei. He first stipulated that

> All annually appointed Tendai Lotus students, from this year 818 to all eternity, shall be of the Mahāyāna Persuasion. . . . They shall be initiated into the Ten Precepts of Tendai before they become novices, and when they are ordained government seals will be requested for their papers.[9]

In the five regulations that followed, Saichō sought to assure the purity and thoroughness of training received by Tendai monks, the usefulness of those monks to the nation, and the exclusiveness of government sanction for Tendai doctrines.

9. Tsunoda, p. 132.

Saichō's contemporary, Kūkai, also studied in China. He found Shingon doctrine most persuasive. Upon his return he wrote of the texts he wished to promulgate,

The Buddha preached these sutras especially for the benefit of kings. They enable a king to vanquish the seven calamities, to maintain the four seasons in harmony, to protect the nation and family, and to give comfort to himself and others.[10]

Doubtless that sort of argument helped Kūkai win court approval just as Saichō's willingness to link church to state had benefited his cause. Shingon also resembled Tendai in its handling of other Buddhist doctrine. Where Tendai absorbed other practices eclectically, Shingon organized them in a coherent hierarchy of revelation. Kūkai, who was a more profound theologian than Saichō, spelled out at length how other teachings, Buddhist, Hindu, Confucian, and Taoist, all fitted together to form stages of enlightenment that culminated in the final mighty truth of the Buddha Mahāvairocana.[11] This argument was based on the *Mahāvairocana* sutra (*Dainichi-kyō* or *Great Illuminator*), which, Kūkai contended, was superior even to the *Lotus* of Tendai because the latter was only the highest revelation of the living Buddha Sakyamuni while the former was the secret doctrine taught by the timeless Buddha Mahāvairocana. In Kūkai's words,

The doctrine revealed by [Sakyamuni] is called Exoteric; it is apparent, simplified, and adapted to the needs of the time and to the capacity of the listeners. The doctrine expounded by [Mahāvairocana] is called Esoteric; it is secret and profound and contains the final truth.[12]

Kūkai's teachings also contained other attractive qualities that ultimately made them more appealing to Heian aristocrats than those of Tendai. Whereas older teachings had

10. Hakeda, p. 41.

11. Hakeda, pp. 157–224, is a translation of Kūkai's discourse on the ten stages of enlightenment.

12. Hakeda, p. 151.

emphasized that the attainment of enlightenment would come after death or even take eons of time and many reincarnations, Kūkai argued that it could be attained in one's current existence if one practiced the secret teachings of Shingon. Moreover, such practice meant not laborious study and learned discourse but engagement in secret rituals. As Kūkai explained it, Shingon teaching could not be enunciated in writing. Because the Buddha's grace is manifested through religious art, however,

> the secrets of the sūtras and commentaries can be depicted in art, and the essential truths of the esoteric teaching are all set forth therein. Neither teachers nor students can dispense with it. Art is what reveals to us the state of perfection.[13]

From this theological premise Kūkai and his followers developed elaborate religious ceremonies that in due course were emulated even by the Tendai priesthood. During the ninth and tenth centuries, therefore, esoteric practices proliferated in both Tendai and Shingon monasteries, and the continuing appeal of the two sects seems to have been directly connected to esoteric Buddhism's aesthetic richness— its use of secret formulae, gorgeous symbolism, and emotional participation in sacred ritual. It was a religious style that accorded well with the Heian elite's taste and undergirded it with religious values.

Only the elegant few could afford to practice this sort of religion with its heavy demand on time, wealth, and attention to procedure, but only by doing so had one a prospect of redemption. Buddhism in classical Japan thus established a religious distinction between the fortunate few who evidently were worthy of Buddha's grace and the many who were not. The aristocrats in Heian were able to perpetuate these favorable religious arrangements because with principles of doctrinal correctness and error elaborately articulated and with the procedures for ordination spelled out, religious thought and procedure meshed with the institutional ar-

13. Tsunoda, p. 142. Another translation is in Hakeda, pp. 145–46.

rangements of the Taika-*shōen* system to sustain central control of Buddhist establishments throughout the country.

The aristocratic character of Tendai-Shingon is ironic because, in contrast to the elitist doctrines (Theravada) found in Hossō teachings, the *Lotus* sutra of Tendai embodied one of the clearest statements of the populist doctrine (Mahāyāna) that all sentient beings, including all men and women, can attain enlightenment. In a key passage of the *Lotus* sutra Sakyamuni reputedly said that he first employed lesser truths to lead "the dull" to Buddha-wisdom because,

> Not yet could I say to them,
>
> "You all shall attain to Buddhahood,"
>
> For the time had not yet arrived.
>
> But now the very time has come
>
> And I must preach the Great Vehicle [Mahāyāna].[14]

Within the context of Heian society the Tendai doctrine of universal salvation and the Shingon doctrine of enlightenment during this existence did not lead to the emergence of a religion of the masses. Rather, the doctrines seem to have contributed to the spread of Tendai-Shingon among the elite by making them seem, in their combined offer of salvation now even for the dull, surer religious vehicles than the older sects. And the complexities of Shingon and the eclectic nature of Tendai fostered intermingling of religious practices. Monasteries of those sects accommodated a variety of other religious practices, including a wide range of simple superstitions and local customs, while Tendai and especially Shingon practices were adopted by many other sects and religious groups.

The comfortable eclecticism of Heian aristocratic religion is suggested by this excerpt from a nobleman's last testament of ca. A.D. 960.

> When you arise in the morning chant seven times the name of the star for the year. Next look at yourself in a

14. Tsunoda, pp. 121–22.

mirror. Next consult the calendar to know the fortune for the day. Next use your toothpick and face west to wash your hands. Next chant the name of the Buddha. At the same time you may also chant the names of those Shintō shrines to which you are affiliated.

He went on to speak of various other rituals and practices that one ought to follow, suggesting that

As to the frequency of this form of worship, use your own discretion. However, if you do not believe, your lives are likely to be cut short, as demonstrated by many former examples.[15]

A century and a half later that eclecticism was evident during the painful death of the Emperor Horikawa (1078– 1107). One day all life signs of the ailing monarch ceased, and distraught attendants hurriedly summoned a Tendai prelate and two Tendai priests skilled in the ascetic practices of Shugendō (the mountain cult). Their efforts failed to help, but an exorcist who was then called managed to lure the evil spirit from the emperor's body and he revived. A few days later the emperor worsened again, and he requested readings from the *Kannon* (*Avalokiteshvara* or Goddess of Mercy) chapter of the *Lotus* sutra. The pain only intensified, however, and he began reciting the *nenbutsu*, an appeal to the grace of Amida Buddha that hitherto had been taboo in the palace. Subsequently he called for more reading of sutras, and a group of twelve mountain ascetics (*yamabushi*: practitioners of Shugendō) were summoned to pray. As life ebbed from his body, Horikawa continued calling the *nenbutsu*, interspersing it with the cry "May the Ise Shrine help me," but all was to no avail and the twenty-nine-year-old emperor died.[16]

15. David John Lu, *Sources of Japanese History* (New York: McGraw-Hill Book Company, 1974), I, pp. 67–68. Quoting the last testament of Fujiwara Morosuke, ca. A.D. 960, Ivan Morris, *The World of the Shining Prince* (Baltimore: Penguin Books, 1969), pp. 103–52, is an extended discussion of elite magico-religious practice.

16. Fujiwara no Nagako, *The Emperor Horikawa Diary*, trans. Jennifer Brewster (Honolulu: University Press of Hawaii, 1977), pp. 59–73. The Shintō invocation is on p. 72.

As Horikawa's experience indicates, the influence of Tendai-Shingon eclecticism reached well beyond Buddhist sects to touch other religious traditions, most notably Shintō and the mountain cult of Shugendō. Shugendō was a body of magico-religious practices performed by people known as *yamabushi*. They were men who guided pilgrims and made their own pilgrimages to sacred mountains where they engaged in ascetic practices and other religious rituals. During the Heian period these mountain ascetics added a variety of Tendai and Shingon practices to their arsenal of magico-religious techniques and used their powers to bring good fortune and ward off evil, illness, and hardship among both the general populace and aristocrats.[17]

Shintō also absorbed Tendai-Shingon influence. Whereas Buddhist theologians argued that the gods of Shintō were avatars or manifestations.of the Buddha nature, Shintō priests found it useful to assert that their gods were protectors of Buddhism in Japan. Buddhist monasteries gradually began the practice of erecting small guardian shrines on their premises, and by the tenth century a syncretic doctrine called Ryōbu Shintō had taken form, making the two religions mutually reinforcing elements that supported the political claims of the imperial institution and its associated corporate aristocratic bodies.

By the late classical age, Japanese religion, like Japanese government, was characterized by complexity and overlapping that served to sustain the established order and its beneficiaries. It achieved this end most obviously by embodying a set of religious practices that were accessible only to the elite and by sustaining a belief that they were the chosen few. Less obviously it helped sustain the aristocratic bureaucratic order by validating complexity, in contrast to simplicity. The multiple titles and relationships of the elegant few were earthly equivalents of the multiple names and associations of the gods and Buddhas.

Classical Buddhism also helped sustain the elite by es-

17. H. Byron Earhart, *A Religious Study of the Mount Haguro Sect of Shugendō* (Tokyo: Sophia University, 1970), is a study of Shugendō with a brief overview of its historical development.

tablishing the proposition that the proper order of things, and hence proper behavior, could be known through reference to authoritative texts as expounded by a properly trained monastic leadership. The way in which religion could validate secular values and practices was nicely expressed ca. A.D. 1000 by the great authoress, Lady Murasaki Shikibu in her fictional masterpiece, *Genji monogatari* [The tale of Genji]. At one point she had her hero explain how the writer of fiction illumines life. She has him poke fun at "the old romances" and then acknowledge that despite their fictional character they can be very moving and instructive.

> If the storyteller wishes to speak well, then he chooses the good things; and if he wishes to hold the reader's attention he chooses bad things, extraordinarily bad things. Good things and bad things alike, they are things of this world and no other. . . . There are differences in the degree of seriousness. But to dismiss them as lies is itself to depart from the truth. Even in the writ which the Buddha drew from his noble heart are parables, devices for pointing obliquely at the truth. To the ignorant they may seem to operate at cross purposes. The Greater Vehicle is full of them, but the general burden is always the same. The difference between enlightenment and confusion is of about the same order as the difference between the good and the bad in a romance. If one takes the generous view, then nothing is empty and useless.[18]

Just as Buddhist teachings may reveal partial truths so as to lead people to higher insights, so a writer of fiction reveals unworthy qualities so that the reader may better distinguish good from bad. Proper earthly conduct, like proper religious conduct, can be known and recorded. Authoritative texts to guide future generations can thus be established, and should the unenlightened not understand, the wise, such as Prince Genji, can set them straight.

18. Murasaki Shikibu, *The Tale of Genji*, trans. Edward G. Seidensticker (New York: Knopf, 1976), I, 437–39.

Arts and letters

The monasteries of the seventh and eighth centuries introduced to Japan much more than just Buddhism. They also contributed mightily to several other major aspects of higher culture that set the classical age clearly apart from both the earlier Yamato and later medieval ages.

The construction and furnishing of buildings required the introduction and development of architectural skills. Learning rapidly from immigrant craftsmen, Japanese artisans mastered advanced techniques of woodworking, bronze-casting, and painting. And their talents were put to use on behalf of the ruling elite in the construction and furnishing of sumptuous monasteries, shrines, palaces, and mansions whose size and accommodations contrasted sharply with the rude huts and hovels of the masses.

Initially monasteries, like cities, were laid out as in China on flat land and in simple geometric patterns, but beginning in the ninth century, buildings were erected in secluded hilly areas, their size, shape, and positioning more irregular and complex because they were determined by considerations of topography and function. Similarly, early monastic sculpture and painting followed the formal and spare lines of continental art, but later softer lines and more sensuous, elaborate, and elegant arrangements and decoration became common. In secular architecture, symmetrical Chinese styles of mansion, palace, and landscape architecture were dominant at first, but later Heian aristocrats developed their own more delicate and informal patterns of layout and construction.

Painting of the early classical period was almost entirely religious in content. However, by the tenth and eleventh centuries the aristocrats found their own lives worth representing, and a vigorous tradition of secular scroll painting developed. Called *Yamato-e* (Japanese painting), it utilized rich colors, bold schematic variation, and unique modes of delineation and perspective to portray landscapes, to illustrate the lives of notable people, and to represent the taste and times of the aristocracy. *Yamato-e* achieved this objective most impressively in one of Japan's greatest artistic achievements, the twenty or so twelfth-century scrolls based on Lady Mura-saki's *Tale of Genji*. These long word-and-picture scrolls follow with great skill the unfolding lives of Genji and his descendants, thereby giving vivid visual expression to an idealized version of courtly life.

The monasteries made a more fundamental historic contribution through their role as the principal vehicles for the introduction of the writing that was basic to the whole political and social order of classical Japan. A Chinese report of about A.D. 580 stated of the Japanese that

> They have no written characters and understand only the use of notched sticks and knotted ropes. They revere Buddha and obtained Buddhist scriptures from Paekche [in Korea]. This was the first time that they came into possession of written characters.[19]

Because Koreans were at the time writing in Chinese, this meant that Japanese began writing in the Chinese language and that before they could give effective literal expression to Japanese thought they would have to abandon written Chinese or somehow modify it so that it could represent a language radically dissimilar in sound, syntax, and syllabication. The latter process was the one that occurred, and it was long, slow, and arduous. Various techniques were tried, and in due time a solution was found in combining selected Chinese characters (*kanji*), chosen for their meaning, with a set of symbols (*kana*) denoting the sounds of Japanese. The latter dominated the literature of Murasaki's day, but later they came to be used primarily as copulas and indicators of inflection, and they served to form sentences using the concepts embodied in the characters.

With Chinese writing, as we noted earlier, came Chinese customs, such as historical scholarship. It led to a series of Japanese dynastic histories during the eighth and ninth centuries, of which the *Kojiki* and *Nihongi* were two of the earliest. By the eleventh century, histories had evolved from factual (or putatively factual) chronologies written in Chinese

19. Tsunoda, p. 12. From the *Sui Shu*.

to highly literary works written in Japanese. They were rich in aesthetic texture but of uncertain reliability in historic detail. One of the best known is the *Eiga monogatari* [Tales of glory], a celebratory history of the great regent, Fujiwara Michinaga. Whereas the earlier histories had validated imperial authority, the obvious purpose of *Tales of Glory* was to celebrate Michinaga's rule and thereby strengthen the political claims of his descendants.

These histories also disclose much about the taste and values of the ruling elite. The *Ōkagami* [Great mirror], a history of Michinaga's age written in the tradition of the *Nihongi*, is more measured in tone than *Tales of Glory*. Its author presents Michinaga not as a prettified dandy but as a vigorous leader, tough and politically ambitious. We hear nothing about his diabetes, his other ailments, his irritability, or his occasional irrational rages, all of which would weaken the author's case.[20] We learn instead that he was a forceful man who could icily humiliate his rivals and one whose courage was of the most exceptional sort. That uncommon courage was particularly demonstrated on one occasion when he, unlike two other courtiers, accepted fearlessly the emperor's dare to spend a rainy summer night by himself in a darkened building at court.[21] In the small aristocratic world of Heian, whose members were tormented by angry spirits and demonic forces, his performance that night, nonchalantly sitting in the dark, was seen as one of the highest measures of bravery.

The author of *Ōkagami* clearly considered Michinaga's political ambition and toughness key factors in his rise to power, but he devoted much more ink to recapitulating the ranks and titles of Michinaga's ancestors, the bountifulness of his rule, and his courtly polish. For example, we learn that Michinaga was adept at archery and horsemanship, but we learn it almost in passing. The writer happened to describe Michinaga's skill with the bow while illustrating his ambition

20. G. Cameron Hurst III, "Michinaga's Maladies: A Medical Report on Fujiwara no Michinaga," in *Monumenta Nipponica*, xxxiv, no. 1 (spring, 1979), pp. 101–12, discusses Michinaga's health.

21. Edwin O. Reischauer and Joseph K. Yamagiwa, *Translations From Early Japanese Literature* (Cambridge, Mass.: Harvard University Press, 1951), pp. 337–39.

and icy self-control, and he mentioned his horsemanship while describing a visit to the Kamo shrine:

> the snow was falling especially heavily, so that he let out the sleeves of his unlined inner garment, raised his fan high [and shielded himself with it], but since [the snow] was falling very white upon it, he said, "Oh, how grand!" and his actions, as he swept [the snow] away, were very pretty. His over-garment was black and his red inner garment was gay. To this combination the color of the snow added its beauty too, and it was something that was indescribable. [The Emperor had] a certain horse of great fame named something or other, and it was an exceedingly bad horse [but on that day], ah, [Michinaga] broke it for him.[22]

As further evidence of Michinaga's extraordinary stature, the author had one courtier suggest that he was master of both the Confucian heavenly way and the teachings of Buddhism. He wrote,

> This lord is a man who has been accepted both by heaven and by earth. Whenever he undertakes anything, even though a great wind may blow and continuous rains fall, still, from two or three days before, the skies clear and the earth seems to dry up. Since this is so, one may even say perhaps that Prince Shōtoku has been born [again] or that Kōbō Daishi [Kūkai] had been born [once more] in order to have the Buddhist Law flourish.[23]

In Heian Japan, as in any society, political power required strength of character. But it was buttressed by one's mastery of the canons of good taste and the higher wisdom of society, and it was certified by favorable comparison with culture heroes of the past.

Characteristics of the classical age are also reflected in more purely creative literature. It consisted initially of poetry

---

22. Reischauer and Yamagiwa, p. 341.
23. Reischauer and Yamagiwa, p. 365.

modeled on Chinese precedents, but within decades Japanese poets were investing works with their own sensibilities. This achievement was preserved in the *Man'yōshū* [Collection of a myriad leaves], ca. A.D. 760, which contains poems of emperors and unknowns alike.[24] Some are long, many are short, and they cover a variety of matters, speaking of life, love, and the land. Thus an emperor wrote,

> Countless are the mountains in Yamato,
>
> But perfect is the heavenly hill Kagu;
>
> When I climb it and survey my realm,
>
> Over the wide plain the smoke-wreaths rise and rise,
>
> Over the wide lake the gulls are on the wing;
>
> A beautiful land it is, the Land of Yamato!
>
> *(Emperor Jomei)*

Generations later an official traveling in a distant province wrote,

> Before me on my track
>
> Lie the sounding waves of the sea;
>
> Behind me, my wife and children—
>
> All left at home!
>
> *(Kisakibe Isoshima)*

A princess wrote,

> I thought there could be
>
> No more love left anywhere.
>
> Whence then is come this love,

24. *The Manyōshū* (New York: Columbia University Press, 1969). Poems selected from pp. 3, 256, 92, 280, and 281, respectively.

That has caught me now

And holds me in its grasp?

(Princess Hirokawa)

And two unknown poets recorded bits of their lives in this way:

See neighbour,

Washing morning greens in the river,

Your child and mine are well-matched

In years—give me yours!

(anonymous)

My hands so chapped from rice-pounding—

To-night again, he will hold them, sighing,

My young lord of the mansion!

(anonymous)

As the classical age advanced, poetry became more standardized in theme and form. The two great compilations of later years, the *Kokinshū* [Collection of ancient and modern poetry], A.D. 905, and *Shinkokinshū* [New collection of ancient and modern poetry], A.D. 1205, show how it focused beautifully but narrowly on scenes that would evoke aristocratic sensibilities, such as love and longing, loneliness, regret, beauty, aging, and the brevity of life.

Classical aristocrats developed other literary genres, and they, too, increasingly directed the attention of the elite to their own lives, reinforcing their conviction that the matters of consequence were those relating to their own small circle of acquaintances. Building on anecdotal poem-tales, folk tales, and private diaries, they fashioned ever longer, more elaborate fictional works. The process culminated in the eleventh-century masterpiece, *The Tale of Genji*, Lady Murasaki's monumental account of the life and times of the elegant Prince Genji. Written in Japanese by an attendant to the imperial consort during the age of Michinaga, it is a landmark in world literature because of its cohesive narrative construction, subtle treatment of personality, and consistent and credible tone and perspective.

The main social implications of this aristocratic literacy and of such literary output as the *Genji* hardly needs enunciating: the aristocrats had acquired an awesome set of skills that increased immensely the distance separating themselves from the untutored masses, and those skills were used in ways that reinforced their inclination to see themselves as superior beings. Less apparent is one of the unusual consequences of this particular pattern of literary development; namely, that it opened up temporarily an aperture in higher culture through which aristocratic women in the Heian court were able to make a major historic contribution to Japanese belles lettres and aesthetics. The literary development of the tenth century occurred during decades in which male courtiers continued to believe that they properly wrote only in Chinese or in clumsy hybrid styles. Court ladies were not similarly inhibited and found the new syllabic writing techniques very effective for composing poetry and prose, essays as well as fiction. Court men as well as women enjoyed and encouraged such writing, and under this impetus ladies-in-waiting such as Murasaki Shikibu and Sei Shōnagon produced literary masterpieces that were to inspire all subsequent generations of Japanese authors. In later centuries women lost this unusual literary advantage because the genre of court literature became stereotyped and uncreative, because newer literary motifs emerged from a military experience that was known mostly to men, and because men abandoned the Heian prejudice against writing in the vernacular. During that brief summer of late Heian, however, female artistic creativity enjoyed a moment of flowering that may be unparalleled in the history of humankind.

In their writings the ladies tell us much about the values of their day, and the undying popularity of some of their works made them important texts sustaining the social values of future generations of aristocrats. One of the most informative literary works was *Makura no sōshi* [The pillow book] of Sei Shōnagon. It is a vast collection of personal notes assembled by a peer and contemporary of Murasaki Shikibu. In her *Pillow Book* Lady Shōnagon spelled out through myriad examples the qualities in life and people that the aristocratic few cherished or despised.[25]

Giving voice to a thought shared by many women in many ages, she expressed her appreciation of her own good fortune in this way:

> When I make myself imagine what it is like to be one of those women who live at home, faithfully serving their husbands—women who have not a single exciting prospect in life yet who believe that they are perfectly happy—I am filled with scorn. Often they are of quite good birth, yet have had no opportunity to find out what the world is like. I wish they could live for a while in our society, even if it should mean taking service as Attendants, so that they might come to know the delights it has to offer.

Concerning the importance of status, she noted, in a long list of "hateful things,"

> It is most improper to address high-ranking courtiers, Imperial Advisers, and the like simply by using their names without any titles or marks of respect; but such mistakes are fortunately rare.

And in a list of "unsuitable things," appears this: "A woman of the lower classes dressed in a scarlet trouser-skirt. The sight is all too common these days." In a similar spirit she noted that praise from a servant had the same effect as criticism from one's peer, and "Besides, people of that class always manage to express themselves badly when they are try-

25. Ivan Morris, trans., *The Pillow Book of Sei Shōnagon* (New York: Columbia University Press, 1967), vol. 1. The passages are from pp. 20, 28, 51, 250, 65, 183, 57, 90, *seriatim*.

ing to say something nice." Perhaps that helps explain why Shōnagon mentioned among "rare things," "A servant who is pleasant to his master."

There doubtless was good reason to respect status in a society where status determined office and office brought perquisites. For example, Shōnagon described how an inconsequential cleric would suddenly find himself fawned upon when promoted to high office. And she wrote of a man who had just been appointed governor,

> In the past everyone treated him with rudeness and disdain; but painful as it was, he bore it all patiently, realizing that he had no choice. Now even his superiors respect the man and play up to him with remarks like, "I am entirely at Your Excellency's service." He is attended by women and surrounded by elegant furnishings and clothing that he has never known before.

In comment after comment the importance of style is evident. "Nothing can be worse than allowing the driver of one's oxcarriage to be poorly dressed," because if one's driver is "badly turned out, it makes a painful impression." Among "splendid things," on the other hand, she mentions, "Chinese brocade. A sword with a decorated scabbard. The grain of the wood of a Buddhist statue." Whatever other function they might have in life, to the courtly elite the clear obligation of people and objects was to be aesthetically pleasing. The issue at stake was not the ox-cart driver's competence as a driver, the sword's sharpness, or the statue's religious efficacy, but whether they were gratifying to the sensibilities of those about them.

As Shōnagon's notes suggest, the classical literature that these court ladies developed to perfection found its inspiration in the rituals and routines of aristocratic life itself, and a central element in that aristocratic life was music. Music played a key role in the formal rituals of the court, Shintō shrines, and Buddhist monasteries, and it was conspicuous in the cultured leisure life of the aristocrats themselves. Before the seventh century the Yamato elite had used a simple bamboo flute and a type of cittern (*wagon* or *Yamato-goto*) to accompany their singing, but early in the classical period a number of other instruments were introduced along with Chinese musical theory. The instruments included various flutes, lutes, drums, clappers, bells, other percussion instruments, and various larger dulcimer-type instruments known as *koto*. Classical musicians composed solo and orchestral pieces, refined musical techniques, modified and enriched their musical theory, and by late in the age had developed several major music traditions. Of those the most remarkable was *gagaku* or court music.

Gagaku was an orchestral form based on several continental traditions that were systematized during the ninth century by a retired emperor and his musical followers and then preserved relatively unchanged down to the present. It was eminently suited to classical Japan because it required the cooperation of skilled musicians who were well-trained in their art, free to practice, and intimate enough to play together the complexly polyrhythmic music of the day. The heart of the *gagaku* orchestra was the wind section.[26] A double-reed woodwind, the *hichiriki*, dominated with its strident, piercing tone. An exquisite instrument, the *shō*, a small hand-held seventeen-reed pipe organ, produced sustained ethereal chords of a poignant beauty. Flutes complemented the *hichiriki*, and a set of drums, a lute (*biwa*), and two *koto*-type stringed instruments provided supporting sound. The instruments were combined in different ways, depending on whether the music was played in concert form, as accompaniment to dance, or occasionally with voice.

In music, as in the other higher arts, the classical age transformed the Japanese scene. Because *gagaku* music has been preserved in such pure form, we can appreciate the magnitude of that achievement even today. As William P. Malm has written,

> Listening to *gagaku* is a history lesson in sound and a transmigration back into the soul of the Heian courtier. As it stands it is a shadow of its former self and yet it is

---

26. William P. Malm, *Japanese Music and Musical Instruments* (Rutland, Vt.: Charles E. Tuttle Co., 1959), pp. 78ff.

still one of the clearest adumbrations left of the grandeur and artistic taste of the court of ancient Japan.[27]

Even nature was forced into the mold of aristocratic grandeur and taste. Most metropolitan patricians knew it only through their gardens, their short trips beyond the city gates, and their occasional pilgrimages to famous monasteries, nunneries, and shrines. It was portrayed in their art in soft colors accented by gold and silver. The violence of storm and sea came through as disciplined artistry. The hard and unlovely worlds of animals and working people were far away, as far as the rustics whose taxes and later *shōen* rents supported the aristocrats in their metropolitan oasis. War, violence, and physical privation seemed almost unknown, or if known, unworthy of examination. The center of life was occupied by elegant polished people whose lives were so intimately linked that they could be fully evoked by artistic and literary techniques of psychological subtlety and the most restrained suggestion.

At its zenith that culture reflected and helped sustain the world of its makers. In all its parts, its religion, art and architecture, belles lettres, and music, it validated complexity and elegance and directed attention of the aristocratic few to themselves and their attainments. It set an immense gulf between the "good people" (*yoki hito*), who were the cultured chosen few at court, and the unworthy, fostering a value system that reinforced the narrow exclusivism of the aristocracy. Aesthetics and ethics became one: to be beautiful was to be good; to know beauty was to know the good. But to know true beauty and be truly beautiful required the most intense cultivation and attention to detail. Thus in her diary Murasaki described one incident at a court gathering,

"On that day all the ladies in attendance on His Majesty had taken particular care with their dress. One of them, however, had made a small error in matching the colours at the openings of her sleeves. When she ap-

27. Malm, p. 104. The music may be heard on a number of recordings, such as Murray Hill Album S-4743, *Musical Treasures of Japan* (five-record set).

proached His Majesty to put something in order, the High Court Nobles and Senior Courtiers who were standing nearby noticed the mistake and stared at her. This was a source of lively regret to Lady Saishō and the others. It was not really such a serious lapse of taste; only the colour of one of her robes was a shade too pale at the opening.[28]

It had been a lapse of sufficient seriousness, however, to merit the hard stares of reproach. True beauty had to be so deeply internalized as to spring from the very soul, and only the elegant few could attain such mastery of taste. By the time of Murasaki it was assumed that only those born to culture could know it and thus be worthy. In one episode of *The Tale of Genji* the writer puts these sensibilities into the mind of her hero Genji, who, while resting with his beloved concubine, Murasaki, had just received a letter from his new wife, the thirteen-year-old Imperial Princess Nyosan. To Genji's delight the letter was written on fine crimson paper and folded tastefully.

But when he examined the writing he found it extremely childish. He wished that he could stop Murasaki from seeing it for the time being—not that he really wanted to keep anything from her, but in view of Nyosan's rank it seemed a shame that anyone should know how unformed her hand still was.[29]

Secular virtue, as evidenced in aesthetic refinement, had thus come to be associated with high caste. That idea is probably best seen as a secular manifestation of the Buddhist argument that people were born to high status because of a good *karma*, the result of exceptional virtue in prior incarnations. As Emperor Horikawa lay dying in A.D. 1107, the Buddhist prelate who was praying at his bedside said,

Since this person received the Ten Precepts in a former life, and did not break one of them, he was reborn into

28. Translated by Morris in his *Shining Prince*, p. 206.
29. Ibid., p. 197.

this supreme position of emperor, which position he has long upheld.[30]

By the twelfth century the Japanese aristocracy, which as of A.D. 600 had no great traditions of architecture, sculpture, literature, music, or scholarship, had contributed to the world one of humanity's greatest cultural epochs. It had utilized and digested a set of continental precedents, combined them with a range of domestic tastes, and forged a fresh and unique higher culture, one that was to underlie all future epochs of Japanese civilization. At the heart of this highly refined urban aristocratic culture were a vibrant feel for beauty, a keen sensibility, a mordant irony, and an introspective melancholy. Later, after powerful forces of historic change had destroyed the insular world of the status-conscious Heian elite, those tastes would be enriched and modified by others, but they would persist as core elements in Japanese higher culture even to the present day.

THE LARGER SOCIETY

The cultural glory of classical Japan would have been impossible without the establishment and flourishing of a metropolitan center in which the creative energies of the elegant few could commingle and cross-fertilize. The existence of that metropolis depended, in turn, on the Yamato elite's success in constructing and then adapting a centralized political order that enabled it to control and tax effectively the growing productivity of the general population. And what is perhaps most noteworthy about that achievement is that the elite did it in a way that maintained or even increased rather than reduced the cultural distance separating metropolitan patrician from hinterland pleb. On the face of it one wonders how an aristocratic elite so divorced from its foundation could have endured for half a millennium.

Yamato society had consisted of an agricultural population bound together by bands of leaders gathered in head-

30. *Horikawa Diary*, p. 69.

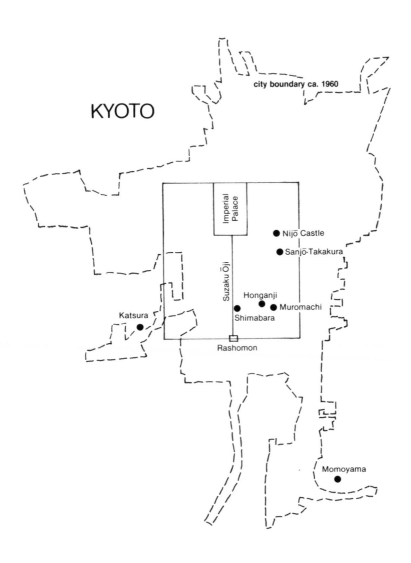

KYOTO

city boundary ca. 1960

Imperial Palace

● Nijō Castle

● Sanjō-Takakura

Suzaku Ōji

Honganji

Muromachi ●

Shimabara

Katsura ●

Rashomon

Momoyama ●

quarters settlements that frequently moved from place to place in the Yamato region. That pattern ended with the introduction of continental political and religious ideas and the subsequent establishment of Nara and later Heian. Those planned geometric cities were big. Each was bisected by a great boulevard, Suzaku Ōji, that ran northward from the south gate, called Rashomon, to the imperial palace. Suzaku Ōji in Heian was a tree-lined avenue some two and a half miles long and nearly three hundred feet wide. A contemporary poem celebrated its beauty in this way:

> Light green they shine,
>
> Dark green they shine,
>
> Stretching into the distance as far as the eye can see,
>
> They glitter like jewels.
>
> Oh, how they glitter—those low-hanging boughs
>
> Of the willows on Suzaku Ōji![31]

From the imperial palace, street after street led off south, east, and west. The main thoroughfares were bordered by mansions of the aristocracy. The narrow back streets were lined with simple houses of the plebs. In the age of Fujiwara Michinaga the population of Heian may have numbered about one hundred thousand, making it one of the greatest cities in the world of its day. Of these hundred thousand, perhaps five thousand were aristocrats,[32] and the rest ran the gamut from influential and elegant but untitled subordinates, clerics high and low, and attendant personnel, down through the merchant, artisan, and employed-laborer segments to marginal entertainers, gamblers, the honorable poor, and the unfree of various sorts.

31. Translated in Morris, *Shining Prince*, p. 39.

32. Morris, *Shining Prince*, p. 93. Yazaki, p. 34, speaks of Nara having 200,000 inhabitants at its peak in the eighth century, of whom 10,000 were in officialdom. John W. Hall, "Kyoto as Historical Background," in Hall and Mass, p. 10, gives the figure as 100,000, of whom 10,000 were "nobles and lesser officials," in ninth-century Heian.

Most serving people, attendants, and craftsmen were in the employ of aristocratic families, monasteries, and shrines, but there was also an appreciable number of independent entrepreneurs and artisans. Their activities were centered on two great market places that accommodated the city's needs. In them several scores of shops sold a great variety of goods, from animal hides, vegetables, and bean products to ceramic ware, medicine, and iron utensils.[33]

Most eleventh-century Japanese lived in the provinces. There the populace ranged from a handful of titled provincial officials, regional administrators, and well-established clerics to subordinate administrators of regional government offices, monasteries, shrines, and *shōen*, and leaders of local constabulary forces, and from local notables such as village chiefs or substantial peasant proprietors to itinerant merchants, artisans, menial servants, lesser peasants, and common laborers.

The peasants were mostly settled in close-knit village communities. There they lived in small, thatched-roof houses, tilled their fields, paid their taxes or rents in produce and labor services, and traded some goods locally. They marked the progress of the seasons and coped with the difficulties of life by means of a number of regular celebrations and ceremonies, many of which were associated with local Shintō shrines. Their positions being legally identified by Taika regulations and later by *shiki* arrangements, they were formally bound to the soil. Doubtless, too, they generally preferred to stay put, living among neighbors and kin, sharing the vicissitudes of life, the years of sufficiency and the years of famine, among people who would help them if necessary and possible. Exceptionally severe hardship or disorder could precipitate flight, however, as individuals, families, or even whole villages decamped, secretly fleeing to another *shōen*, another valley, or another province in search of a better life.

Such a move in quest of a better life was a plausible act because classical Japan was a growing, expanding society.

---

33. Takao Tsuchiya, "An Economic History of Japan," in *The Transactions of The Asiatic Society of Japan*, Second Series, 15 (Tokyo, 1937), pp. 84, 87–89, lists many goods sold in Heian.

The most basic form of growth was expansion of the realm itself. Throughout the classical period government agencies, monasteries, shrines, *shōen* holders, and peasant cultivators steadily hacked away at the forest land, forcing their way up the hillsides and back into less accessible valleys and uplands. In the northeast, Japanese settlers pressed ahead in the face of resistance by the Ezo, arboreal tribes of uncertain ancestry who lived in northeast Honshū. The northward advance was spearheaded by military forces who compelled the Ezo to retreat in a long, erratic series of struggles that spread imperial influence to the northern reaches of Honshū by the tenth century. By the twelfth, the realm of Japan had come to embrace the three islands of Honshū, Shikoku, and Kyūshū, and also the southern tip of Hokkaidō, then called Ezo after its inhabitants.

The opening of ever more land and the vigorous extension of riparian works increased agricultural output. The introduction of new crops and tools from the continent permitted better use of drier hillsides, more intensive paddy tillage, more efficient use of manpower, and greater variety in the public diet. More specifically, with government encouragement peasants gradually replaced wooden hoes with metal ones and began erecting drying racks for rice that theretofore had been cured on the ground. Government edicts encouraged the use of water-powered mortars for grinding grain and water wheels and irrigation projects for increasing paddy acreage and yield. The use of water wheels and water-powered mortars did not become general until much later, but whereas grain had been pounded in Yamato-era mortars, it was ground in the classical age, with a consequent reduction in loss of grain and improvement in palatability. Both government and *shōen* owners sponsored large-scale riparian projects, and the government constantly admonished landholders to keep their irrigation systems in good repair. The frequency of those admonitions suggests, however, that the government's success was not great. The government also encouraged crop diversification, urging tillers to grow more wheat, millet, barley, buckwheat, mulberry and lacquer trees, hemp, pears, beans, peas, turnips, and other vegetable crops.[34] Peasants continued to prefer rice, which yielded a higher return per hectare, but as the classical age progressed, the volume and variety of foodstuffs steadily increased. In part this increase reflected widespread double-cropping, the summer rice crop being followed by a winter dry-field crop such as the recently introduced wheat. Throughout the classical period, yield per hectare slowly increased, and that, together with the large increase in tilled area, permitted the sixth-century population of perhaps two to three million souls to grow by the eleventh century to nearly five million.[35]

Compared with that of prior eras, the populace of classical Japan was noteworthy for its size, diversity, and productivity. What most distinguished it from the populace of later ages, however, was the magnitude of the cultural gap that separated the few thousands of aristocrats from the millions of plebs. Doubtless that gap dated from the Yamato age or earlier. However, it was broadened and perpetuated rather than reduced by the introduction of literacy because the classic aristocracy acquired its literate higher culture as part of the process of reforging and perpetuating its leadership role in society and succeeded in making the new culture an element of hereditary privilege.

There were several reasons why they could do this. Buddhist monasteries were best equipped to spread learning through the populace because they were the principal vehicles of education and embraced teachings favoring mass religion. However, as noted earlier, the people who dominated the monastic orders were not advocates of mass proselytism and instead promoted an elitist religion. They behaved that way partly because the government encouraged it but also because the monasteries adhered to principles of celibacy, and monastic leadership was not self-renewing. Instead the priesthood became an accepted career prospect for surplus members of aristocratic families who had access to no secular

34. Tsuchiya, p. 68.

35. Morris, *Shining Prince*, speaks of five million in ca. A.D. 1000. Hanley, p. 45, speaks of five or six million in the eighth century. George Sansom, *A History of Japan to 1334* (Stanford: Stanford University Press, 1958), p. 486, suggests a population of five million in ca. A.D. 1300.

positions. As abbots, monks, and nuns they preserved an aristocratic orientation in the Buddhist establishment. Moreover, the administrative structure of monasteries was such that as the education of promising acolytes progressed, they were steadily promoted upward from provincial monasteries toward the main monastery of their sect. They were inevitably absorbed into the aristocratic milieu rather than forming an effective outward-oriented linkage between metropolis and hinterland. In religion, as in government, to think outward was to think downward, and to get ahead one looked inward, toward Heian. As a result, the Nara sects and later the Tendai and Shingon monastic organizations were operated by and for the few, and the new religion did not close the cultural gap between patrician and pleb.

The religious element in that cultural gap should not be misconstrued. It did not deprive the masses of religion. The ruling elite had succeeded in preserving monastic Buddhism as an aristocratic pursuit, but itinerant evangelical Buddhist monks or "holy men" (*hijiri*) and nuns (*bikuni*) joined Shintō priests, mountain ascetics (*yamabushi*), and others in providing a multiplicity of religious services to the general public. Plebeian religion in classical Japan therefore contained many elements of Buddhism, Shintō, and other traditions of magic, superstition, healing, and spiritual celebration.[36] The elegant eclecticism of elite Heian religion was thus paralleled by the variety of magico-religious practices of the common folk. This elemental similarity of religious styles is important because in later centuries it would facilitate the bridging of the cultural gap between class and mass. During the classical age, however, this similarity of religious style was concealed by the difference in patrician and plebeian religions. What distinguished the two was essentially the difference between a largely literate elite whose religion was expounded by formally educated monks who might be well versed in sophisticated religious thought and a largely illiterate mass whose religion was communicated by unlettered practitioners whose magico-religious insights were mostly grounded in folk wis-

36. Hori, pp. 40, 77, 93.

dom and custom rather than in the study of sophisticated texts.

The secular provincial arrangements that emerged from the Taika Reform also worked to preserve the distinctiveness of class and mass. Offices were closely tied to hereditary rank, and vertical mobility and exchange were sharply restricted. Structure and process were highly formalized and so arranged as to minimize the real human contact between metropolitan, provincial, and district levels of administration. For example, the highway system that was created included rest stations along the way. But their use was restricted to officials, and barrier points on the highways were maintained to prevent unauthorized travel. As a consequence of such arrangements the administrative structure that linked Heian to the hinterland helped keep patricians and plebs apart.

Two other main aspects of the Taika system also separated pleb and patrician. According to law the lands of all peasants were to be reallocated at periodic intervals, the redistribution being made in accordance with the numbers and types of people in a peasant household. These arrangements were designed to assure a tolerable living situation for all producers, but as long as they functioned, they also worked to deny any producer the means of accumulating enough wealth to buy learning and social advancement. Similarly the Taika militia system was designed to recruit commoners in a regularized manner. However, it restricted command duties and rank to people of appropriate aristocratic lineage and thereby kept commoners distinct from their hereditary betters. As long as the militia functioned, it returned those recruits who had completed terms of service to their place of origin simply honored and safely unadvanced.

The original religious and secular ideas and arrangements of the classical order thus kept the masses in their place, sharply separated from the educated few, humanely governed—the aristocrats presumed—but undeniably bound to their customary stations in life. The cultural gulf that separated the elegant few from the inelegant many reinforced the former's sense of exclusiveness. It prompted them to huddle in their civilized metropolitan oasis, isolated from the hinterland whose production underlay their very survival. Men named to provincial posts were reluctant to venture into the provinces to govern. More and more they let others handle civil and military affairs there, often men from the provinces whose own interests were not necessarily served by enforcement of imperial regulations. It was a situation that on the face of it seemed bound, even as early as the ninth century, to wreck the elite position before many generations had passed. Yet that did not happen for centuries. Why?

Surely a crucial part of the answer lies in the aristocrats' success in keeping a monopoly on literacy. Although that monopoly broadened the gulf between them and their social base, it also deprived potential rivals of skills necessary for the direct manipulation of government. Instead such potential rivals as local notables and leaders of private military bands found themselves serving their literate betters, habitually accepting *shiki* rights of income in return for service. They were well rewarded for their efforts, and in due course those rewards led to political power, but their service helped perpetuate the advantages of the urban elite well into the twelfth century.

Strengthened by their monopoly of literacy—and aided by their access to imperial legitimation, secular and religious prestige, and inherited wealth—the aristocracy succeeded in replacing the faltering Taika government mechanisms with the more adaptable and more satisfactory *shōen* arrangements. It is true that the transfer of tax lands to estates undermined the imperial fisc. However, the more relevant truth here is that the *shōen* system, as we noted earlier, served to keep control of the land in the hands of the imperial family, the other great aristocratic families, monasteries, and shrines.

Controlling the *shōen* from their city, the classical aristocrats retained control of society's resources, perpetuated their own advantages, and created the higher culture that reflected their world and helped sustain its courtly, refined, and insular values. They were able to turn the expanding production of a growing populace to advantage, and to maintain until the twelfth century an aristocratic order whose leadership's physical, cultural, and social separation from its power base had seemed destined to ruin it as early as the ninth.

THE WANING OF AN AGE

In due course the aristocratic bureaucracy of classical Japan was destroyed. It was not ruined, as have been so many regimes, by foreign invaders. Nor was it destroyed by subversion from within the classical aristocracy. Rather, it was undone by complex processes that gave rise to new social groups within Japanese society that in due course challenged and finally overwhelmed the ruling elite at Heian. Central to those complex processes were some of the very mechanisms that had helped perpetuate the classical order.

This is not to suggest, of course, that the classical age had at any time been a pristine haven of total tranquility. From the time of the Taika Reform itself there had been malcontents here and there, ambitious local leaders, embittered members of the elite, desperate people seeking relief, gangs of bandits, or other breakers of the peace. For centuries, however, such people and groups had been relatively easy to coopt or suppress. Even the slow and sometimes disorderly evolution from Taika bureaucratic order to *shōen* system had not created lacunae of control of sufficient magnitude to permit an effective challenge to the established order.

Finally, however, those lacunae did appear and the classical order was supplanted. Two aspects of the original Taika system itself contributed to this outcome. First, the Taika Reform had mandated the creation of a conscript militia, but it never flourished. The militia system placed onerous burdens on the peasantry, and the aristocrats who were supposed to provide its leadership were insufficiently motivated. By the ninth century the militia system no longer functioned, and the task of peace-keeping was taken over by local constabulary groups, often semiprofessionals who were under command of provincial or other governmental officials. These groups were spread widely across the country, but they tended to be most influential in the Kantō and northeast, where they became the principal element in the frontier wars with the Ezo and major figures in the opening and settlement of northeastern Honshū.

Second, the Taika reformers knew from harsh experience that the proliferation of imperial-family members could trigger a struggle for power and thus disrupt the imperial succession and undermine political stability. To limit the size of the imperial family, the Taihō Code of 702 stipulated that descendants six generations removed from their imperial sire would lose their princely status. Upon declassment these ex-imperial-family members were granted one of two family names, Taira or Minamoto. Like superfluous members of prolific aristocratic families, some of them found no satisfactory positions in Heian and left the city in hopes of building careers in the provinces, often through provincial office-holding. Probably because of their aristocratic ancestry and advantageous connections at court, some of these imperial scions and their descendants were able to command substantial respect and acquire power and prestige as local officials or leaders of postmilitia constabulary. Or they served as representatives of powerful *shōen* owners, provincial governors, or high court officials, most notably Fujiwara family members. In the process they received income rights and accumulated military followers. The most successful were awarded distinguished court titles and posts and even *shōen* of their own, in time acquiring practically all the characteristics of regular Heian aristocrats. However, these Taira and Minamoto leaders usually made their gains through military performance rather than the mere accident of birth. That colored their outlook on life and caused them to be placed in an entirely separate social category. They came to be known as *bushi* or military families, as distinct from the *kuge* or noble houses, as the regular Heian aristocrats were designated. They were unable and sometimes unwilling to merge completely into the established elite, and *kuge-bushi* relations were often marked by envy, disdain, and resentment.

The failure of the Taika Reform's militia system created a need for alternative peace-keeping arrangements, and descendants—or putative descendants—of the imperial family emerged as key figures in the military organizations that replaced the militia. They thus became potential rivals of the *kuge*.

Then aspects of the *shōen* system combined with these developments to undermine the political order of classical Japan. As aristocrats acquired *shōen*, they became ever less dependent on income received from the imperial treasury and so less insistent on the maintenance of central control over government tax lands. Provincial governors found themselves, willingly or not, granting more and more authority to local officials, and as the eleventh and twelfth centuries passed, they lost control of the income from newly opened land and the corvée services of growing village populations. These resources were becoming available for the use of local leaders, often enough men of *bushi* status.[37]

The growth of *shōen* did not only erode aristocratic interest in the imperial bureaucratic order. It also gave rise, as earlier noted, to disputes over ownership and income rights that were ultimately resolved through administrative adjudication and the issuance at Heian of official documents of title. The procedures of settlement were routine, but the nature of each settlement tended to reflect the configuration of power at court. As long as the center of power was reasonably stable, this system of dispute resolution preserved the classical order. During the eleventh and twelfth centuries, however, that central stability was lost, and thereafter armtwisting and even threats of force acquired ever more political value in advancing the interests of disputants. Ironically it was members of the imperial family itself who most contributed to the central instability that ruined the classical order.

What happened was that the imperial family undertook to escape Fujiwara control by acquiring enough *shōen* of its own to offset Fujiwara landed power. In doing so the imperial family "eventually became the largest private landholder in the country."[38] The imperial estates were held by retired

37. Nagahara Keiji, "Landownership Under the *Shōen-Kokugaryō* System," in *The Journal of Japanese Studies* No. 2 (spring, 1975).

38. G. Cameron Hurst III, *Insei: Abdicated Sovereigns in the Politics of Late Heian Japan, 1086–1185* (New York: Columbia University Press, 1976), p. 256.

emperors, who managed them through their own household offices and used their power as landholders to give the imperial lineage more real influence at court than it had known in centuries. Although designed to reassert imperial primacy, however, what the imperial resurgence seems to have done was to push the political process out of manageable channels and into disorder. Fujiwara hegemony gave way to a stalemate in which powerful individuals and groups, including imperial-family members, resorted more and more to military force to achieve their objectives.

Bushi provided that military force. *Shōen* owners and administrators who earlier had relied on Taira and Minamoto leaders for protection of their estates and implementation of their provincial duties found them useful for promoting family interests in Heian itself. By the eleventh century, members of the Taira and Minamoto families, despite their identification as *bushi* or military men, were able to exercise an influential role in court politics, most commonly as the military arm of others. The disruptive potential of this emerging military power had been foreshadowed as early as A.D. 940 when Taira Masakado, a powerful *shōen* holder in the Kantō, proclaimed himself emperor and launched a rebellion. His venture was crushed, and later outbursts by others were also quelled, but by the eleventh century the growth of rural disorder was beginning to have a debilitating effect on society as a whole.

The general disorder hampered tax and land-rent collection, undercutting the fiscal base of the metropolitan elite. By the eleventh century the population of Heian was declining and the city was beginning to decay. Abandoned mansions went to rack and ruin, and parts of the western side of the city reverted to scrub brush and farm land. In the hinterland, as well, the growing disorder brought suffering to many as marauding bands pillaged and destroyed. Citing a document of the time, George Sansom says of a rebellion by Taira Tadatsune in 1028–31,

> In Kazusa [province in the Kantō] women and children were dying for want of food and shelter. The three provinces were like dead countries. Great effort would be

needed to revive them. Fortunately, we learn, by the end of the following year fugitive peasants were beginning to return, and more land was being brought back to tillage.[39]

More and more the Heian aristocrats found themselves calling on one or another Taira or Minamoto chieftain to suppress the marauders, who often enough were other Taira or Minamoto chieftains. It was Minamoto Yorinobu who led the suppression of Tadatsune. The Fujiwara and imperial families continued to employ military men successfully throughout the eleventh century, but their success always entailed a price, most commonly in the form of land grants, titles, and military authority. By A.D. 1100 the numbers of Minamoto holding high court office was a cause for alarm to some Fujiwara leaders. In 1102 one such leader complained that fully half the senior nobility consisted of Minamoto family members.[40]

These *bushi* gains from above were matched by gains from below as landed peasants commended their farms to successful military leaders in return for protection, and as lesser warriors swore allegiance to those who seemed able to deliver them glory and gain. By the twelfth century those military leaders who were sustained by substantial *shōen* in the countryside and able legally to move about Heian were capable of playing segments of the old *kuge* elite off against one another. The stage was set for basic political change.

Military leaders of the day were well aware of both their inferior status vis-à-vis *kuge* and the crucial political role they had acquired. In the year 1159 Minamoto Yoshitomo, a fifth-generation descendant of Yorinobu, described his family's responsibilities in these terms:

> For seven generations since [receiving the family name Minamoto], through our skill with bow and arrow have we until now banned rebellious groups and, transmitting the art of military strategy, repulsed outlaws.[41]

39. Sansom, *Japan to 1334*, p. 249.
40. *Horikawa Diary*, p. 25.
41. Reischauer and Yamagiwa, pp. 405–6. From the *Heiji monogatari*.

Taira leaders, too, claimed that peace-keeping role, however, and a few months later Yoshitomo was slain by his rival, Taira Kiyomori, in fighting that erupted around Kyoto. After defeating Yoshitomo and his supporters, Kiyomori exploited his ties to the retired emperor to establish himself as the most powerful figure in the land. He commanded fighting men more effectively than did his rivals. He was better connected than they to influential members of the court and more skillful than they at politico-military maneuver. Kiyomori's rise marked the arrival of military men at the center of the historic stage.

The long era of aristocratic hegemony was ending as a new sector of society acquired the skills and resources necessary to play a role in shaping the destiny of Japan. *Bushi*, men who were discriminated against by the Heian elite and yet were expected in the end to serve aristocratic interests, had constructed an image of self and world based upon the hard demands of their rural military heritage. That image subverted their respect for their literate superiors and prompted them to challenge aristocratic primacy. Once they had gained a landed base in the *shōen* system and a legitimate military role at the center, they were able to do so, and in the process they became the vanguard of a new age.

Before looking at the world the *bushi* built, it may be useful to relate their rise to the Taika Reform and our opening themes of "evolution and revolution." Whereas the makers of the Taika order were an important segment of the preexisting Yamato elite, the emerging military men were people who, despite their claims to an illustrious ancestry, were for generations separated from the Heian elect and compelled to make their way in life as a separate sector of society. Consequently they are rightly viewed as a new force in history, a force bringing onto the historic stage values that would in time lead to a major change in the character of the social order and its higher culture.

The *bushi* emergence was an "evolutionary" phenomenon in regard to such themes as long-term growth of social intricacy, political elaborateness, and cultural sophistication. Before their rise, only a few thousand aristocrats and clerics had been consciously engaged in affairs of the realm. Military men added thousands more who participated—more or less by choice—in the political process. Politics remained an activity of the select few, but the number of participants increased dramatically. In their rise, moreover, military men added, as we shall see, new techniques to governance, new dimensions to higher culture, and new conditions to the economy. The rise of the *bushi* was part of the longer process leading toward "nationhood," that is, toward that condition in which the populace in general perceives itself as participants in the historical fortunes of the realm.

The *bushi* rise also involved patterns of disruption and displacement. It was "revolutionary" in the sense that it led to the displacement of one historic configuration by another. In this sense, military men and Taika founders played similar historic roles. Both groups forged new orders by quite comparable patterns of creative adaptation, selective innovation, and willful preservation. Much as the political system developed by the Taika reformers had been constructed through selective use of continental precedents and creative adaptation and deliberate preservation of Yamato practices, so the *bushi*, as will be noted later, developed their system by selective and creative use of classical precedents and deliberate preservation of warrior practices. In both cases old elements were recombined to form distinctive new systems.

What this suggests is that military men and Taika reformers had in common something that determined their behavior more than did their social rank. What they had in common, perhaps, was a shared perception of the existing order as unresponsive to their wants and inadequate to its self-assigned task of ordering society. They had a shared conviction that that existing order could rightfully be changed in substantial respects to remedy those failings and that they could properly initiate those changes. Finally, they shared strategic places in their societies, enabling them to translate perceptions into policies.

3

Medieval Japan: An Age of Political Fluidity

The *kuge* or classical aristocracy had devised a system of governance that gave enduring stability to an age. It accommodated substantial social growth and made possible the elegant Heian life style. That same system, however, fostered development of a new social stratum, the *bushi*, military men or samurai, which during the twelfth century was able to shove the civil aristocrats aside and usher in a new age. Whereas the classical age had been noteworthy for its continuities and enduring order—which made possible its characterization in structural terms as aristocratic bureaucracy—the medieval age was remarkable for its change, which prompts its characterization in terms of process as an age of fluidity. That fluidity touched all levels of society and all facets of human activity: political, cultural, social, and economic. During the medieval age, various political alternatives appeared and were tried at one or another place in society until finally political techniques were developed that enabled the most astute and fortunate of their practitioners to impose their will on society at large.

The political experience of medieval Japan was strikingly different from that of the classical period. Not only did the order and continuity of the aristocratic age contrast with the disorder and change of the samurai age, but the civil nature of the one contrasted just as sharply with the military nature of the other. The medieval polity was military both in the formal sense that the main participants were identified as *bushi* rather than *kuge* and in the functional sense that they relied openly on military organization, values, and measures in their exercise of power. Furthermore, whereas the court nobility had governed through an aristocratic bureaucracy, the medieval samurai relied heavily on feudal techniques of governance, making personal and reciprocal leader-follower relationships central to their rule. Granting that feudal systems are bureaucratic in greater or lesser degree and that bureaucratic systems rely heavily on personal relationships, still the differences between the classical and medieval political systems are sharp enough to warrant the verbal distinction.

These fundamental systemic differences appeared slowly. They were not caused by the abrupt, willful, and violent destruction of one system by another. On the contrary, the old structure of power was changed in an almost backhanded way, in which *bushi* leaders made administrative adjustments at the end of the twelfth century partially as a way to prop up the Taika-*shōen* system by supplementing it with a few new institutional arrangements. Although those new arrangements did restore the fiscal foundation of the classical elite, they also served from the outset to shift decisively the locus of power. As the medieval period advanced, power relationships evolved in ways that slowly but inexorably destroyed every vestige of the *shōen* system. The process also eroded all the residual elements of the Taika state, leaving naught but a vocabulary of formal titles, a few impoverished aristocratic families, a threadbare imperial institution, and the entrenched principle of an inviolable imperial title.

In place of the Taika-*shōen* order, medieval samurai developed a system of feudal ties between a military leader, known as the shogun, and his vassals. During the Kamakura period (1192–1333) the shogunal government or *bakufu* was based at Kamakura in the Kantō. During the Muromachi period (1334–1573) the *bakufu* was situated in the Muromachi section of Kyoto ("the capital") as Heian came to be called. As the centuries passed, shogunal fortunes fluctuated and eventually decayed. Regional and local military leaders acquired more autonomy and attempted by various strategies to govern their domains. They recruited supporters, commonly rewarding them with fiefs, and used samurai ideals of hereditary loyalty, service, and obligation to reinforce ties of mutual interest. Their success in stabilizing affairs was limited, however, and by the sixteenth century, warfare was widespread in Japan.

The medieval political experience can thus be described in terms of changing patterns of *bushi* rule because samurai were the most influential element, dominating both central and regional politics. Moreover, when political fluidity ended during the late sixteenth century, men of *bushi* status still held their superior position. It is important to recognize, however, that samurai of the early medieval period were so different from those of the sixteenth century in terms of origins and military and political behavior that they can usefully be viewed as different social groups. The former were a relatively small and stable number of men who warred and ruled through comparatively simple institutions and claimed, often with considerable validity, descent from imperial scions. By contrast the latter were vastly more numerous, fought and governed through much more complex, labor-intensive institutions, and mostly rose from obscure origins during the centuries of medieval disorder. They had learned much from the age of fluidity in which they rose to power, and they used that accumulated knowledge to establish the integral bureaucratic order of early modern Japan.

The changing character of this military class was only part of broader patterns of change. Medieval Japan experienced the emergence of a truly popular and dynamic indigenous Buddhism. A new, exciting, and sophisticated higher culture was forged, one that combined, many would affirm, the finest elements of classical Japan, select new influences from China, and the best of *bushi* taste. More significantly from our perspective, it embodied values that both shaped and reflected the social activity of the medieval populace, not just nobles, but also samurai, clerics, and some commoners. There occurred rapid growth in the economy, proliferation of small towns, and emergence of a much more elaborate commercial-artisan sector of society. The age also witnessed basic changes in the character of warfare, changes that drew vast numbers of commoners, willingly or not, into the political process. Indeed, all social groups participating in these developments—nobles, samurai, clerics, merchants, artisans, peasants rich and poor—undertook many sorts of political action that added to the diversity and fluidity of medieval governance. Finally, this whole transformation took place while the population was growing rapidly and society's productivity was rising commensurately.

By the sixteenth century, Japan was a much bigger and more complex society than it had been in the twelfth. Organizational patterns that had once been adequate had become obsolete. In a sense the political history of sixteenth-century Japan was the history of a society whose whole tradition of government—Yamato–Taika-*shōen*–early medieval *bushi* —had been outgrown. The political process had become one of trial and error in which aspirants to power, or simply security, tried combinations of procedures, in the process learning how to organize power locally, then regionally, and finally, at century's end, nationally. When that process was successfully completed, Japan passed from an age of political fluidity into an age of integral bureaucracy.

THE EMERGENCE OF *BUSHI* RULE

Taira Kiyomori was on the winning side in armed struggles between rival court factions in 1156 (the Hōgen incident) and again in 1159–60 (the Heiji incident). Exploiting the preeminent military position he thus acquired in Kyoto, he gradually gained a dominant political role by continuing to play more successfully than his rivals the established game of *bushi* support for *kuge* factions. Where he eventually differed from earlier practitioners of the art was essentially in the openness with which he acceded to ever higher positions until he had acquired titles hitherto restricted to court nobles. Also, in a way that was thoroughly unprecedented for powerful military figures, he formed his own marriage ties to the imperial family, eventually having his own grandson designated emperor. When the need arose, he had no qualms about humiliating and destroying rivals or expanding the *shōen* and raising the status of his followers. Yet, for all his dictatorial ways, he remained near Kyoto, ruling as had the Fujiwara through the institutions of the Taika-*shōen* system, differing from them primarily in terms of his social origins and the openness of his use of force.

In his rise to power, Kiyomori had destroyed many rivals, including Minamoto Yoshitomo. He had spared Yoshitomo's sons, however, being content to exile them to the provinces. By the late 1170s, those lads, of whom the eldest survivor was named Yoritomo and a younger one Yoshitsune, had grown to maturity, and they were eager to avenge their father. By then, too, Kiyomori's governance had won him many enemies in Kyoto. One of those enemies was Minamoto Yorimasa, a distant relative of Yoritomo and an aged man-about-court who had long been ridiculed by Taira rulers. In 1180 he began plotting his revenge. In the opening words of the *Azuma kagami* [Mirror of the east], the official history of the Kamakura regime, we are told that Yorimasa had long schemed to overthrow Kiyomori.

> But realizing the difficulty of accomplishing this long-cherished ambition by his stratagem alone, he, together with his son Nakatsuna, the governor of Izu, secretly called this evening on Prince Mochihito, the second son of the ex-sovereign, at the Sanjō-Takakura Palace and urged him to join in the destruction of the Taira and to assume the rule of the country himself. He would be aided in the effort by Minamoto Yoritomo, the former assistant captain of the Military Guards, Right Division, and his followers of the Minamoto clan.[1]

The insurrection, thus consciously plotted and legitimized by connection with a claimant to the imperial throne, was soon launched and raged for years. Initially the Taira re-

---

1. Minoru Shinoda, *The Founding of the Kamakura Shogunate, 1180–1185* (New York: Columbia University Press, 1960), p. 149. The entry is for 1180, fourth month, ninth day.

pulsed their challengers, and Yorimasa committed suicide. However, in 1181 Kiyomori died. Subsequently his followers lacked resolute leadership, whereas the insurgents received skillful guidance from the young and ruthless Yoritomo, who had assumed leadership of the Minamoto forces. By 1185 he and his collaborators, notably his brother, Yoshitsune, had triumphed in a series of dramatic battles that swirled from the Kantō westward as far as Kyūshū.

Victory in war established Minamoto primacy, but it was Yoritomo's political actions during and after his triumph that perpetuated that primacy. Far more boldly than Kiyomori, he broke with Fujiwara political tradition and gave visibility to the new *bushi* order. He had risen to power in the Kantō and decided to establish his seat of government there. His headquarters were installed in the small, defensible seaside town of Kamakura, rather than in Kyoto. He founded his power solidly on his own *shōen*, which he multiplied at Taira expense, and on his own vassals, called *gokenin* or "housemen," whose numbers he also increased rapidly.

Yoritomo recognized that to perpetuate his family security and political effectiveness on the national scene, his personally controlled power must somehow be joined to the legitimizing authority of the imperial institution. There were two reasons why such a joining was necessary. First, his power was regional, based on loyal supporters in the Kantō and sustained in the face of rivals and would-be rivals elsewhere. Second, his power was rooted in a set of human relationships—feudal lord–vassal ties—that had no national legitimacy. Whereas all the human relationships of the *shōen* system had ultimately been sanctioned by imperial edicts, feudal ties were personally arranged between lord and vassal and had no higher sanction. By gaining imperial legitimation of his actions, Yoritomo would obtain tacit approval of his vassalage arrangements and their application across the country. He could hope thereby to conceal the true character of his role as the insurgent chief of a regional band of personal followers and present himself instead as the legitimate preserver of sanctioned traditional principles and interests.

Yoritomo chose to achieve the linkage of intrusive personal power and customary imperial authority by leaving the Heian court structure intact and working through the established forms of the Taika-*shōen* system. Utilizing intermediaries and justifying his requests in terms of military necessity, during the 1180s and 1190s he won imperial approval for the appointment of his *gokenin* as supervisors of *shōen*, entitled *jitō* (land steward), and as provincial-level commanders of military forces, entitled *shugo* (constable). He obtained court titles legitimizing his control of these officials and court approval for funding arrangements that assured them a stable, enduring, and legal economic foundation. While preserving the institutional arrangements of the classical age, Yoritomo thus also assured that he and his *gokenin* would have income rights and authority sufficient to regulate fiscal and judicial affairs in the *shōen* and to preserve the peace in the provinces. These moves helped legitimize his new regime's power, and many courtiers found them hateful. However, given the success of Yoritomo's armies, all in Kyoto knew they held office only on sufferance of Kamakura, and only once, in 1185, was he forced to drive antagonists from office.

Yoritomo's stabilizing measures served to control rivals from below as well as rivals from above. During the decades of the Minamoto rise, many other ambitious warriors tried to gain wealth and power, usually by encroaching on the income and administrative rights of *shōen* holders. Yoritomo invoked established authority to justify the suppression of such challengers and the reimposition of order on the land. In the process he won a measure of gratitude from those monasteries, shrines, and nobles whose perquisites he preserved. For example, in 1186 he apparently learned that the lands of a shrine in western Japan had been plundered by a local samurai and also by one of his own retainers, who told a sceptical court that he was collecting an authorized military tax. In response Yoritomo denounced their actions, ordering, "Henceforth their outrages are to cease, and the shrine's authority shall be obeyed. It is commanded thus."[2] Yoritomo, the regional insurgent, thus spoke in support of imperial authority

2. Jeffrey P. Mass, *The Kamakura Bakufu, a Study in Documents* (Stanford: Stanford University Press, 1976), p. 53.

and on behalf of an established shrine interest and against the depredations of other samurai, even his own vassals.

Yoritomo also sought to control rivals from below by transforming his regional band of followers into a national caste of elite warriors. He carefully restricted access to the status of *gokenin*, requiring those admitted to take personal oaths of allegiance to himself, rewarding them with suitable lands, and subsequently knitting them into his band by marriage and adoption arrangements that perpetuated the fictive kinship character of his following even after *gokenin* were situated in many parts of the country and included many men who in fact were neither kin nor original followers. Moreover he (and his successors) tried to limit the size and character of the broader samurai caste, establishing it too as an elite body, by insisting that a *gokenin* could promote a retainer from the general ranks of foot soldiers to the elite status of samurai only with shogunal approval. The *Azuma kagami* credits one shogun with saying this to a prominent *gokenin* who sought permission to promote a retainer to samurai status:

> If you make a samurai of this man who is not a samurai, then one day he will forget his origin, and try to become a [go]kenin. This cannot be permitted.[3]

By such careful attention to legitimation without and control within, Yoritomo successfully extended his power beyond the Kantō. Within a decade of the insurrection's beginning in 1180 he had ruined the Taira, restored order, and fashioned most of the political arrangements that would assure Kamakura solid and legitimate control of all Minamoto lands and much of the rest of central and northern Japan. In 1192 the court saw fit to grant him the title of shogun (*seii taishōgun* or "barbarian-subduing generalissimo"), and in later years his governing apparatus at Kamakura became known as the *bakufu* (tent government).

Seven years later Yoritomo died. After a few years of uncertain leadership under his hapless sons, the Kamakura *bakufu* came into the hands of an able vassal family, the Hōjō.

3. Sansom, *Japan to 1334*, pp. 350–51. Italics added.

The Hōjō chief, Tokimasa, had been the guardian of young Yoritomo. His gifted daughter Hōjō Masako (1157–1225) had become the Minamoto leader's wife. In 1203 Tokimasa assumed the post of regent (*shikken*) to Yoritomo's son, and subsequently, his offspring, who proved as effective as Yoritomo's had proved inadequate, made the position hereditary. Thereafter shogun at Kamakura were powerless title-holders whom the Hōjō regents selected from high-ranking families of the court. In 1221, Emperor Go-Toba gathered a small army and revolted. However, the Hōjō, prodded into offensive action by the vigorous representations of Yoritomo's aged widow, Masako, crushed his forces decisively and seized the opportunity to solidify Kamakura rule. They established a more powerful representative group in Kyoto, assigned *gokenin* as land stewards to much of the rest of Japan, and took over more *shōen* for themselves. With those changes the Hōjō position became unassailable.

Yoritomo and his successors had thus superimposed a new system of control on the cumbersome arrangements of the Heian elite. A small group of samurai-administrators at Kamakura, working directly or through branch offices in Kyoto and Kyūshū, actually dominated the polity. They did so through central organs of governance that had been enlarged and rationalized sufficiently to retain *bakufu* effectiveness despite extraordinary growth in the scope of their responsibilities. Through these offices they were able to keep track of the *bakufu*'s scattered vassals, settle those legal disputes that could not be resolved locally, manage estates and other property during peacetime, and deploy forces in war. Out in the countryside, Kamakura's control was exercised directly by *gokenin* on their own estates or through appointed land stewards in most other *shōen*. These stewards participated in the general management of *shōen*, resolved disputes among inhabitants, and supervised the collection and forwarding of land rents to *shōen* holders after taking their own authorized portion as salary. Also out in the hinterland were the constables, who were charged with the arrest of criminals and insurgents and, in times of mobilization, with the summoning to arms of *gokenin* and other military men in their provinces.

These new posts supplemented but did not displace most of the offices of the Taika and *shōen* systems. Members of the classical elite continued to staff the central and regional offices of the old imperial bureaucracy and the *shōen* administrative hierarchies. However, the former were little more than ceremonial titles. And the power of the latter steadily eroded as Kamakura leaders extended their administrative and judicial authority over the whole country, especially following Go-Toba's ill-fated attempt to destroy the new regime in 1221.

In the year 1232 the spirit of this samurai administration was codified in the Jōei Code (Jōei *shikimoku*). It consisted of fifty-one articles that specified guidelines to be followed in settling legal disputes relating to property, vassalage, official duties, and criminal acts. The code contained little that was strikingly new in terms of specific criteria of justice. Nevertheless it was important as a simple, lucid, and public statement of reasonable legal principles and as the first major codification since the early classical age. Conscientious adherence to the principles of the Jōei Code by Kamakura justiciars gave the regime a unique reputation for equitable governance that contributed to its success in keeping the peace for another century.

It would be misleading to regard the heart of the historic transformation as lying in the creation of new institutions. The *bakufu* preserved most of the older Taika-*shōen* institutions and interest groups. Moreover, many of the institutional arrangements of the *bakufu* itself were simply outgrowths of familial arrangements of the Minamoto, which consisted of organs, such as the *mandokoro*, that were akin to those of aristocratic *shōen* governance. Minamoto estates were *shōen* held in the same legal manner as classical *shōen*. The posts of land steward and shogun both had pre-Kamakura antecedents. Finally, the rights and duties that Kamakura assumed were nearly all assumed as supplements to and not replacements of prior institutional arrangements. Rather, the heart of the transformation lay in what might be called a changing political ethos that enabled a new segment of society to challenge the established order and bend old arrangements to its own needs. Having acquired over the years legitimate control of land and experience in large-scale political operations, the new samurai rulers—who were unawed by *kuge* pretensions, who considered their own relatives and vassals the core of their organizations, and who treasured horsemanship, swordsmanship, valor, and toughness rather than diplomacy, subtlety, and polish—had expanded and modified those older arrangements in unprecedented ways so as to impose their own values on society and forge a new political order.

By 1232 the new order had been formulated and a new age ushered in. As with the Taika Reform, the new order was built upon the old, but this time the scope of change tended more to be minimized by rhetorical disclaimers than exaggerated by bold schemata and braggadocio. Nevertheless in both cases the changes were major, and they did succeed in ending a time of disorder and reestablishing governmental effectiveness.

EVOLUTION OF THE POLITICAL ORDER, A.D. 1250–1500

In a manner reminiscent of the classical development from Taika to *shōen*, medieval Japan developed from the relatively integrated Kamakura order of the thirteenth century to the relatively decentralized Muromachi order of the fourteenth and fifteenth centuries. Both cases involved erosion of imperially sanctioned elements of government, expansion of alternative arrangements, and a shift in the locus and exercise of power within the established ruling elite. In all these aspects the medieval changes were more extreme. Taking place within a context of rapid and fundamental social change, however, they were less successful than the *shōen* system in perpetuating political order and elite stability. The turmoil that marked the end of the medieval period was more profound and punishing than that of the twelfth century and gave rise to more fundamental efforts at reconstruction.

Several circumstances converged to destroy the Kamakura regime. The Hōjō regents turned their hegemonial position to familial advantage by designating many relatives *jitō* and *shugo*, and in the process of enriching their own they alienated other vassals of the Minamoto. Over the generations, descendants of *gokenin* proliferated, but they received no commensurate increments of income from the *bakufu*. Finding that service to Kamakura offered no adequate rewards, they blamed their poverty on *bakufu* leaders. Left to their own devices, they became accustomed to running their own family affairs, and by the late 1200s many thought of themselves more as local notables than as Minamoto vassals. It was a shift in self-image that boded ill for the regime.

Late in the century Kublai Khan and his Mongol conquerors of China launched two massive invasions of Japan. The samurai repulsed both attempts and spent years maintaining a burdensome alert, but when the heroes of national defense turned to Kamakura for reward, the *bakufu* had little to offer. Samurai from western Japan, who had done most of the fighting and guarding, were particularly displeased and began looking elsewhere for more substantial benefactors.

Concurrently a succession dispute arose in the imperial court. For several decades the Hōjō pacified the two claimant parties in the dispute by alternating the imperial title between them. However, in 1326 the Emperor Go-Daigo defied the Hōjō by naming his own son heir. Protests were made, but the ineffective Hōjō regent of the time failed to settle the matter, and Go-Daigo's supporters multiplied. Five years later he raised the standard of revolt. The Hōjō dispatched Ashikaga Takauji, the leader of a powerful *shugo* (constable) family, to suppress the insurrection. He and other commanders switched sides, however, and destroyed the Hōjō position in both Kyoto and Kamakura.

In 1334, Go-Daigo proclaimed a restoration of imperial rule, the Kenmu Restoration as it is called, but he governed ineptly. A year later Takauji turned against him and put another person on the imperial throne. Claiming descent from Minamoto Yoritomo, Takauji shortly thereafter established his own *bakufu* in the Muromachi district of Kyoto. Go-Daigo retreated into the Yoshino mountains south of Nara and with the support of various samurai and noble families established a rival imperial throne. For several decades central Japan was rent by civil war as families struggled for land and power, legitimizing their ventures as actions in support of one or the other imperial line. As they struggled, *bushi* chieftains—Ashikaga relatives most notably—forged semi-independent domains of their own. They formed and broke tactical alliances of convenience and in the process gave rise to a coalition among the greatest warrior families in central Japan.

Takauji's grandson, Ashikaga Yoshimitsu, became shogun in 1368. Utilizing the support of major military families, he resolved the imperial-succession dispute, asserted fuller authority over feudal subordinates, and initiated nearly a century of political stability in central Japan. The legitimacy of Yoshimitsu's regime derived from the Ashikaga claim to be successors to the Minamoto. Takauji and his descendants styled themselves shogun, called their government a *bakufu*, and organized it on Kamakura lines. They designated their supporters vassals, gave the greatest of them titles as constable, and encouraged them to live in Kyoto where they could be more easily controlled. Like Kamakura leaders before them, Ashikaga shogun saw to it that the court certified all constable appointments, sanctioned land arrangements as they were made, and awarded honors and titles in accordance with classical precedents.

Constables cooperated with shogun because they needed shogunal support as much as shogun needed theirs. They had acquired much land by the rude displacement of residual imperial authority, other *shōen* interests, or rival samurai perquisites. As they seized land, they incorporated local warriors into their vassal bands and tried to retain their support by granting their leaders fiefs. By comparison with Yoritomo's day the lord-vassal relationship was much more often an ad hoc one of immediate convenience that broke down as soon as a vassal saw better prospects in rebellion. Hence constables were not securely in control of even their own lands, which usually covered much smaller areas than the provinces they were officially supervising as *shugo*. In their roles as *shugo*, moreover, the regional barons were expected to control local warriors who were not even their own vassals. And these men, who often had lands and followers of their own, were especially inclined to revolt when opportunity seemed ripe. Constables cooperated with the *bakufu*, therefore, to obtain shogunal and imperial support against such challengers from below.[4]

As this description of the Ashikaga order suggests, it was the weakest of Japan's post-Yamato systems in terms of legitimacy. It was also the most decentralized. The real locus of power was situated uncertainly in the field of interaction between regional barons and the local leaders of small, tightly knit warrior bands who were ultimately in control of most rural production and manpower.

The uncertainty of the order fostered attempts at self-strengthening by its component elements. At the lowest political levels, commoners undertook a variety of political initiatives, as we note later in examining the broader process of social change. Leaders of warrior groups persistently maneuvered for advantage, and at higher levels constables repeatedly intrigued and bargained to advance their interests. At the highest level both Yoshimitsu and his son the shogun Yoshinori (r. 1428–41) attempted to strengthen the *bakufu* position. Yoshimitsu did so by forging solid ties to selected powerful constables and by developing an independent economic base for the *bakufu*; namely, fostering a lucrative trade with China and taxing the growing commerce around Kyoto. Yoshinori tried to strengthen his position by assigning more tasks to *bakufu* officials, by pitting constables against one another, and by encouraging lesser warriors to rebel against powerful constables. In 1441 a constable who felt threatened by Yoshinori's maneuvers contrived to have him murdered, and the resulting war of revenge added to the tension.

Then the whole edifice of power ruptured in 1467 with the outbreak of the Ōnin war. That war was basically a power struggle between major regional barons. However, it was

4. This topic is nicely explored in Kawai Masaharu, "Shogun and Shugo: The Provincial Aspects of Muromachi Politics," and Miyagawa Mitsuru, "From Shōen to Chigyō: Proprietary Lordship and the Structure of Local Power," in John W. Hall and Toyoda Takeshi, ed., *Japan in the Muromachi Age* (Berkeley: University of California Press, 1977), pp. 65–105.

waged within the city of Kyoto because the fighting erupted there in the wake of a disputed shogunal succession whose outcome the rivals had been seeking to influence by threats of force. It proved to be a horrendously destructive war. The massive opposing armies, "which at one time numbered 160,000 on one side and 90,000 on the other,"[5] engaged in intense street fighting, threw up barricades, dug trenches, burned out blocks to protect their lines, and then struggled indecisively to dislodge one another. After five months of terrible fighting the worst had been done. Wrote a *bakufu* official,

> The flowery capital that we thought would last forever to our surprise is to become the lair of wolves and foxes. In the past there have been rebellions and disasters, but in this first year of Ōnin the laws of gods and kings have been broken and all the sects are perishing.[6]

Little remained of the city, but the opposing armies fruitlessly held their lines for a decade. By the time they left the ruined capital, the *bakufu* had been reduced to little more than a barony among baronies, and warfare had spread widely through the provinces, where it continued for a century in the form of endemic turmoil. That turmoil had the general effect of destroying the *shugo* domains that had arisen earlier. In a process commonly called *gekokujō*, "those below toppling those above," local warrior leaders overthrew their lords, forged larger domains, and, in turn, were overthrown by some of their own vassals and other challengers. Despite its negative connotations, however, *gekokujō* was a creative historical process that led during the late sixteenth century to a new political order. The new order, that of early modern Japan, ended the political turmoil and tied Japanese society together more thoroughly than had the arrangements of any preceding age.

5. Hayashiya Tatsusaburō, "Kyoto in the Muromachi Age," in Hall and Toyoda, p. 27.

6. George Sansom, *A History of Japan, 1334–1615* (Stanford: Stanford University Press, 1961), pp. 225–26.

HIGHER CULTURE

Just as the higher culture of classical Japan was an inseparable part of the enduring supremacy of an urban civil aristocracy, so the higher culture of medieval Japan shaped and was shaped by the creativity, vicissitudes, and compromises of a samurai elite that occupied the shrinking social space between the old patricians and the increasingly diverse, turbulent, and visible plebs. Medieval Japan's higher culture is intrinsically interesting for its remarkable aesthetic qualities, but our principal concern in examining it is to gain insight into the character of the age, to see how cultural production reflected the age, influenced it, and gave some degree of coherence to it. Moreover, mindful of the political disorder of medieval Japan, one wonders how such extraordinary aesthetic achievements could have been realized in a society characterized by so much political turmoil. One also wonders how this conjunction of creativity and disorder related to the larger historic processes of growth and change.

There were several noteworthy forms of medieval arts and letters. A new literary genre, the war tales or *gunki monogatari*, revealed the souls and justified the actions of the *bushi* builders of the new age. Works of philosophical and religious exegesis gave vitality and order to new religious movements of profound historic significance. The creative dynamism of the new age was also evident in sculpture, painting, and architecture. During the Muromachi period a new aesthetic unity was articulated that displaced the classical elite's cult of beauty, and it was manifested in painting, architecture, landscape architecture, the Nō drama, and the tea ceremony.

The *bushi* ethos

The *bushi* ethos dominated the higher culture of the Kamakura period and remained a major influence throughout the medieval age. It lay at the heart of the change from classical to medieval Japan and was embodied initially in oral tales that recounted the struggles of Taira and Minamoto. Recited to the accompaniment of the *biwa* (lute), those tales of samurai exploits were recorded, celebrated, embellished, and made into the foundation myths of a new age. The war tales became the formative texts that spelled out the values of samurai society and reified them in the remembered performance of glorious forefathers. In terms of symbolic founders, they established successors to Shōtoku Taishi, the seminal culture hero of classical Japan.

The aristocratic norms of the classical age had been evinced in such works as the fictional *Tale of Genji* and the historical *Tales of Glory* and *Ōkagami*. We earlier noted how the author of *Ōkagami* presented Fujiwara Michinaga as a tough ruler, and yet even in his most "manly" aspects, he appeared very unlike the samurai of medieval literature. The Heian courtier's fascination with elegance and the use of past precedent to suggest the magnitude of present worth was very different from the *bushi* ethos evinced in the war tales.

The overt values pervading the war tales were those of heroism, self-discipline, simplicity of taste, devotion to duty, honor, pride of name, and an awareness of the brevity of life. They came to be epitomized in one of the most celebrated of the founders, the tragic hero Minamoto Yoshitsune (1159–89). Yoritomo's younger brother, Yoshitsune was a gifted warrior who fought valiantly in his service and played a central role in two of the most celebrated battles of Japanese history. He led a bold cavalry charge into the center of the Taira encampment at Ichinotani in early 1184, routing them and driving them from central Japan. Subsequently he led his small band of cavalry in hot pursuit, driving the Taira westward to Dannoura and defeat at sea. Yoshitsune's prowess and achievements won him much popularity at court, doubtless fed his own ambition, provoked Yoritomo's distrust, and finally prompted the Minamoto leader to have his younger brother hounded and hunted across Japan and driven to commit suicide. By the fifteenth century Yoshitsune had become lionized in song, story, and stage play. A major figure in the famous thirteenth-century war tale *Heike monogatari* [Tales of the Heike], he became the central figure in the fifteenth-century work, *Gikeiki* [Annals of Yoshitsune]. That tale recounted in serial fashion moving and heroic incidents in his life, and it ended with his tragic death. In closing, the raconteur saw fit to make his message explicit. He wrote of those whose actions had led to Yoshitsune's suicide,

> By wickedly betraying their lord in defiance of their father's last wish, they forfeited their lives, destroyed their family, and allowed their hereditary lands to become the treasured possessions of other men. Nothing is so important in a warrior as loyalty and filial piety. One can but pity them.[7]

Besides these overt values, one can see other attitudes of the medieval period taking shape in the war tales. One prominent feature was the ready acceptance of willfulness as legitimate motivation. We earlier noted how the *Azuma kagami* matter of factly reported Minamoto Yorimasa's long-term wish to overthrow Taira Kiyomori. In the early war tales, those of the thirteenth century, ambition and willfulness tended to be constrained by a sense of proper place, or at least proper title. Thus in the *Heike monogatari*, Minamoto Yoshinaka, a formidable warrior and victor over the Taira, antagonized Yoritomo and was destroyed by him. To illustrate Yoshinaka's uncouthness and overweening ambition, the narrator had him say this after he had terrorized Kyoto and subdued resistance there.

> [Yoshinaka] having also taken the daughter of the Kwampaku Motofusa and made her his wife, he assembled his retainers and gave his opinion thus: "I, Yoshinaka, have confronted the Sovereign Lord of this Empire in battle and have conquered. If I would, I might become Emperor or I might become Hō-ō (retired Emperor): but I don't want to become Hō-ō, for I must become a shaven priest; and how can I become Emperor, for I should have to be a child. Very well then, I will become Kwampaku." At this his official scribe, Taiyū-bō Kakumei, stood up and said: "A Kwampaku must be of the princely house of Fujiwara, of the stock and lineage of the great Kamatari; Your Excellency is of the Genji

7. Helen Craig McCullough, trans., *Yoshitsune: A Fifteenth-Century Japanese Chronicle* (Tokyo: University of Tokyo Press, 1966), p. 294.

line, and therefore cannot hold such office." So it ended by Kiso [Yoshinaka] consoling himself with the title of Groom of the Stables to the Retired Emperor, and appropriating the province of Tanba as his fief.[8]

Although propriety of title could thus be used to constrain ambition, achievement could also be invoked to justify it. Especially in later tales, willfulness and bald political ambition became ever more acceptable, even being appropriate for emperors. In the *Taiheiki* [Chronicle of grand pacification], which recounted the fighting of the Kenmu Restoration, we are told that Go-Toba, leader of the earlier insurrection of 1221, had sought to destroy the Hōjō because "it was hateful to his heart that the government of the court was set aside by the power of the military."[9] The tale went on to report that although successive Hōjō regents had governed well,

> The generations of emperors thought always, "Would that the eastern barbarians might be struck down!" For it was in their hearts to comfort the spirit of the imperial exile of Shōkyū [Go-Toba]; likewise, they sorrowed to think upon the court's power, how it wasted and became as nothing.

In the later *Ōninki* [Chronicle of Ōnin], which told of warfare in the 1460s, willfulness and anger were even more openly cited in explaining behavior. Thus the feudal baron Yamana Sōzen, the most celebrated figure in the tale, was at one point outraged by what he regarded as abusive behavior by the Ashikaga shogunate. He proposed to take revenge. In reply his vassals urged self-restraint on the ground that his ethical position was weak. It was, they said, based on a "private," i.e., self-serving, agreement while that of the shogun was based on the principle of obligation to one's master. Yamana replied to his vassals in this way:

8. A. L. Sadler, trans., "Heike Monogatari," in *Transactions of the Asiatic Society of Japan*, 49, Part I, 1921, pp. 107–8. (Vol. 8, ch. 12, of the *monogatari*.) "Kwampaku" is an older romanization of *kanpaku*.

9. These two translated passages are from Helen Craig McCullough, trans., *The Taiheiki: A Chronicle of Medieval Japan* (New York: Columbia University Press, 1959), pp. 4, 5.

Such loyal words are beyond reproach. But it is not in my nature to command according to "the way." They say if water is muddy on top, then the current below will not be clear; and when government is disordered, the people will find no peace. I will ride forth and vent my anger by striking down those fellows who plot against the Shiba. And even though I violate the wishes of the shogun, it should cause me little harm.[10]

Yamana's propriety-be-damned attitude characterized much of the conduct of figures in *Ōninki*. It suggests how fully such behavior, which would have won the most haughty denunciation from a Heian courtier, even from the coolly ambitious Michinaga, had come to be seen as normal and acceptable.

In other ways, as well, the war tales showed movement away from classical norms of explanation and argumentation. In the early tales, such as *Heiji monogatari* [Tale of the Heiji incident], the raconteurs told their stories in official tones, replete with references to Chinese precedents and principles of righteous governance. The works of the Muromachi period, such as the *Taiheiki* and *Gikeiki*, were much more creative. In them magical powers were invoked more freely, and bombast and hyperbole were more common. And since the larger stories in these two tales were stories of ultimate failure—which samurai did not celebrate—the raconteurs focused on the moments of the hero's success and the villain's reverses. *Gikeiki*, for example, was ultimately the tragic story of Yoshitsune's destruction. But what in fact stands out in the narrative time after time was the vitality of Yoshitsune and his vassal Benkei and the repeated defeats of his enemies, defeats that were recorded with dry satisfaction. For example, at one point Yoshitsune and his men had repulsed an attacking force led by a warrior named Tosa, whom Yoritomo had dispatched to destroy Yoshitsune. As the raconteur told the denouement,[11]

10. Translated by H. Paul Varley in *The Ōnin War* (New York: Columbia University Press, 1967), pp. 148–49.

11. This and the following translated passage are from McCullough, *Yoshitsune*, pp. 153, 293.

In time, the men who had escaped made their way back to Kamakura. "Tosa blundered. Yoshitsune cut off his head," they told Yoritomo.

"I won't tolerate the seizure and execution of a man who was acting as my representative!" Yoritomo exclaimed. Among themselves his warriors said, "Why shouldn't Tosa have been executed? Wasn't he personally leading an attack on Yoshitsune?"

Near the end of the tale, Yoshitsune was dead and his loyal vassal Kanefusa was helping end his family's life honorably. Kanefusa fired the building in which the bodies lay, made one last sally against the besieging enemy, and dragged one attacker named Nagasaki Jirō into the burning house with himself, where they both died. The raconteur's parting comment on that incident was this:

> When one stops to consider, it was a frightful thing to do—the act of a very demon. Kanefusa, to be sure, had been determined from the outset to die in the fire, but poor Nagasaki Jirō was indeed to be pitied! Instead of receiving rewards and lands from a grateful court, he was snatched up willynilly and roasted alive.

In much the same spirit, although Go-Daigo's restoration attempt failed, the *Taiheiki* only acknowledged as much by occasional oblique references. It filled its pages, instead, with celebrations of triumph and willful heroics. In contrast to the Heian period, battlefield success and heroic behavior, regardless of one's origins or political position, were sufficient to legitimize one's conduct.

In the presentation of heroics it also seems possible to detect other changes in the medieval *bushi* world. In the pages of the early tales, as heroes charged into battle, those who called out their names and lineages were men of elegant, or at least respectable, samurai descent. Thus, Minamoto Yoshihira, hero of the *Heiji monogatari*, identified himself in this way.

> He who speaks is one called Kamakura no Akugenda Yoshihira, descendant in the ninth generation of the

Emperor Seiwa and eldest son of the Director of the Stables of the Left, Yoshitomo.[12]

By the time of the Kenmu Restoration more warriors were engaged in the fighting, and fewer could claim—or even cared to claim—elegant ancestry. And the fifteenth-century *Gikeiki* featured prominently the irreverence toward authority and propriety and the nonchalance toward danger of Yoshitsune and his mighty vassal, Benkei. Even the calling out of a hero's name was a ritual that could by then be mocked. Thus, in the incident mentioned above, in which Yoritomo's man, Tosa, was slain, the fighting had started badly for Yoshitsune. The previous evening he had gotten drunk and sent Benkei and his other retainers away so he could dally with a courtesan. While he was in drunken sleep, Tosa's men had attacked. One nondescript manservant kept them at bay while Yoshitsune dressed, and later Benkei arrived. It was still dark, and as Benkei approached, Yoshitsune did not recognize him and feared he was an assailant. As the enemy force readied to attack again, Yoshitsune called out to Benkei in this way:

"Who are you? Name yourself or be cut down," he demanded, advancing toward Benkei.
[Benkei] proclaimed aloud, "Let those who are far away listen to what is said of me! You who are close, behold me now with your own eyes! I am Saitō Musashibō Benkei, the eldest son of the Kumano abbot Benshō, who traces his ancestry to Amatsukoyane. I serve Yoshitsune, and I am a man in a thousand!"
"Very amusing," said Yoshitsune. "You should save your jokes for more suitable occasions."
"Very well—only you told me to identify myself, so I did," Benkei replied, not in the least abashed.[13]

---

12. Reischauer and Yamagiwa, p. 441. Many of these points are also brought out in the "Hōgen Monogatari," the tale of the battles of 1156, which is translated by E. R. Kellogg in *Transactions of the Asiatic Society of Japan*, 15, part I, 1917, pp. 27–117.

13. McCullough, *Yoshitsune*, pp. 148–49.

By the time of the *Ōninki* this sort of battlefield self-promotion, even when satirical, seemed to have gone out of style, perhaps because the armies were too large, the number of combatants too great. In fact, the raconteurs of *Ōninki* seemed to have their hands full just listing noteworthy people involved in all the battles and maneuvers.

Perhaps, too, *Ōninki* raconteurs dispensed with superfluous heroics because the ethics of all had become so unambiguously tied to the advantage of the moment that it simply was no longer possible to embroider reality enough to establish who were the superheroes to be credited with extraordinary virtue and bravery. Instead the realpolitik was allowed to stand on its own merits. Thus at one point in the fluid political situation the regional baron Hatakeyama Yoshinari and his forces had been defeated by a coalition of rivals while Yamana Sōzen had stood aloof from the fray. Yoshinari had fought bravely, however, and when Yamana heard of his courage in adversity, he was moved to tears, blaming himself for Yoshinari's misfortune. Then, drying his eyes, he mused,

> "Yet even though his House has come upon these evil days, he remains steadfast. Who can match him in military prowess? If Yoshinari and I should come to an understanding, no one in the Capital would be able to raise a hand against us." Meanwhile Yoshinari was speculating along similar lines. Among the families aligned against him, he could find no soldier who was the peer of Yamana Sōzen. If, perchance, he and Sōzen should become allies, who then could challenge them?[14]

Doubtless the absence of moral pronouncements of a consistent sort in *Ōninki* also reflected the fact that no clear winners or notable losers emerged from the fray. In the early-thirteenth-century tales, Minamoto heroes had earned praise by triumphing over the Taira. And in the Muromachi tales, *Taiheiki* and *Gikeiki*, the unsuccessful supporters of Go-Daigo and the heroic Yoshitsune were celebrated for their unflinching constancy. It was clear who was to be deemed good and

14. Varley, *The Ōnin War*, p. 155.

who bad, and the attributions of motive and worth reflected those clear judgements. By contrast the ethical inconsistency of figures in *Ōninki* was strikingly apparent. Earlier we saw Yamana speaking lightly of his defiance of the shogun. Later, however, when the shogun was cooperating with him, Yamana and a group of supporters denounced their major rival on the ground that he had allied with another military leader, "to disturb the peace. Now these two have gone against the shogun's order and have sown the seeds of treason."[15] Had "treason" in fact been a significant ethical category to the raconteur, Yamana's conduct would have been presented differently in other places. But it had become a rhetorical posture because social status was not sacred and position did not determine proper conduct. Terms such as treason served pragmatic purposes whose real justification lay in the acceptability of forceful action and the sanction that derived from success.

Religious thought and action

The contrast between the secular values of Heian aristocrats and medieval samurai is no more dramatic than the contrast between classical and medieval religion. Whereas sophisticated religion of the classical age was restricted to the aristocracy, in the medieval era it became accessible to the general populace. Whereas classical aristocratic religion involved elaborate ritual and complex theology, medieval religion minimized ritual and simplified thought. Whereas classical religion tried to achieve an integrated hierarchy of doctrine, medieval religion rejected the notion of an all-embracing structure of thought and instead was pluralistic and discordant in both philosophy and sectarian practice. In this pluralism, medieval religion offered new avenues of access to truth and hence new ways to explain and legitimize action. In the process of articulating new doctrinal positions, medieval religion gave rise to new institutional arrangements. Those new arrangements were crucial to the development of popular religion, and they turned religious institutions into mech-

15. Ibid., p. 158.

anisms of popular social and political action whose effects were felt at all levels of society.

Classical Buddhism, with its elaborate ritual, doctrinal complexity, and concern for aesthetic sensibility, hardly responded to the *bushi* need for a religion that validated willfulness and performance as basic indicators of merit. In the principles and practice of Zen Buddhism, samurai found a doctrine that did meet their needs. The basic scriptures of Zen had been present in Japan for centuries, but it was the two monks Eisai (1141–1215) and Dōgen (1200–53) who established Zen in Japan as an independent doctrine and an organized sectarian movement. Both had studied at the Tendai monastery on Mt. Hiei, and both subsequently went to China in quest of more satisfying religious experiences. They brought back the principles and practices of meditation and enlightenment as developed in the Zen (Ch'an) monasteries of China. Those principles can be stated succinctly:

A special transmission outside the scriptures,

No dependence upon the written word,

Direct pointing at the soul of man,

Seeing one's nature and attaining Buddhahood.[16]

By requiring dialogue with a master ("special transmission") rather than textual study ("no dependence"), and self-discipline and meditation ("direct pointing" and "seeing one's nature") rather than ritual and good works, Zen offered a religious experience unlike that of most Nara and Heian Buddhism. The teachings were propagated, moreover, by prelates whose unpretentious life style was itself strikingly different from the worldly, ritualistic, and elegant monastic style characteristic of the classical age.

What these teachings offered was a new way of knowing, and through that a new ground of action. A student was encouraged, in effect, to know himself and to find the necessary guidelines for life within himself. To grasp religious

16. Sansom, *Japan: A Short Cultural History*, p. 337.

truth required neither high birth nor the wealth and cultivation necessary to participate in the elegant practices of Tendai and Shingon. Rather, it required the mental vitality and self-discipline necessary to penetrate the inner recesses of one's own mind. Whether or not one was capable of doing so could only be discovered in the doing. And so Zen doctrine opened religion to anyone in the general populace who had sufficient resolve to try his hand at the pursuit of enlightenment and sufficient courage to accept the outcome of his effort as evidence of his merit.

As the earlier and more political of the two, Eisai had greater influence on the new rulers, in his day becoming the most influential Buddhist prelate in Kamakura. He and his successors developed the Rinzai sect of Zen into a major monastic organization with large centers in both Kamakura and Kyoto. However, it was Dōgen's Sōtō sect that proved the more durable because he kept it aloof from the medieval regimes of Minamoto and Ashikaga. In consequence it was not tied to the vicissitudes of those governments, and Sōtō monasteries flourished in the hinterland even into the twentieth century.

Dōgen also was a more powerful thinker than Eisai. His intellectual rigor and insistence on the sustained self-discipline of *zazen* (meditation) appealed to dynamic figures throughout the medieval period.[17] One reason for this was that while he called for discipline, he also held that in principle all could attain enlightenment. Thus in one conversation he reminded his disciples that the study of Buddhism required diligent attention and that in Zen that basically meant practicing *zazen*. Then he added, "*Zazen* is suitable for all people, whether their capacities be superior, mediocre, or inferior."[18] In sharp contrast to Tendai-Shingon, Dōgen was advocating a very simple religion, one that he considered potentially accessible to all, and one whose value was solely dependent on the will of the practitioner.

17. Hee-Jin Kim, *Dōgen Kigen: Mystical Realist* (Tucson, Ariz.: University of Arizona Press, 1975), is a scholarly examination of Dōgen's teachings.

18. Reihō Masunaga, trans., *A Primer of Sōtō Zen: A Translation of Dōgen's Shōbōgenzō Zuimonki* (London: Routledge and Kegan Paul, 1972), p. 16.

In practice the universalistic potential of this doctrine was diminished by Dōgen's insistence that monastic discipline, not secular life, provided the ideal conditions for attaining enlightenment.[19] And in any case *zazen* required time, and that requirement reduced the accessibility of Zen to the masses, who scarcely could afford to spend their waking hours sitting in single-minded meditation. In consequence, although Zen met samurai needs, it was other sectarian movements that provided a religious experience appropriate to the general populace.

The religious doctrine that did most to bridge the cultural gap between patrician and pleb was the Buddhist doctrine of Amida. From the Nara period, sutras expounding Amidist teachings had existed in Japan, and both Saichō and Kūkai had included them in their systems of theology. The core element of Amidist doctrine was Amida's vow to save all sentient beings. Specifically, the *Muryōju-kyō* [Greater *sukhavati-vyuha*; Sutra of infinite life] enumerated forty-eight vows by Amida, of which the eighteenth is crucial. There Amida vowed to assure that "all beings in the ten quarters" should "desire in sincerity and trustfulness to be born in my country [the Western Paradise or Jōdo]," and "be born there by only thinking of me for say, up to ten times."[20] This vow offered a simple and assured means of salvation to all who would believe. During the later Heian period the practice of calling upon Amida's saving grace by uttering the *nenbutsu* (the invocatory phrase *namu Amida butsu*) became a popular religious practice among both the aristocratic elite, who learned it in their monasteries and nunneries, and commoners, who heard of it from itinerant monks and nuns (*hijiri* and *bikuni*).

Amidist doctrine gained favor among late Heian aristocrats because it seemed to constitute a proper religious solution to the problems of disorder and decay that characterized the elite experience of the day. It seemed proper because it provided a solution to the problem posed by the Buddhist

19. Kim, p. 53.

20. D. T. Suzuki, *Collected Writings on Shin Buddhism* (Kyoto: Shinshū Otaniha, 1973), p. 45. Whether "entering Jōdo" was itself enlightenment or whether it placed one in a position from whence to attain enlightenment was an issue of doctrinal disagreement among proponents of Amidism.

doctrine of *mappō*, the "degenerate age" of the "latter law." That doctrine spoke of an age (*shōbō*) in which Sakyamuni's teachings could be understood by all, a later age (*zōbō*) in which only the gifted few could understand, and finally a "degenerate age" (*mappō*), in which chaos would prevail and none could understand Buddha's word. Calendrical calculations suggested that Japan had entered that "degenerate age" from about A.D. 1050, which seemed to explain the disorder of the day. With enlightenment beyond the capability of all sentient beings, it seemed evident that only faith in the saving grace of a spiritual titan would suffice. Amida had offered that grace.

In this situation, where theology offered not only an explanation for the crisis of the age but also a solution to it, evangelical Amidism began to prosper. During the eleventh and twelfth centuries, evangelists propagated the message of Amida's grace among patrician and pleb alike.[21] They maintained that other doctrines were unhelpful in the "degenerate age" because they depended on self-power (*jiriki*), which would no longer suffice. Only reliance on the power of another (*tariki*), specifically Amida, would assure one's escape from the painful cycles of existence. The most influential of these evangelists was Genshin (942–1017), whose treatise, *Ōjōyōshū* [Essentials of rebirth], became a seminal exposition of Amidist faith. By way of conveying his message effectively to people of all classes, Genshin illustrated his ideas with "horrendous pictures of the suffering of the doomed and the delights of the blessed." His book "grasped the imaginations and emotions of the people of his age and succeeding ages."[22]

By the twelfth century, many among the Heian elite were adherents of Amidism. As the classical age dissolved in urban decay and rural turmoil, the established sects discredited themselves by engaging actively in the politico-military brawling that terrorized Heian and confused the hinterland. In this situation salvationist teachings, and preachers who repudiated their ties to established monasteries, became

21. Hori, pp. 92ff.

22. Both quotations are from Alfred Bloom, *Shinran's Gospel of Pure Grace* (Tucson, Ariz.: University of Arizona Press, 1965), p. 18.

the more persuasive. At the end of the twelfth century the monk Hōnen (1133–1212) articulated with new clarity and intellectual rigor the unique and universal saving grace of Amida. Like Eisai and Dōgen, Hōnen had studied on Mt. Hiei and left it to propound his own faith among the general populace. According to Ichirō Hori,

> [Hōnen] never built one temple of his own. He believed and declared that any place where people practiced Nembutsu—any small farmer's or fisherman's hut where a few persons gathered to pray and repeat the name of Amida—was his temple or seminary.[23]

In later years, Hōnen's disciples, following the *hijiri* tradition of itinerant evangelists, carried his salvationist message far beyond the aristocratic few to samurai and commoners in the hinterland. Their activities led to the formation of congregations of the faithful to established Jōdo temples in which Amidist doctrines were taught more or less to the exclusion of all other Buddhist thought.

Of Hōnen's several fervent disciples, it was Shinran (1173–1262), who also had studied at Hiei before turning to Amidism, who left the most enduring legacy. His teachings were institutionalized as Jōdo Shin (True pure land) Buddhism and developed into the single most important Amidist sect. Shinran argued that only absolute faith in Amida could assure rebirth. Any willful religious exercise interfered with its attainment, he held, because such constituted an assertion of ego. Any special religious practices were therefore counterproductive. He is reputed to have said that[24]

> All the sacred books devoted to the explanation of the truth of the Other Power [*tariki*], show that every one who believing in the Original Vow, recites the *nembutsu*, will become a Buddha. Excepting this, what learning is needed to be reborn in the Pure Land?

---

23. Hori, pp. 129–30.

24. These three quoted excerpts are from Suzuki, *Collected Writings*, pp. 212, 207, 220, in that order, and are quotations from *Tannisho*. Italics added.

Similarly, "deeds of morality are not required," and "No matter how valuable offerings be which are made to the Buddha, or to the teacher, they are of no use, so long as the donor lacks in faith."

In doctrinal terms Amidism and Zen were very dissimilar. The one was based on utter faith, the other on intense self-discipline. They differed also in that one appealed to samurai in particular whereas the other appealed to the populace as a whole. Historically, however, they had important similarities insofar as they both contributed to a massive broadening of the population that was touched by organized, intellectually sophisticated religion. They also had a similar impact in that they challenged and destroyed the doctrinal pretensions of Tendai-Shingon universalism, replacing it with a religious pluralism that was to persist throughout the medieval period. Dōgen, for example, was sharply critical of the religious merit of other doctrines, Amidism in particular. And Shinran responded to criticisms of his teachings by insisting on the right of Amidist believers to pursue their own way. Proponents of Zen and Amidism, like Kūkai before them, used dichotomous logic to distinguish their teachings from all other Buddhist doctrines (i.e., *tariki* vs. *jiriki* and esoteric vs. exoteric), but unlike Kūkai they did not attempt to gather all teachings into one integrated order. Their concern was with religious simplicity and philosophical clarity, and the result was to create sectarian doctrinal bases for religious discord.

This religious pluralism was not everywhere welcome. One who attempted to overcome it was Nichiren (1222–82), another seminal figure in medieval Japanese Buddhism. He studied at Hiei, as Eisai and others had done. However, instead of repudiating Tendai, as they had, he found in the *Lotus* sutra the supreme all-embracing statement of Buddhist truth. Like Saichō he saw an intimate connection between his teachings and the state and believed that the purpose of his mission was to preserve Japan and make it the fountainhead of a dynamic revival of universal Buddhism.

It was symptomatic of the age, however, that whereas Saichō had seen other doctrines as lesser in value but still of use to some seekers, Nichiren denounced other sectarian teachings. He regarded Zen and Amidism in particular as heretical views that propagated error and half-truth and hence threatened to destroy Japan and damage Buddhism. Driven by doctrinal intolerance and a passionate sense of national identity, Nichiren struggled to save Japan from false doctrine and foreign invaders. In the process he proved to be the most militantly sectarian and divisive of the medieval evangelists. While his noisy intolerance created many enemies, however, the fire of his conviction won him equally fervent supporters. By the latter half of the thirteenth century he had an appreciable following. Then the Mongol invasions seemed to demonstrate his unique prescience and greatly enhanced his reputation. During the next two centuries Nichiren's Lotus sect flourished, becoming one of the major popular religious movements in Japan.

In the end Nichiren failed to establish a universal faith and, like Dōgen and Shinran, only added to the pluralism of medieval Japanese religion. In other ways, as well, his Lotus sect had basic similarities to Zen and Amidism. Like them his teaching required total personal commitment. Where Zen called for single-minded meditation and Amidism called for utter faith in Amida's grace, Nichiren called for complete trust in the *Lotus* sutra. He said,

> If you desire to attain Buddhahood immediately, lay down the banner of pride, cast away the club of resentment, and trust yourselves to the unique Truth. . . . Has not Buddha declared, "I alone am the protector and savior"? There is the power! Is it not taught that faith is the only entrance [to salvation]? There is the rope! . . . Devote yourself wholeheartedly to the "Adoration to the Lotus of the Perfect Truth," and utter it yourself as well as admonish others to do the same. Such is your task in this human life.[25]

Like Amidism and Zen, the Lotus sect thus placed the person of the practitioner at the center of his religion. Priests, temples, and religious practices were utilitarian adjuncts, and the crucial dialogue of religion bypassed them all. The

25. Tsunoda et al., pp. 222–23.

ultimate religious act was a private one of the individual, whether experienced as an act of faith or of introspection, whether in solitude or in communal service. In consequence of these doctrinal orientations, samurai and commoners of all sorts found religious fulfillment in the doctrines of Zen, Amidism, and the Lotus, and as the thirteenth century advanced, temples and monasteries sprang up all over the country.

There was one particular doctrinal element in Amidism that helped give temples a radically new social function as autonomous centers of local power. On the premise that special religious practices were counterproductive, Shinran rejected monastic customs, including celibacy. He and his successors encouraged Jōdo Shin priests to marry and lead normal private lives. In consequence priests of that sect did marry, did raise their own successors, and thus brought the common Japanese institutional pattern of patrilineal organization into the priesthood. This arrangement helped overcome recurrent problems of leadership succession and gave Jōdo Shin temples, later known as Ikkō temples, an especially solid organizational core. It served to "indigenize" temple leadership and break down the older ecclesiastic promotional pattern that had caused the talented and educated to drain away from rural monasteries. In due time other sects adopted the same custom, and as a result popular Buddhist doctrine gained a solid institutional base in a highly autonomous, self-perpetuating local leadership.

High-ranking clerics had to devise mechanisms to control these more self-sustaining local temples. Mostly they relied on religious constraints such as ordaining and defrocking priests, giving and withholding religious talismans and sacred texts, and asserting special doctrinal ties to the founders of the sect. During the late fifteenth century Rennyo (1415–99), the leader of the Ikkō sect's main temple, the Honganji in Kyoto, strengthened his position in a new way, namely, by issuing "pastoral letters" (o-fumi) in colloquial Japanese. These, he explained, would be comprehensible to all.[26] As never before, the content of religious faith as well as the

---

26. Stanley Weinstein, "Rennyo and the Shinshū Revival," in Hall and Toyoda, p. 347.

institutions that embodied it were to be common property shaping the lives of all who believed.

The proponents of Zen, Amidism, and the Lotus, together with some revitalized older sects, had accomplished in Japan a religious revolution with important secular ramifications. They had brought Buddhism to the public, giving the general populace several widely shared faiths and dotting the countryside with temples and temple towns large and small. They also had developed a new instrument of political action, a form of local sectarian organization in which hereditary local leaders could advance the material interests of their families, their temples, and even their congregations by relying upon the fervent support of a local population organized by the temple and united in its faith.

By the time of Rennyo both Ikkō and Lotus temples were actively engaged in politics. They were running affairs locally, maintaining armies to oppose rival authorities, and battling one another and other sects, including a rejuvenated Tendai at Mt. Hiei. During the era of *gekokujō*, temple-led forces were an important element in the national disorder. For example, in Kyoto there were about twenty-one Lotus temples, some of them surrounded by moats and earthen walls and supported by the neighborhood populace, for whom they were a refuge in time of battle. There were other Lotus temples in nearby cities such as Nara and Sakai. In the year 1532, Ikkō forces from near Kyoto attacked and captured a major Lotus temple in Sakai. In retaliation the Lotus temples in Kyoto mobilized, attracted allies, and launched an assault on the Ishiyama Honganji, a great fortified Ikkō bastion at Osaka. After an unsuccessful siege the combatants worked out a compromise, but in subsequent decades these and other religious groups continued to play a role in national politics.[27]

The great monasteries of classical Japan had also engaged in politics, but they had done so as aristocratic institutions. Armies of monks and mercenaries in Nara and Heian had used their numbers and their religious prestige to advance monastic interests. But their efforts neither depended upon the manpower of a faithful popular following nor ad-

27. Hayashiya, pp. 31–33.

vanced the interests of those whose land rents supported the monasteries. The political action of popular medieval Buddhist organizations was much more a politics of, by, and for the supporting congregation. It was a new and potentially revolutionary phenomenon in Japanese history.

The patterns of sectarian fragmentation and popularization so evident in medieval Buddhism also were apparent elsewhere in the medieval religious experience, most notably in Shugendō and Shintō. In the classical age, mountain ascetics (*yamabushi*) seem to have devoted themselves mainly to going or guiding others on pilgrimages up sacred mountains for the purpose of practicing ritual austerities. During the medieval age, however, they developed their own Shugendō headquarters, religious hierarchy, and standardized sectarian organization and procedures. They spread their practices widely among the people, and sometimes lived in temples as hereditary priestly families, administering to local followers and assisting pilgrims from afar. In the words of H. Byron Earhart,

> The *yamabushi* often was looked on as a healer, because his magico-religious connection with the sacred mountain gave him both the personal power and sacred techniques for curing sickness. . . . His magical power made the *yamabushi* well suited for exorcising persons possessed by animals or evil spirits.[28]

These practitioners of Shugendō made regular rounds of their parishes to recite protective formulas, distribute charms, and undertake to heal the ill. On occasion they performed funeral services, though that usually was a task of Buddhist priests. By the Muromachi period, these mountain ascetics had established bases of support among their local followers and become active sectarian rivals of Buddhist priests.

Shugendō, like sectarian Buddhism, thus contributed to the doctrinal pluralism and political fragmentation that characterized medieval Japan. Developments in medieval Shintō ultimately had the same effect even though some proponents

28. Earhart, p. 33.

of Shintō attempted, as did Nichiren, to overcome those trends by presenting their teachings as the focal point of a revitalized social cohesiveness. During the classical age Shintō priests had appropriated Buddhist customs and gradually developed an integrated body of practices known as Ryōbu Shintō. During the medieval period there was a significant movement to reverse this development and "purify" Shintō, thereby establishing it as a body of doctrine and practice that was purely Japanese, uncompromised by exogenous influences, and hence uniquely fitted to protect the nation and serve as its religion.

The elite national awareness implicit in this "purification" of Shintō—which we also noted in Nichiren's rhetoric—was fostered by renewed contact with China and then by the two Mongol invasions. The invaders were met by appeals to the gods and Buddhas as well as by appeal to arms. When fortuitous typhoons, subsequently celebrated as "divine winds" (*kamikaze*), helped crush the invading forces on both occasions, the gods, Buddhas, and their earthly representatives all gained merit as protectors of the country.

Subsequently the Kenmu Restoration gave rise to an outpouring of concern with the imperial institution as the center of the national heritage. One of the most vigorous proponents of the imperial cause was the Shintō scholar Kitabatake Chikafusa (1293–1354), an advisor to the Emperor Go-Daigo and an apologist for the anti-Ashikaga imperial line ensconced in the Yoshino mountains. He opened his major opus, *Jinnō shōtōki* [Records of the true imperial succession], which he composed in 1339, with this passage:

> Great Japan is the divine land. Its foundations were first laid by Kunitokotachi-no-mikoto and it has been ruled since time immemorial by the descendants of Amaterasu Ōmikami. This is true only of our country; there are no examples among foreign lands. It is for this reason that we call our land the divine land.[29]

29. H. Paul Varley, *Imperial Restoration in Medieval Japan* (New York: Columbia University Press, 1971), p. 36. Varley discusses Kitabatake on pp. 96–112.

Kitabatake then sought to establish criteria by which the legitimate holders of imperial authority could be established for all time. He did so by reinterpreting the entire genealogy of the imperial line so as to show that a self-correcting system of heavenly determinism was always at work, weeding out baneful imperial trends when they appeared and constantly steering the imperial title back into the hands of virtuous and able rulers, such as Go-Daigo. Thanks to that heavenly determinism, he argued, the destiny of Japan was assured so long as people abstained from meddling in the imperial succession and instead placed their trust in imperial rule.

Kitabatake then went on, in a spirit similar to that of Nichiren, to extol the special merit of Japan as compared to China, India, and other lands. His efforts did not bear fruit in terms of political consolidation, but they did help sustain interest in Shintō and strengthen its claims to a doctrinal life of its own. In succeeding decades that claim was further strengthened, most notably by proponents of the Yuiitsu Shintō school that took form in the fifteenth century. Because of primitive Shintō's signal lack of sophisticated thought, these proponents in fact borrowed heavily from continental traditions, but in the process of converting them to Shintō use, they worked out elaborate arguments demonstrative of Shintō universal significance and intellectual self-sufficiency. Their attempts at doctrinal purification, like that of Nichiren, also resulted in further sectarian fragmenting rather than religious consolidation. By the end of the Muromachi period, Shintō, like Buddhism, was characterized by the existence of hereditary sects based on supportive populations, a self-sustaining priesthood, and legitimizing bodies of doctrine.[30] Thus this effort to bring about religious unification, like that of Nichiren, eventuated not in unity but in more diversity of thought and organization.

Within the diversity of medieval thought there were nevertheless consistencies central to the value system of the age. At the heart was a pervasive belief that performance was

30. D. C. Holtom, *The National Faith of Japan* (London: Kegan Paul, Trench, Trubner & Co. Ltd., 1938), pp. 21–52, traces the history of Shintō briefly.

more important than formalities—whether in attaining enlightenment or salvation, establishing one's undying secular glory, preserving the nation, or rising to power. Performance, in turn, was grounded in one's own effort or, in the case of the popular faith sects, in the spiritual grace of a transcendent force (Amida or Lotus) that could manifest itself only through the individual's expression of faith. It was a set of core values sharply at odds with the classical ideal of propriety based on status and precedent.

Arts and letters: a new aesthetic unity

The medieval ideal of performance grounded in personal effort was manifested in the visual and performing arts, just as it was in the war tales and religious literature. It became in turn part of a new aesthetic ideal that eventually replaced the classical cult of beauty. Sometimes spoken of as a "Zen aesthetic," it was actually more cosmopolitan than that label suggests. Like classical higher culture, it merits notice for its intrinsic aesthetic worth, but more important here is the pattern of its articulation with society at large.

The central role of monks in this medieval aesthetic development cannot be ignored. They were freed from the unyielding hand of Heian tradition by the doctrinal pluralism of medieval religion and were sustained in their vitality by the new temples that enjoyed widespread popular support. Thus favored, they were instrumental in developing during the Muromachi period a new integrated cultural vision that accommodated much more human choice and movement than had the Heian cult of beauty. It was a vision rooted in a philosophical premise common to Buddhism, Taoism, and Confucianism. That premise was

> the principle of the fundamental unity of man, nature, and society and of political-ethical, religious, and artistic concerns.[31]

31. John M. Rosenfield, "The Unity of the Three Creeds," in Hall and Toyoda, p. 207. In his essay, Rosenfield is discussing a central theme in ink painting of the Muromachi period.

This principle of unity gave Muromachi higher culture an aesthetic universalism that countered the fragmenting tendency of medieval religious and political pluralism. Hence an internal coherence ran through Muromachi art, architecture, drama, music, and the tea ceremony. The principle of unity also permitted monks to engage in politics and trade, shogun to become hermits, and all and sundry to become aesthetes.

That new unifying cultural principle emerged only gradually as creative persons combined artistic elements derived from classical Japan, China, and the newly risen *bushi* to forge distinctive new patterns. We have already noted the samurai contribution of vigor, discipline, and willfulness as manifested in the war tales. From China came new religious influences, notably Zen, and also a renewed Confucian scholarship and new styles of art. From the classical age of Japan came the highly cultured aesthetic of the *kuge*. Out of the interaction of these influences in the particular nexus of medieval Japan arose that new unified vision of aesthetic perfection.

The *kuge* contribution was facilitated by Minamoto Yoritomo's decision to preserve aristocratic interests. That decision had the corollary effect of preserving in Kyoto, in attenuated form at least, most of the arts and letters of the classical age. The routines of court life continued to be followed. *Gagaku* music still was played. Poetry continued to be written and compiled. Diaries, memoirs, histories, and fictional accounts still were produced. One of the finest of those memoirs, *Towazugatari* [The confessions of Lady Nijō], was written in about 1307.[32] It evidenced the enduring influence of Lady Murasaki's *Tale of Genji* as well as the continuing style of aristocratic life in the old capital.

As the Heian period receded into the past, it became romanticized. In part it was a romantic view of the classical political order that inspired Go-Daigo to attempt his restoration in 1334. The *kuge* tendency to contrast the ugly present with a glorious past was most poignantly evinced in the *Tsurezuregusa* [Essays in idleness], a collection of epigrammatic essays written in about 1330 by the court official, poet, monk, and

32. Karen Brazell, trans., *The Confessions of Lady Nijō* (New York: Anchor Press, Doubleday, 1973).

aesthete Yoshida Kenkō. Kenkō sought to record all the facets of what he saw as a dying civility, and against those he juxtaposed the many instances of crassness that seemed to mark the decadent today and foreshadow the dreadful tomorrow. He wrote,

> A familiarity with orthodox scholarship, the ability to compose poetry and prose in Chinese, a knowledge of Japanese poetry and music are all desirable, and if a man can serve as a model to others in matters of precedent and court ceremony, he is truly impressive. . . . Poems of recent times occasionally seem to contain an aptly turned line or two, but I wonder why one never senses in them as in the old poetry overtones going beyond the words.[33]

Kenkō delights one with the diversity of his interests, the refinement of his taste, and the incisiveness of his judgements. Doubtless, too, he appeals to the disgruntled oldster in everyone.

The *kuge*, however, did much more than pine for a dead past. From the time of Yoritomo some aristocrats cooperated with military leaders, and as a group they furnished a behavioral model for warriors who often were untutored ruffians from the countryside and ill prepared to create arts and letters of their own. Through association with courtiers, samurai were able to exploit the traditions of the classical age. And much as Yamato aristocrats had utilized Chinese influences to form a higher culture uniquely their own, the new rulers infused classical traditions with their own spirit to create new cultural monuments. The result is evident in the war tales themselves insofar as the very act of writing them down depended on mastery of the written language and a belief that the stories could better be transmitted in writing than in telling. The result of this *kuge-bushi* linking was not a bland compromise, however. The rough edges of samurai conduct were smoothed and the technical skills of the nobility were perpetuated and even disseminated to a larger

33. Donald Keene, trans., *Essays in Idleness: The Tsurezuregusa of Kenkō* (New York: Columbia University Press, 1967), pp. 4, 13.

sector of the populace. But the samurai commitment to accomplishment without regard for the dictates of hallowed custom prevailed, and it was manifested not only in the war tales but in the plastic arts, music, and the tea ceremony.

One of the most authentic visual representations of the medieval ethos was the sculpture of the Zen monk, Unkei (fl. 1200–10), "whose name sounds in Japanese ears as the name of Michelangelo sounds in our own." [34] Unkei was the outstanding artist in his discipline. He formed vigorously lifelike figures that stand in sharp contrast to the idealized, normative Buddhistic forms of Nara-Heian sculpture and instead fairly speak to the observer of humble dignity, integrity, and self-discipline. The basic technique of Unkei's craft was a major departure. Abandoning the customary practice of carving out logs and attaching projecting limbs to them, he utilized a rare technique in which sculptors and apprentices working as a team sculpted to shape and fitted together in hidden ways large numbers of small pieces of wood. By this procedure they gave themselves the plastic freedom necessary to present dynamic, lifelike figures of superb design. The technique enabled Unkei to say what he wanted, namely, that the individual he was representing was significant for his own self, for the qualities and attainments that sprang from within and were particular to him even while universal in implication.

The notion that individuals were significant in themselves and not simply as embodiments of customary virtues was also found in painting. There secular figures, both the famous and not-so-famous, were portrayed in somber and stately, yet realistic fashion. More grandly the active individual, his life, and his times were celebrated in paintings of the *Yamato-e* style, which recounted war tales, Buddhist didactic tales, travelogues, and stories of adventure. These experiences could be accessible to anyone who pursued them with sufficient resolve. They were a world apart from the cloistered, elegant realm of Fujiwara Michinaga, whose imputed glory prompted comparison with Shōtoku and Kūkai and whose wisdom and understanding were accessible only to the fortunate few born to the Heian elect.

34. Langdon Warner, *The Enduring Art of Japan* (New York: Grove Press, 1958), p. 45.

The medieval principle of "the fundamental unity of man, nature, and society and of political-ethical, religious, and artistic concerns" permeated the arts of the Muromachi period. The medieval religious flowering promoted a prodigious amount of temple construction. Chinese and Japanese architectural styles mingled in eclectic variety, and religious and secular purposes became thoroughly entwined. The architectural developments of the age turned the Muromachi *bushi* residence into an appropriate setting for experiencing the principle of artistic unity, making it fit for such activities as religious meditation, tea ceremony, poetry parties, and banquets. Sedge mats (*tatami*), which had been limited to sleeping areas of classical *kuge* residences, were spread over the board floors to make them more comfortable for the prolonged sitting of both tea ceremony and meditation. Alcoves (*tokonoma*) were developed for the display of treasured art works, including paintings in the ink-line (*sumi-e*) style. *Sumi-e*, which sometimes used only ink tones but more often included some color, was brought to new heights of sophistication by such fifteenth-century Zen monks as Shūbun (1414–65) and Sesshū (1420–1506). They used it effectively to convey the Zen precept of enlightenment through intuitive apperception of the Buddha nature.

The new residences utilized sliding doors (*fusuma*) that could be decorated with large murals. Late in the medieval period the Kanō school of painters combined *sumi-e* with the colorful tradition of *Yamato-e* to form a new and lively artistic style of great power and subtlety that was appropriate to the large expanses of the sliding doors. Those sliding doors made possible the conversion of small rooms to large, facilitating gatherings of various sizes. They also permitted the easy opening of chambers to the outdoors. New styles of small, enclosed gardens, some consisting only of sand and stone, were integrated with buildings by way of corridors, windows, and enclosing walls, thus promoting an habitual intimacy of man and nature.

Another exciting new element in medieval higher culture was the Nō drama. Older traditions of religious theatre and folk dance had acquired considerable popularity by the early Muromachi period, drawing crowds in Kyoto that included both commoners and members of higher officialdom. During the fourteenth and early fifteenth centuries the playwrights Kan'ami (1333–84) and his son Zeami (1363–1444) built upon that popular tradition. They wrote a large number of librettos, prepared theoretical treatises on the principles and procedures of the Nō drama, and converted it into a highly sophisticated dramatic medium that embodied the integrated ideals of Muromachi higher culture. The creative vitality that distinguished war tales and medieval religion was shared by Nō librettists. Their art, in Donald Keene's words, was noteworthy for

> the extraordinary freedom permitted the dramatist in both the language and the structure of the plays. Surely no other theatre has disregarded so completely the normal considerations of time and space.[35]

In content as well as form, Nō was adventurous. It plumbed the depths of personal experience, examining madness, religious ecstasy, compassion, hatred, and the calm of redemption. It also expressed the liberating ideal of self-derived insight as clearly as did any Buddhist tract. In one of his most dramatic dialogues Kan'ami makes a tragically demented old woman, the former court beauty, Ono no Komachi, the vehicle of transcendent insight in a religious debate with monks. The monks find her sitting on a religious figure and criticize her for behaving irreverently. She retorts defiantly and the dialogue is on:

Komachi: It [the religious figure] was on the ground already. . . .

First Priest: Just the same it was an act of discord.

Komachi: "Even from discord salvation springs."

---

35. Donald Keene, ed., *20 Plays of the Nō Theatre* (New York: Columbia University Press, 1970), p. 8. Another series of Nō plays in translation is Arthur Waley's *The Nō Plays of Japan* (New York: Grove Press, 1957).

Second Priest:	From the evil of [the wicked disciple] Daiba
Komachi:	Or the love of [the goddess of mercy] Kannon.
First Priest:	From the folly of [the witless disciple] Handoku
Komachi:	Or the wisdom of [the god of wisdom] Monju.
First Priest:	What we call evil
Komachi:	Is also good.
First Priest:	Illusion
Komachi:	Is Salvation.
Second Priest:	"Salvation
Komachi:	Cannot be watered like trees."
First Priest:	"The brightest mirror
Komachi:	Is not on the wall."[36]

Properly humbled by her mastery of Buddhist dialectics, the monks are reminded that even the most wretched can attain Buddhahood and that the outward appearance is not the inner reality. Religious insight derives from within, and from a madwoman as surely as from a man of the cloth. It is expressed directly, willfully, and by one whose worth is individual and demonstrable in verbal combat. Nō thus shared the practitioner-centered values of other medieval arts and letters, values dramatically at odds with those found in Heian thought.

In its music, Nō gave voice to the medieval ideals of simplicity, discipline, and experiential unity. The complex polyphony and elaborate instrumentation of *gagaku* had been replaced by a highly disciplined and austere musical style. Actors and chorus shared the chanting of the Nō text and three or four instruments provided musical support and emphasis. The singing of librettos derived from popular musical forms and Buddhist chanting techniques that were spare in melodic style and solemn in tone. Accompaniment was by a

36. Donald Keene, ed., *Anthology of Japanese Literature* (New York: Grove Press, 1955), p. 267. Another translation is in Waley, *The Nō Plays of Japan*, pp. 154–55.

single flute played forcefully and supported by two or three drums. There was no waste motion, no waste sound, only the essentials, and they were presented with incomparable dignity.

In the Nō drama, medieval music was a culmination of earlier themes, but it was a culmination that followed decades of development. In other ways medieval music continued to change, as did the values evident in the war tales, and it was noteworthy as a harbinger of glories yet to come. The *biwa* music that accompanied raconteurs of war tales and Buddhist tales of mystery and grace later evolved into the popular musical tradition of the samisen, a long-necked lute. And the story-telling itself evolved into the librettos of the seventeenth-century kabuki drama. The flute music of wandering medieval beggar priests anticipated the introspective music of the *shakuhachi*, a large bamboo flute. In Malm's words,

> the Muromachi period was a time of musical potential; a material and psychological build up for a flood of activities that was soon to burst upon the artistic world in a torrent of color and sound.[37]

In other ways, too, medieval higher culture foreshadowed early modern Japan. The Kanō school of artists gave rise to greater artistic triumphs. The Nō contributed to the development of kabuki. Landscape architecture flourished in later centuries. Moreover, the basic principle of the unity of man, nature, and society was later elaborated in thought and applied to social practice with unprecedented pervasiveness.

On balance, however, it is the fruitions, the successful departures from Heian, the articulating and legitimizing of ideals of willfulness and performance, and the forming of new integrated cultural statements, that hold our attention. By the end of the fifteenth century, medieval Japanese had forged a brilliant new higher culture. Its core elements even today remain central to the global image of Japan's traditional civilization. At its highest level of philosophical insight that

37. Malm, p. 33.

culture aspired to realize direct human apprehension of existence by utilizing fully the senses of taste, smell, sight, sound, and touch. The ideal of a universal human capacity for total intuitive apprehension of being was expressed in the famous opening lines of the *Heike monogatari*.

> In the sound of the bell of the Gion Temple echoes the impermanence of all things. The pale hue of the flowers of the teak-tree show[s] the truth that they who prosper must fall. The proud ones do not last long, but vanish like a spring-night's dream. And the mighty ones too will perish in the end, like dust before the wind.[38]

One can know the truth of being through one's ears, through one's eyes, through one's very dreams. Even wind-blown dust through its touch upon the skin, its odor in the nose, its taste in the throat emphasizes the evanescence of life. And these senses that illuminate the nature of being are an endowment of all humanity; they are not the possession solely of an aristocratic few.

The ideals of total sensory engagement and its accessibility to all were most perfectly realized in the tea ceremony. Like *sumi-e* or Nō, it could be both an aesthetic and a religious experience. In its simple fashion—friends sitting amiably and quietly in a small, sparely decorated room while the master heated the water and mixed and served the tea—it combined the art and architectural developments of the day with principles of cuisine and meditation to form a unique experience of quietude and beauty. Seeing the tea service, hearing the water boil, holding the cup, smelling and tasting the tea, engaged all the senses and required the most intense self-discipline and refinement. It was, one might say, the ultimate expression of the medieval cultural ideal of aesthetic unity.

In examining the fruitions of medieval literature, plastic arts, drama, and tea ceremony, we have seen how the emergent samurai class repudiated the aesthetic and intellectual norms of the Heian elite. They proclaimed in their stead that

---

38. Donald Keene, *Japanese Literature* (New York: Grove Press, 1955), p. 78.

knowledge was accessible to all of sufficient vigor, regardless of his or her station in life. In consequence any person had the right to act, if he or she—whether Hōjō Masako, Lady Nijō, or Ono no Komachi—chose. And a person of sufficient resolve could participate in the drama of history not merely as a passive element in the background—not merely as a peasant whose production feeds his betters or a dutiful spear-carrier whose obedient weapon sustains the ruling elite—but as an active participant. He could be guided by his own judgment, pursue his own goals even in defiance of established norms and legitimate authority, and in the end be judged by his accomplishments and by the strength of character he or she has displayed.

Having said this, we are brought again to the initial paradox of a brilliant higher culture in a context of political disorder. How could arts and letters have acquired such aesthetic excellence, and how could they have survived the harrowing disorder of the day? After all, the informing political vision of the age could have been limited to the crude egoism of a Minamoto Yoshinaka or the angry calculation of a Yamana Sōzen. And the accomplishments could have been destroyed in a rage of unbridled nihilism. But somehow the desperateness of struggle and the destruction of war were offset by moments of reflection and places of tranquility sufficient to link this newly released social energy with ethical and aesthetic considerations that enabled it to achieve sophisticated expression in a whole range of highly demanding artistic arenas.

We have hinted at the answer to this paradox in the references to new forms of Buddhism, to the commoners' contributions to Nō, and to the varieties of medieval music. In essence, changes in the city of Kyoto, in the cultural interests of samurai, and in the character of the commoner class served to increase greatly the numbers of those patronizing arts and letters, both as creators and as consumers. These patrons maintained many islands of tranquility in the sea of political turmoil that was Muromachi Japan, and in those islands the creative arts flourished. In contrast to the classical age, higher culture was not dependent on the survival of one city or a handful of aristocrats. Places of nurture and refuge could be found for cultural treasures and their creators, and despite fearful destruction of artifacts, artistic creativity survived the disorder of the day.

At the heart of it all, Heian the imperial city of classical Japan gave way to medieval Kyoto, a religious center studded with wealthy temples of the new Buddhist sects that became powerful patrons of the arts. In Kyoto, moreover, there developed an important population of wealthy merchants whose resources supported higher cultural activities. Feudal lords also fostered the arts, and some, such as the shogun Ashikaga Yoshimitsu, supported talented people with minimal regard for their social origins. Kan'ami of the Nō, for example, was a commoner who enjoyed Yoshimitsu's favor. Many other commoners with intellectual, artistic, poetic, musical, or acting talents won samurai or noble patronage, often rising by way of a position in the priesthood. Nor was the samurai contribution to higher culture limited to Kyoto. They also exerted great effort to develop the arts in their own provincial headquarters towns, sometimes even aping the customs and duplicating the temples and shrines of Kyoto.[39]

Elsewhere in the provinces, as well, heads of temples, shrines, and successful merchant houses enhanced their prestige by hiring craftsmen, building libraries, tea houses, and gardens, and cultivating the tastes of their associates and subordinates. Traveling storytellers, secular and religious, contributed to the diffusion of higher culture. These jongleurs used music, puppets, and chanting to tell tales of Buddhist mystery and war tales such as *Gikeiki*, and in so doing they gave their audiences vicarious experiences far removed from the tedium of daily life. In the words of Barbara Ruch, those jongleurs "altered the course of Japan's literary history," giving rise to Japan's first "national literature," meaning "a certain core of literary works the content of which is well known and held dear by the majority of people across all class and professional lines, a literature that is a reflection of a national outlook."[40]

The glories of medieval higher culture survived the disorder of the day because they embodied a view of life that

39. Hayashiya, p. 24.

40. Barbara Ruch, "Medieval Jongleurs and the Making of a National Literature," in Hall and Toyoda, pp. 286, 291.

was widely attractive. Those cultural monuments therefore not only enjoyed the patronage of a dispersed elite but also were nurtured and sustained by a broad, if only semiarticulate, base in society. The cultural creativity of the rapidly expanding medieval elite is best viewed as but the tip of an iceberg of cultural activity. It was fostered even more than it was injured by the disorder of the day because that very disorder smashed the grip of custom, allowed noble, samurai, cleric, and commoner to commingle, and made cultural inventiveness and dissemination possible. Even more basically, the creativity was encouraged by the very elemental factors that gave rise to political disorder itself; namely, the extraordinary and pervasive growth and change that Japanese society was experiencing throughout the medieval period.

SOCIAL CHANGE: THE EARLY PHASE OF A METAMORPHOSIS

In a manner of speaking, medieval Japan was characterized by a condition of societal *laissez faire* that released creative and productive powers throughout the whole population. The creativity of the central elite was only part of an all-pervading experience that was remaking the face of Japan and propelling it into the future at an unprecedented rate. The great cultural gulf that had separated classical patrician and pleb was being closed, and Japan was acquiring some of the cultural solidarity and social infrastructure characteristic of nationhood.

This process was to continue into the twentieth century, but it was not a simple linear development. As will be noted later, the passage from medieval to early modern Japan involved important discontinuities. Nevertheless one can see most aspects of this overall nation-building process developing during the medieval period. Considering its commercial aspects, medieval development involved several things: a substantial increase in agricultural production; the emergence throughout the country of consumer demands that could not be satisfied locally; the development of widespread domestic trade and a substantial overseas trade; the corollary development of money use; the growth of a vast number of markets and market towns; and, as all this implies, the appearance of an appreciable and widespread population of independent artisans and merchants.

These are the main elements of commercial development, but the social change of medieval Japan also had other major dimensions. One was the establishment of a popular Buddhism that was, as mentioned earlier, of both religious and secular importance. Another was the development of mass military techniques and activity. A notable result of these commercial, religious, and military changes was the emergence of many expressions of popular political participation. A more basic area of social change was the rapid growth of total production and aggregate population. And a corollary to those changes was growth in the diversity and complexity of both the populace and its activities. Together, these changes amounted to the first stage of a metamorphosis. By the sixteenth century they had launched Japan well on the way to a new age.

Economic trends

Earlier we noted how the spread of popular sectarian Buddhism gave rise to patterns of autonomous local temple organization that had important political consequences. The spread of Buddhism also had economic implications and was surely an essential element in the economic development of medieval Japan. Reminiscent of its role in the Taika Reform, Buddhism met a fundamental need for expanded literacy. The priests themselves and many samurai had to be able to read to handle their duties. Increasingly, merchants and village leaders also needed literary skills to keep ledgers, manage household and business affairs, and handle village and town matters. The temples of popular Buddhism were a major source of basic education in mathematics and language as well as religion and ethics. They gave commoners a window on the world, and commercial development gave them reason to use what they learned there.

Buddhist monks played one other important but less fundamental role in economic development. One facet of that development was a renewal late in the twelfth century of contact with China. That contact involved substantial trade. And because Zen monks had studied in China, knew the country and its language, and had useful connections there, they participated actively as both intermediaries and beneficiaries in the trade. This overseas commerce had domestic ramifications. It generated a need for more money, provided a market for Japanese products such as swords, and opened up a source for luxury goods such as the brocades sought by newly risen *bushi*.

This very phenomenon of newly risen *bushi* itself contributed mightily to economic development. When the Kamakura *bakufu* deployed constables, land stewards, and ordinary *gokenin* across the country, it unwittingly created a widely distributed consumer class that was eager to reap the benefits of power. Much as widespread samurai interest in religion helped spread Buddhism, their interest in fineries created a market and fostered the use of coins. Then during the fourteenth and fifteenth centuries the rise of local barons accelerated commercial development in the hinterland. It increased the power of regional rulers, whose ambitions and pretensions rose commensurately. As decades passed, they and their followers lived better lives in larger, more elegant residences, surrounded by more commodities and their fabricators. They were entertained in ever more varied and expensive ways by artists, dancers, musicians, raconteurs, Nō troupes, and tea masters. Their pursuit of success led to a quest for wisdom, the support of temples, and the accumulation of scholars, books, and the learning they presumably brought. This whole process spread consumer demand widely through the country and fostered the use of money as a medium of exchange.

To accommodate the growing demand in the provinces, the numbers of itinerant merchants grew, thus gradually giving rise to a large number of trading centers. Markets initially met periodically, once, twice, or three times a month. As demand grew, they opened more frequently and for longer periods. Eventually entrepreneurial artisans began to settle at favorable locations, and the market sites turned into permanent trading communities.

These trading communities were only one form of urbanization. The spread of popular Buddhism was fostering the growth of more and more temple towns. Similarly the emergence of regional barons was leading to the development of settlements around fortified headquarters, forerunners of the later castle towns. The increase in transportation needs that accompanied all this social activity resulted in the creation of port and highway towns. To be specific, during the late medieval period Uji-Yamada, a town that developed around the imperial shrines of Ise, and the temple town of Tennōji near Osaka each had a population of over thirty thousand. Several other temple towns with ten to fifteen thousand inhabitants were scattered about central Japan, and ten to twenty towns of several thousand each developed at fortified temples of the Ikkō sect. Among port and highway towns, the most notable were Sakai, the gateway to Kyoto, with some thirty thousand and Onomichi to the west with five thousand. Smaller ports were scattered all along the coastline of Japan. By the 1570s, castle towns included large ones such as the Uesugi headquarters (in Echigo on the coast of the Japan Sea), with thirty thousand inhabitants, and a number of others in the five-to-ten-thousand range.

Of these several urban forms, the castle towns were the most complex. To quote Yazaki Takeo's description of the sixteenth-century town at Hachigata castle in northern Musashi in the Kantō,

> The main castle fronted on a river bank, the other sides being protected by moats and embankments. Around the castle were the dwellings of samurai, merchants, and craftsmen (especially those engaged in arms production), and peasants. The inner sector of the town was filled with inns, markets, and shops, while on the edges of the town were temples and shrines. Thus did such a castle town exhibit a more complicated structure embracing the multiple functions of [local rule], market economy, travelers' facilities and religious institutions.[41]

41. Yazaki, p. 104.

By the late Muromachi period the spatial demographic pattern that had perpetuated a gulf between classical aristocrat and commoner had been destroyed. The gulf was being filled by local warriors, clerics, village leaders, and the members of a burgeoning commercial class. Not surprisingly, the growth of a commercial class and of population centers in which they could pursue their trades was accompanied by the growth of commercial organizations. During the thirteenth century, entrepreneurial craftsmen dealing in goods such as vegetable oil, silk, salt, dyes, dried fish, iron utensils, wood, and lumber had developed guilds or *za* under official patronage to protect themselves from undue taxation and other business hazards.[42] In the course of the next two centuries the functions of craft production and merchandising gradually were separated and merchants and artisans became distinct social groups. This role differentiation occurred during centuries when entrepreneurs had to cope with the exigencies of civil disorder, however, and it did not lead to a sharp social separation. Members of both groups developed ever-closer ties to effective patrons such as feudal lords, temples, or leaders in Kyoto, with skilled artisans and successful merchants working together for material advantage. When regular patrons failed to protect, as they did increasingly after 1467, some merchants and craft groups worked out communal defense and management arrangements of their own, most notably in the port town of Sakai.

This widespread commercial growth depended, of course, on the availability of an adequate medium of exchange. Although barter continued to account for a great deal of the trade, especially local transactions, money was essential to an ever-larger proportion of the whole. This money was obtained during the Ashikaga heyday by imports of currency from China that amounted to hundreds of millions of coins. The demand for coins was even sufficient by the fifteenth century to support domestic counterfeiting operations. By then the participants in this monetized trade had

42. Yazaki, p. 79. For an example of this medieval economic development, see the concise essay on "Sakai, From Shōen to Port City," by V. Dixon Morris, in Hall and Toyoda, pp. 145–58.

spread far beyond the *bushi* elite and had come to include people in most strata of the general population, especially in central Japan. Peasants, for example, were selling some produce for cash and paying some taxes and rents with the receipts, and market prices had become a factor determining the level of rent payments.[43]

The sharp growth of domestic economic activity was paralleled by an increased role of economics in Japanese foreign relations. During the classical age the most persistent form of foreign relations had been frontier relations with the Ezo, the arboreal occupants of northeastern Japan. By the ninth century they had been driven back to the northern end of Honshū, but the pacification there remained incomplete. During the medieval period samurai leaders in northern Honshū attempted to govern the area and also established some frontier settlements and penal colonies on southern Hokkaidō. However, the settlers repeatedly clashed with residents of the island, and the latter's resistance was sufficient to stall completely the northward advance of the frontier, so that Japan ceased to expand territorially. Instead, spatial growth assumed a new character, involving the beginnings of commercial settlement in southeast Asia.

Japanese continental trade during the Muromachi period consisted of an official China trade carried on by authorities in Kyoto and also a substantial private trade carried on by regional barons, temples, and enterprising merchants. Mostly the private traders were content to engage in peaceful commerce wherever they could. At times they were unable to do so satisfactorily, however, especially during the fourteenth century, when all of eastern Asia was in political turmoil. At those times some were not averse to drawing their swords and indulging in rampant piracy, plundering warehouses, taking slaves, and terrorizing the coasts of Korea and China. From the early fifteenth century on, political affairs stabilized in east Asia. Piracy declined, trade expanded, and the Japanese participants extended their commercial activities far beyond Korea and China, well down into the kingdoms and islands of southeast Asia.

---

43. See, for example, the document in Lu, vol. 1, p. 159.

Some of this trade was carried on by people whose regular livelihoods had been disrupted by civil strife. From time to time political turmoil even led groups to flee Japan permanently. In an earlier age such groups might have headed northeastward to uncultivated land. But with Honshū settled and Hokkaidō effectively closed to settlement, they had to go elsewhere. Neither Korea nor China had accessible lands available for occupancy, and so most Japanese refugees, emigrants, and adventurers settled in "Japan towns" scattered across southeast Asia. By the latter part of the sixteenth century there were several such settlements in the area. They were well situated, it appeared, to serve as effective intermediaries in a growing net of long-term east Asian trade relations. The economic development that was changing the character of domestic society thus seemed also to be changing the character of Japan's relationship to much of Asia.

Military trends

Change in the medieval economy was paralleled by change in medieval military affairs. There is a wealth of evidence concerning those affairs, but it is mostly in the form of anecdotal war stories and is difficult to evaluate. The relevant generalizations that one can make seem to be these.

The samurai armies of the Taira-Minamoto age were centered upon mounted horsemen. They enjoyed great mobility, and the battles of the heroic age ranged from northern Honshū to Kyūshū, with commanders such as Yoshitsune leading their flying squadrons of a few scores or hundreds of cavalry long distances in dramatic pursuits, escapes, and flanking movements. Unmounted forces of pikemen added to the numbers, and in a few engagements during the 1180s large armies of tens of thousands were assembled. These functioned rather like the large monastic armies that Mt. Hiei and other monasteries used in their political activity in and around Heian, and they do not appear to have remained under arms for long periods of time.

By the fourteenth century, warfare was changing, probably because the politics of war had changed. The habitual object of combat was to expand one's domain at the expense

of one's neighbor, not to lead a flying column to Kyoto to co-
erce the court or conversely hundreds of miles into the hinterland to suppress a rampaging warrior-bandit. In this new
situation, larger, less impressively equipped armies of foot
soldiers could handle both offensive and defensive operations, even though they could move only short distances. Because protection of one's established position had become a
key purpose of warfare, techniques of defense also acquired
an unprecedented value among the *bushi*. During the decades after Go-Daigo's ill-fated restoration of 1334, when one
imperial court was lodged in the Yoshino mountains and another in Kyoto, *bushi* developed primitive techniques of hill-
top castle defense, relying on terrain features and supple-
mental barriers of brushwood and stakes. As generations
passed, more elaborate masonry castles were erected. By the
mid-sixteenth century they were developing into major bas-
tions surrounded by moats, bounded by the walled residences of vassals, and overlooking broad agricultural basins
whose production sustained the castle-town population.

During the last decades of the sixteenth century, Europeans introduced firearms, both muskets and cannon, to
Japan. Their advent had two consequences. First, the cannon
gave impetus to more elaborate castle building, thus escalating a trend that was already underway and helping determine the size and shape of the massive castles of early-modern Japan. Second, the muskets proved to be superior field
weapons and determined the outcome of certain battles.
They thus helped to sort out the winners and losers, bringing
victory to those who had access to the weapons and skill in
deploying them. In short, the introduction of firearms did
not radically alter larger political and military trends but
rather fitted into those trends and served to accelerate them.

By the end of the medieval period, Japan had many
more men bearing arms than in Yoritomo's day. The country
was dotted with a large number of standing armies based on
formidable castles and fortified temples, villages, and towns.
Those armies could be reinforced rapidly with peasant or
townsman conscripts who would serve as pikemen and service personnel, enabling feudal lords and religious commu-

nities to field large armies on short notice. Where Taira and Minamoto had ordinarily fielded hundreds or thousands of combatants, late-medieval armies commonly numbered tens of thousands. In the 1460s Ōuchi from western Japan reportedly deployed twenty thousand, Hosokawa of central Japan sixty thousand and Yamana thirty thousand.[44] After the Ōnin war, battles involving thousands occurred periodically, some forces fighting for feudal lords, others for religious organizations. By the late sixteenth century, armies of tens of thousands were again marching as great lords struggled for national hegemony. Perhaps as many as two or three hundred thousand were engaged in some of the decisive battles and campaigns, and the Japanese armies that invaded Korea in the 1590s were of that magnitude.[45]

The proliferation of armies reflected the fragmentation of the polity and the diffusion of power widely through the populace. Moreover it perpetuated that condition because the size and character of those armies weakened their effectiveness as anything more than local forces, thereby making the task of national reconsolidation all the more difficult.

This evolution from the relatively small twelfth-century armies of a few thousand swordsmen to large sixteenth-century armies of tens of thousands of pikemen had political implications for the masses that resembled the implications of popular Buddhism and economic development. These trends all encouraged commoners to participate in larger social affairs by drawing them into a broader network of activities. They made them more knowledgeable about the world, involved them economically and religiously with more people, and subjected them to military participation. Equally important, these trends created local structures through which an ambitious commoner could act. He could become an active figure in the local religious community and then rise through the clerical order or use the local faithful as a secular power base. He could seize economic opportunities to increase his wealth and influence. Or he could master military techniques

44. Sansom, *Japan 1334–1615*, pp. 221, 223.
45. Ibid., pp. 233ff, 276ff, 305ff, 352ff.

and through skill on the battlefield create his own band of followers and exploit the political disorder of the day to rise in the world.

On the other hand, of course, the commoner could be killed in battle or have his lands and home ravaged by a marauding army. He could lose his livelihood to a usurer, or he could become the dupe of a religious charlatan. Whether for good or ill, however, compared to his counterpart in the classical age, he found it much harder to lead his own life untouched by the actions of the high-born. With the spread of Buddhism and related learning, and the proliferation of towns, commerce, and political activity, patrician and pleb were commingling as never before. The turmoil and opportunity of the one had become to a considerable extent the turmoil and opportunity of the other. In cultural, experiential, and structural terms, the population of late-medieval Japan was becoming an integrated whole. Important characteristics of nationhood had made their appearance in society.

Trends in gross productivity and population

This overview of social change has added new complications to our picture of late medieval Japan. To the seeming contradiction between a brilliant higher culture and a disorderly polity one must add the apparent coexistence of a massive increase in the scope and frequency of warfare and a booming, thriving economy and society in which more and more people were better and better off. Although the coexistence of these phenomena may be seen as a problem, it should not be assumed that war by its nature either promotes or discourages social growth and well-being. Rather, if one assumes that a society can have either, neither, or both warfare and a generally higher standard of living, then the question is why medieval Japan seemed to have both whereas, for example, seventeenth-century Japan had only the latter.

It was suggested earlier that medieval higher culture flourished because it was rooted in a much broader social base, supported much more widely than the arts and letters of classical Japan, and therefore better protected against the disorder of the time. To explain the latter conundrum of war and social well-being also requires us to look beyond the immediate issue to the larger context. To suggest an explanation concisely, it appears that the basic expansion in medieval Japan's population and productivity was so great that it could support both intensified warfare and a generally higher standard of living. Moreover, in contrast to the situation in the seventeenth century, the particular pattern of political change that characterized the age worked to encourage both war and boom rather than merely the one or the other.

This explanation is far from definitive, however, because information about the late-medieval human condition is replete with uncertainties and inconsistencies. For example, the Ōnin war unquestionably ruined Kyoto, and the condition of the city was probably precarious for many years thereafter. Yet it eventually revived, and by the 1560s life there was comfortable and the city thriving. Similarly, there are endless reports of armies marauding, villages being ravaged, peasants rioting, and religious groups warring. But even during the century of warfare after 1467 there is also evidence of continuing vigorous social and economic growth.

Doubtless a basic factor in this situation was the long-term increase in agricultural output experienced by medieval Japan. The elements of that increase were not unusual; indeed most of them were in line with policies the imperial government had been promoting from at least the early classical period, such as use of better tools and crops, opening of more land, and improvement of irrigation techniques. Some of these earlier efforts had only limited effects prior to the medieval age. Then the growth of towns, commercial connections, and consequent marketing opportunities prompted farmers to attempt new techniques of tillage, in the process raising gross agricultural output markedly. This agricultural expansion involved the opening of more land to tillage, the extension of irrigated acreage, the use of more fertilizer, the diversification of crops, development of double-cropping, the improvement of tools, and greater use of draft animals. To cite specific factors, scythes, picks, rakes, and winnowing machines came into use, water wheels became more popular, and more varieties of natural fertilizer were used. The cultivation of grapes and oranges began, and barley and tea, which previously had been cultivated only in a limited way, became major crops. These changes increased substantially the productivity of hillsides and nonirrigable uplands and allowed greater double-cropping. Moreover, Champa rice, which ripened more quickly and was more hardy than older varieties, was introduced from southeast Asia. Its use increased the reliability of harvests and permitted rice cultivation farther northward.

Such a notable increase in production permitted a dramatic rise in population. The aggregate number of Japanese seems to have grown from some five million in the eleventh century to nearly ten million by about A.D. 1300 and some eighteen million by about 1600. The growth in total productivity was enough, then, to raise the standard of living of the many who moved up to clerical, commercial, and warrior styles of life while supporting a major increase in total population. This suggests that the social and economic costs of increased warfare were not coming, at the expense of other needs, from a fixed quantity of human capability and output. Rather they were coming from a growing quantity of goods and services, leaving enough untouched to permit substantial social development of other sorts.

Does this mean that medieval Japanese society would have grown even faster had there been no disorder and warfare? Probably not. It is probable that the increase in production was inseparable from armed conflict because two of the basic factors fostering greater production were the very factors that promoted warfare. First, the diffusion of power, commonly called the process of political decentralization, not only fostered warfare but also spurred agricultural output. As previously noted, it took more and more power out of the hands of shogun, *shōen* owner, and *shugo*, and deposited that power in the hands of rural warriors, village leaders, local clerics, local entrepreneurs, and even organized village, town, and religious communities. People of peasant origins and even practicing agriculturalists were acquiring political power. They were more directly dependent on local political support, more conscious of their need for local production, and more disposed to encourage it as best they could than were classical or early medieval rulers. They devoted more effort to improving local trade, encouraging maximum exploitation of the land, and ensuring that crops be properly harvested and stored. Being closer to the source of production and more familiar with it, they were better able than earlier rulers to see that their efforts bore fruit, and better able to turn them to political use.

Similarly the spread of social, economic, and political knowledge and capabilities among the masses, which was essential to the diffusion of power and which contributed to the spread of political disorder, also gave people in general greater technical know-how and greater resilience. It thereby enabled towns and villages to rebuild themselves more rapidly following military devastation. To cite a prominent example, merchants played a key role in the recovery and administration of Kyoto after the Ōnin war, performing a function that the impoverished nobility, powerless *bakufu*, and indifferent barons no longer could or would play. In the absence of merchant knowledge and wealth, Kyoto's recovery would have been much less rapid and complete.

In short, although the sum total of human suffering in late medieval Japan seems to have exceeded substantially that of the waning years of the classical age, the sum total of human capacity to overcome that suffering seems to have increased even more substantially. As the evidence of a booming, thriving society suggests, despite the turmoil and agony, the general quality of life improved rather than deteriorated.

THE LEGACY OF AN AGE

At its peak, medieval Japan was characterized by a fragile political order that made possible the development of a brilliant higher culture in Kyoto and its diffusion to the provinces. The order was sufficiently weak, moreover, that it was unable to prevent socioeconomic changes from proceeding apace; indeed it encouraged them, and in the end they altered radically the character and capabilities of society.

Just as the *shōen* system gave the old Taika aristocracy a new lease on life, so, one could argue, the Ashikaga political configuration accommodated changes in samurai society and gave descendants of the Kamakura elite another century and a half of primacy. However, the weakness of Ashikaga governance tended to encourage the development of political alternatives much as it encouraged other forms of growth and change. Some of those alternatives arose as calculated political ventures and others were simply byproducts of religious, economic, or military trends. In any case, by comparison with both earlier and later ages, the medieval period was an era of political diversity and fluidity, and these qualities were the crucial elements in the medieval legacy for early modern Japan.

In medieval governance there were, to begin with, three major elements of accumulated political tradition. One was the remnants of the Taika system. Go-Daigo's abortive restoration of 1334 breathed new life into the ideal of bureaucratic imperial governance, and then literary celebrations of imperial honor such as Kitabatake Chikafusa's *Jinnō Shōtōki* served to preserve that political ideal. Another element was the *shōen* system, which continued to provide much of the nomenclature and formal legitimization for medieval landholding, especially among temples, long after the true *shōen* system had been destroyed. The third element of political tradition was shogunal governance, with its organs and principles of rule based on precedents of the Kamakura *bakufu*.

These three elements of accumulated tradition did not function very satisfactorily after the Kamakura regime decayed. Ashikaga leaders seem to have recognized their need for new governmental arrangements. In particular the two shogun Yoshimitsu and Yoshinori attempted to establish the principle and arrangements of shogunal monarchy, meaning a shogunal regime that dominated the realm and ruled on its own merit with kingly authority.[46] Yoshimitsu's triumph was brief, however, and Yoshinori's efforts ended in his assassination. In short, the Ashikaga *bakufu* did not provide much of the real government of late medieval Japan.

46. Elements of this position are suggested in articles by Kawai Masaharu and Tanaka Takeo in Hall and Toyoda and in an article by Prescott Wintersteen in Hall and Mass. The thesis of "shogunal monarchy" is advocated more vigorously by Kenneth Grossberg in a volume being prepared for publication. See also Kenneth Grossberg, "From Feudal Chieftain to Secular Monarch," in *Monumenta Nipponica* 21, no. 1 (spring, 1976), pp. 29–49.

Much of that government was exercised by the constables or other regional barons who attempted to rule through a set of personal vassalage and fief arrangements that bound leader and follower together in a reasonably stable manner. Another important element in medieval governance, as we suggested earlier, was Buddhist temples, notably those of the Ikkō sect. During the later medieval period they developed complex internal administrative structures that enabled them to tax and manage their villages and lands almost independently. They combined organizational mechanisms with religious conviction to gain the support of their governed populations and, using that support, engaged in the secular politics of the day.

Another element in medieval governance was commercial organizations. Whereas regional barons and Buddhist temples could function as more or less self-contained governing bodies, much of the regulatory activity of commercial organizations such as the *za* or guilds was carried on in conjunction with other institutions, as noted earlier. By the sixteenth century, however, as larger political units crumbled, merchants in places such as Sakai and Kyoto assumed nearly autonomous control of their own commercial and communal affairs.

As civil disorder spread during the late fifteenth century, *bakufu*, barons, and high-ranking Buddhists found it ever more difficult to manage their lands and people. In the absence of effective rule from above, those below assumed more and more power. Prepared by the socioeconomic changes of the preceding two centuries to handle affairs as never before, they took charge of towns, villages, and localities. Townsmen ran urban affairs through "councils of elders that appeared in cities throughout the country shortly after the Ōnin War."[47] Villagers and local notables such as landholders, merchants, local warriors, or priests organized their neighbors and led the peasantry in political and economic movements, demonstrations, and protests.[48] In some villages, where patterns of

47. Toyoda Takeshi and Sugiyama Hiroshi, "The Growth of Commerce and the Trades," in Hall and Toyoda, p. 140.

48. This issue is explored in David Davis, "*Ikki* in Late Medieval Japan," in Hall and Mass, pp. 221–47.

communal solidarity emerged, village assemblies offered vehicles for self-government by villagers as a group.[49]

To sum up, just as the political condition of medieval Japan both permitted and encouraged socioeconomic change, so it gave rise to several new forms and levels of political organization. The overall picture is that of an age of flux and innovation. The old order of Taika-*shōen*-elite *bushi* governance had been rendered anachronistic and inadequate by pervasive social change. New political configurations were being tested. Insofar as politically engaged sixteenth-century Japanese wished to stabilize affairs, they faced a challenge much like that which the Yamato elite had confronted a thousand years earlier. They had to retain whatever they deemed useful in the grand political tradition, exploit available political alternatives for whatever they might offer in usable techniques and principles, and add whatever else might be needed. Out of that process, successful political participants would develop forms of governance that could handle accumulated growth and change, turn it to political service, and reconsolidate society in a new order. During the sixteenth century, Japan forged the essential elements of that new order. When the process was complete, the age of fluidity came to an end. The disorder ceased, and a new golden age of political effectiveness, cultural brilliance, and far-reaching but orderly socioeconomic change and growth ensued.

49. Nagahara Keiji, "Village Communities and Daimyo Power," in Hall and Toyoda, pp. 115–18.

4

Early-Modern Japan: An Age of Integral Bureaucracy

Early-modern Japan constituted an age as sharply defined as the preceding classical and medieval ages. Its character was largely determined by medieval economic, military, political and intellectual developments. These combined to produce what may be termed an age of integral bureaucracy. The term "integral bureaucracy" has not, to my knowledge, been applied to the early-modern Japanese polity, which customarily is described as "centralized feudalism" or in some other way that suggests that the polity was a samurai institution. The term "integral bureaucracy" seeks to point up the basic proposition that early modern governance in Japan was not merely a samurai institution. From the outset it had a mercantile dimension that shaped its character and its relationship to socioeconomic and cultural developments. The pattern had been foreshadowed in the Muromachi *bakufu*'s relationship to commercial agents and activities, and it matured in the early modern era.

To call the early-modern polity bureaucratic creates no problems. It was bureaucratic—much more so than the classical polity—in the structural sense that political organization was highly articulated and in the functional sense that routinized procedures and fixed structures rather than personal relationships dictated much of the content of political behavior. The term "integral," however, is less familiar in this context and requires comment. The early-modern polity was integral in the sense that it was "composite" or "composed of constituent parts making a whole." There were two main elements—two social orientations and eventually two social groups—in this whole. One was the samurai element, the other, the mercantile.

From their rise in the sixteenth century until their demise in the late nineteenth, early-modern *bushi* saw themselves as following in the Minamoto warrior tradition. That self-image was deserved in the sense that they, like samurai of the late classical age, had risen to prominence as a new force in history, a new sector of society that had come onto the historic stage. It also was deserved in the sense that both groups ruled by working out an awkward political relationship with other power-holders. However, whereas Kamakura *bushi* had evolved a complex pattern of cooperation and conflict with *kuge*, early-modern *bushi* developed an equally complex pattern of cooperation and conflict with *chōnin*, meaning members of the mercantile community that had arisen during the medieval period.

This difference—Kamakura samurai relating upward to aristocrats whereas early-modern samurai related downward to merchants—was central to a more general difference in the two *bushi* groups: from the outset, early-modern samurai had much more extensive ties to the general public than did their Kamakura predecessors. They had such ties when mobilized for war because their armies consisted largely of low-ranking foot soldiers drawn from and supported by the general populace through complex commissariat arrangements. When they were demobilized, samurai became gentry farmers dwelling among ordinary farmers in the countryside or urban dwellers constituting a class of diversified hereditary functionaries. In both situations they found themselves involved in a network of fiscal and social relationships and official duties that placed many in close association with commoners. Both the warfare and politics of the sixteenth century and the routines of the peace that prevailed thereafter thus rendered the "Minamoto" self-image anachronistic.

The importance of that self-image should not be underestimated, however. Early-modern *bushi* were so closely linked to the general populace that they had to make great effort to establish and maintain themselves as a clearly delineated ruling elite. The Kamakura rulers had in fact constituted so small an elite group that they could perpetuate their positions for several decades by maintaining rather simple restrictions on marriage, inheritance, and admission to *gokenin* and *bushi* status. But early-modern rulers had to carry out an intensive, many-faceted policy to establish and preserve their social supremacy. In the end they were more successful than their Kamakura models, but to a significant degree that success was linked to the creation and perpetuation of social fictions that ill fitted the enduring reality of their integral bureaucratic order.

The mercantile element of this integral polity consisted of merchants and artisans who saw themselves as responsible purveyors of essential goods and services. Some were of humble origin, and some were, or at least claimed to be, of samurai origin. Whatever their family background, however, these men of affairs collaborated with samurai in the latter's political enterprises, initially as participants in the polity and from the seventeenth century onward as necessary adjuncts to it. In both positions they helped to link *bushi* to the general public and imposed upon them an awareness that complex economic matters and not merely land taxes were crucial to their undertakings. Because of the samurai relationship to merchants and the broader society in general, the early-modern polity was thus also integral in the broader sense that it linked closely together all major segments of the society and its activities. By comparison with the classical and medieval polities, that of the early-modern age was deeply rooted in and intimately tied to the fundamental structure and values of the entire society. Much of its strength derived from the solidity of that foundation.

This deeply rooted polity did not arise by accident. It

grew directly out of the severe disorder of the post-Ōnin century. As early-modern samurai rose to power by *gekokujō*, they attempted to end the disorder, elevate themselves above the mass of people, and thereby secure their own advantage. They clarified the whole range of human relationships that had been confused by medieval social change. They defined who belonged in what status group, what the functions of each group were, and how each related to other status groups. During the seventeenth century, rulers were able to define with a high degree of clarity relationships within and between the *bushi* stratum, *kuge*, clerics, various types of commoners, outcaste groups, and foreigners. Their success in aligning social structure and values with political structure and principles contributed greatly to the endurance of the new order.

The clarification of social structure did not, however, arrest all processes of change. On the contrary, one of the striking aspects of seventeenth-century Japan was that clarification proceeded during a time of extraordinary social growth and change. In terms of population and production, urbanization and commercialization, and societal sophistication and elaboration, the century was one of unparalleled development. The new order survived that growth and change in part by bending it to political advantage and in part by adjusting to it.

After merchants were reduced to adjuncts of the regime during the seventeenth century, the samurai-merchant relationship became more strained. Nevertheless, the basic character of integral bureaucracy survived, however awkwardly. Both its survival and its awkwardness were reflected in early modern higher culture, in which an initially vigorous warrior activity was soon supplemented by an equally vigorous burgher or *chōnin* culture that was shaped by and for the urban merchant class but that drew inspiration from *bushi* taste and enjoyed considerable *bushi* participation.

As it turned out, the rulers of early-modern Japan did reimpose order on society. They did make that order endure, did cope with extensive change, and did put their own stamp on higher culture. As with the Taika and Kamakura arrangements, however, in due course the effectiveness of the new political configuration declined. By the early nineteenth century the Japanese situation presented a very ambiguous image. Evidence of decline was widespread. The higher cultures of both samurai and townsmen appeared stagnant, and relations within and between the two groups were uneasy. The social situation of both seemed precarious and deteriorating. Intellectual critics of the order were becoming vocal, their criticisms more trenchant and fundamental. In the rural areas an important and populous landlord sector of society appeared to be following in the footsteps of late-classical and late-medieval samurai. It was acquiring the economic resources, social know-how, and political position necessary to begin, perhaps in alliance with disaffected samurai, a thrust for power as rivals of the established elite.

On the other hand, during the late eighteenth and early nineteenth century there was also evidence among the samurai-merchant elite of new thinking and new political strategies that might enable them to reorganize their power position, rather as *shōen* arrangements and the Ashikaga realignment had enabled major segments of earlier elites to resecure their own positions for another extended period. When "Japan before Perry" ended with the arrival of an American naval armada under Matthew C. Perry in 1853, the resolution of these conflicting trends was still pending.

THE FORGING OF INTEGRAL BUREAUCRACY

The Ōnin war and subsequent endemic strife destroyed what remained of the medieval polity. The disorder finally ended at the start of the seventeenth century when the powerful lord Tokugawa Ieyasu imposed his will on the country by force of arms. Ieyasu assumed the established title of shogun and situated his government, the Tokugawa *bakufu*, at his headquarters castle at Edo in the Kantō. From there the *bakufu* administered directly Ieyasu's family domain, which covered about a fourth of Japan, and supervised the activities of the two hundred fifty-odd great lords or daimyo, whose domains occupied the remainder of the country. The daimyo domains ranged in size from a few that covered one or more provinces to many that embraced only a few villages. The smallest of these domains theoretically contained enough productive land to support a minimum population of some ten thousand persons.

Ieyasu and his successors controlled the daimyo through a hostage system called *sankin kōtai* (alternate attendance), a variety of rules and regulations, inspectoral mechanisms, and familial alliances. Both shogun and daimyo governed their own lands and vassal forces according to bureaucratic procedures that determined military and civil organization, personnel policies, judicial processes, tax rates, and the governance of villages and towns.

Emergence of the new structure

Most of the devices by which shogun and daimyo ruled were developed and perfected during the sixteenth century when Japanese leaders and would-be leaders faced the task of forging a new order by trial and error. The task had two dimensions. Externally each leader had to avoid defeat at the hands of neighbors. These were other lords whom each would most commonly know as *tozama daimyō* (outside lords), meaning lords external to one's own organized body of followers. Internally each leader had to retain control of his own body of followers. They included people most commonly known as *kamon*, meaning relatives, and *fudai*, meaning hereditary retainers.

To manage neighbors, or *tozama* lords, required military intelligence and diplomacy. Effective lords knew the capabilities and interests of their neighbors and acted accordingly. They developed advantageous alliances and consummated them by skillful use of marriage and adoption arrangements and by the dispatch or exchange of hostages, commonly one's wife or child, as guarantees of good behavior. As integral bureaucracy developed, those intelligence and diplomatic practices became standardized. During the early seventeenth century, intelligence operations were regularized in a set of organized inspectoral procedures. Marriage and adoption alliances, long staples of Japanese politics, became routine elements of Tokugawa rule. Most important, the hostage custom was systematized in the *bakufu*'s *sankin kōtai* arrangements. These required every daimyo to keep his wife and heir permanently at Edo, and the lord himself had to spend every other year there.

Sixteenth-century leaders were particularly inventive in the handling of their internal resources of land and manpower. In a phrase, their arrangements became increasingly bureaucratic in nature. The process was slow and erratic, but by the end of the century it had become pervasive. For example, lords developed much more elaborate records that enabled them to know how many vassals and rear vassals they had, their weaponry, their land, their productive populations, and their other material resources. Vassals were separated from their bases of power by requiring them to live in castle towns and by supporting more and more of them with stipends rather than fiefs. Military assignments were rotated so as to prevent commanders from developing strong personal ties to the men they led. The size and weaponry of rear-vassal forces were regulated. And the lords carried out "sword hunts" to remove all weapons of war from the general populace, thereby helping to assure that insurgent vassals could not rely on local armed groups in their thrusts for power.

Disarming the general populace was thus part of the strategy for overcoming *gekokujō*. It was also designed to increase domanial productivity by assuring that producers would stay put and produce. To the same end, cadastral surveys were carried out extensively during the 1580s and 1590s to count the people, determine the productive capacity of one's land, and identify available resources. Late-sixteenth-century leaders standardized weights, measures, and money. They encouraged mining, accumulated precious metals, and promoted the production of useful goods. They regulated trade and attracted artisans and merchants to their castle towns, employing them and using them as officials when that seemed advantageous.

Bushi leaders also tried to maximize the effectiveness of their polities by elaborating the organizational structure, processes, and principles of their armed forces and civil administration. They developed structured field-command hierarchies and formed support units of engineer, transportation, supply, and commissary personnel. To administer villages, towns, and districts they appointed reliable officials, whether of samurai or commoner origins. They drew up codes of conduct for officials, issued rules and regulations to guide them, and had other officials check to ascertain that the rules were being enforced.

In this summary description of the emergence of integral bureaucracy, we can see the beginnings of that *bushi-chōnin* relationship that characterized the early modern age. It was grounded in a political need for certain types of skills, not in an alliance of classes. The increased importance of nonmilitary skills is apparent when one compares late-sixteenth-century samurai governance with that of Minamoto Yoritomo's age. Twelfth-century samurai had commanded small bands of warriors and required only modest logistical support in their politico-military operations: primarily blacksmiths, leather workers, armorers, couriers, scribes, and attendants. Because of the medieval change to more elaborate defense systems and the use of large armies of foot soldiers for local offensive and defensive operations, great barons required the much more elaborate logistical foundations we have mentioned. That need created opportunities for both those of military prowess and those with mercantile skills.

As the word *gekokujō* implies, the century after Ōnin was one in which both status and class lines were in utter disarray and opportunities for social movement were exceptionally great for those with valued skills. Given the nature of warfare and politics, men of both military and mercantile skills emerged, meteorlike, into—and out of—the historical record. One finds men of samurai ancestry going into commerce, and men of lesser origins becoming samurai. The intimate connection between successful men of business and successful men of politics is suggested by E. S. Crawcour, who describes the quartermasters of some notable late-sixteenth-century daimyo.[1]

> These official merchant quartermasters, who were usually of samurai origin, were generally granted exemption from taxes and services, given monopoly rights to conduct certain kinds of trade or even all major trade within the baron's territory, and were often appointed as leaders and supervisors of the merchant community.

Even after the Tokugawa victory at Sekigahara in 1600, men of this type continued to be the leaders of Japanese commerce. The three greatest merchants in Kyoto, reports Crawcour,

> had been closely associated with Tokugawa Ieyasu during the campaigns that culminated in the battle of Sekigahara, and all were fully fledged samurai as well as merchants.

Those who succeeded in the new age of baronial politics habitually acquired samurai status. For example, Saitō Dōsan, an oil seller, became a powerful daimyo in the 1540s. And Ōkubo Nagayasu, the son of a comic entertainer, became a powerful domanial administrator and influential advisor to Tokugawa Ieyasu a few decades later. As they rose they became known as *bushi*. Moreover, because samurai ancestry was preferable to most of the alternatives, one finds a considerable number of people discovering or inventing ancestors they had never known about before they rose in the world. Ieyasu himself and his former lord, Toyotomi Hideyoshi, both tried to manipulate their ancestries to advantage. The former discovered a very tenuous link to Minamoto Yoritomo; the latter insisted, to no one's satisfaction, that he was of Fujiwara ancestry. And those who had a claim to warrior ancestry often used it vigorously to establish their own merit while sneering at those more newly arrived on the scene.

1. E. S. Crawcour, "Changes in Japanese Commerce in the Tokugawa Period," in John W. Hall and Marius B. Jansen, ed., *Studies in the Institutional History of Early Modern Japan* (Princeton: Princeton University Press, 1968), p. 191.

Among these was Honda Tadakatsu, one of Ieyasu's more gifted vassals and a formidable warrior of undistinguished but undeniable *bushi* ancestry, who did not conceal his contempt for administrators of non-samurai origins. Referring to them he said,

> There is an old saying that both *daikan* (district administrators) and the neck of a *tokkuri* (sake serving bottle) eventually end up encircled by thongs. The people who serve as *daikan* are (no better than) those who perform comic opera for the daimyo.[2]

In the sixteenth century, then, the emerging pattern of integral bureaucracy continued to be thought of as samurai rule, even though the people involved were diverse in origins and the skills required included mercantile and administrative skills that were neither dependent on nor historically associated with the *bushi* tradition. Historical fictions are important, however. As will be noted later, the fiction that late-sixteenth-century barons were rulers in the grand tradition of Yoritomo helped to determine the eventual relationship of samurai and merchant in the early modern integral bureaucratic order.

The chronology of pacification

By the 1580s the essential structural elements of integral bureaucracy were widely established. By then they had enabled several daimyo to gain solid control over domains that embraced two or more provinces apiece. During the last decades of the sixteenth century, three daimyo in succession exploited and perfected these elements to end the disorder in Japan. First they pacified the area around Kyoto, and during the eighties and nineties they extended that peace outward until all Japan had again become quiet.

The three daimyo were Oda Nobunaga, Toyotomi Hideyoshi, and Tokugawa Ieyasu. Oda was a ruthless lord who imposed his will on the region around Kyoto by destroying

2. Conrad Totman, *Politics in the Tokugawa Bakufu, 1600–1843* (Cambridge, Mass.: Harvard University Press, 1967), p. 247.

all his rivals and placing his own vassals in charge of conquered territories. In the course of imposing his rule he crushed organized forces of the Ikkō sect and of other militant Buddhist groups. Most notably, in 1571 he surrounded and destroyed by fire and sword the three thousand buildings and large population of Mt. Hiei, the great wellspring of medieval Japanese Buddhism that had for so long been a bastion of autonomous military power. Two years later he frightened the last Ashikaga shogun into fleeing Kyoto, and the shogunal title fell into desuetude. The Muromachi *bakufu* had ended even in name.

In one of the last expressions of *gekokujō*, a vassal of Nobunaga killed him in 1582. Another vassal, the gifted commander Hideyoshi, slew the assassin and continued the process of pacification, disclosing in 1583 that control of the whole country was his objective.[3] Within a decade he attained his goal, having subdued the remaining great lords from the southern tip of Kyūshū to the northern end of Honshū. With the country pacified, he undertook two massive, ill-starred attempts to conquer Korea and China. Just why he launched those terrible adventures is unclear, but he had spoken of conquering China as early as 1586, and clearly envisaged it as a heroic and glorious undertaking that would place him in that small band of world-conquering giants among men. During 1592, shortly after his armies had begun their conquest of Korea, in a letter to his ailing mother, he said that

> By now we have taken various castles in Korea and I have sent my men to besiege the capital there. I shall take even China around the 9th month. . . . When I capture China I'll send someone to you in order to welcome you there.[4]

Despite Hideyoshi's confidence that he would shortly host his mother in China, both attempts at conquest failed amidst much blood and suffering. They proved to be the last major

3. Adriana Boscaro, *101 Letters of Hideyoshi* (Tokyo: Sophia University, 1975), pp. 11, 22.

4. Boscaro, pp. 45–46.

expression of Japan's medieval involvement in continental Asia.

When Hideyoshi died in 1598, his heir was a child. The group of great daimyo who tried to govern in his name soon proved unable to cooperate. Rivalries quickly led to a major confrontation between coalitions of western and eastern daimyo, the latter led by Tokugawa Ieyasu, whose domain embraced the entire Kantō plain and was the largest in Japan. In the autumn of 1600, Ieyasu's coalition won a great battle at Sekigahara near Kyoto. In the following months the victors subdued some holdouts, and in subsequent years Ieyasu stripped distrusted *tozama* daimyo of their lands and assigned trusted *tozama*, *kamon*, or *fudai* in their place. The net result was to assure Tokugawa predominance in all but the most distant corners of Japan.

By skillful genealogical sleuthing, Ieyasu was able to claim descent from Minamoto Yoritomo, and in 1603 he could therefore accept the title of shogun from a docile imperial court. Two years later he had it transferred to his son Hidetada, thus establishing a hereditary Tokugawa claim to the position that had once been held by Minamoto and Ashikaga leaders. Through it he established the necessary legal connection between the imperial tradition and the new integral bureaucratic order that had been laboriously constructed over the decades. In 1615 he waged one last successful campaign to destroy the recently matured son of Hideyoshi, and shortly afterward he died.

Ieyasu left the country at peace and the polity effectively organized and in the hands of his mature son Hidetada. The *bakufu* and also the daimyo, whether known as *tozama* or Tokugawa *kamon* or *fudai*, used bureaucratic techniques to administer their domains. The *sankin kōtai* and other diplomatic arrangements that bound *bakufu* and daimyo together gave functional unity to the system and assured that daimyo would abide by terms of the peace. The governing techniques of integral bureaucracy had proven their effectiveness as tools for imposing political order on Japan.

EVOLUTION OF THE POLITICAL ORDER, A.D. 1615–1850

During the seventeenth century, integral bureaucracy was developed to a high level of organizational and conceptual sophistication. It spelled out the character of human relationships throughout Japanese society in vastly more detail than had any earlier polity, and it empowered society's rulers to regulate more aspects of life than had ever been possible before. By the end of the century, moreover, an elaborate ideology had been developed that helped transform the *bushi* into an educated civil elite, rationalized their special status, and reinforced the imperial tradition in legitimizing the political order.

The seventeenth-century evolution of integral bureaucracy led to a redefinition of the central relationship of samurai and mercantile interests. The new relationship was reasonably functional but not very satisfying. Tensions arising from that situation helped to create chronic difficulties for the regime. Consequently the political history of the next century and a half, to 1850, was essentially the history of a frustrating long-term attempt by the rulers to deal with those difficulties.

Elaboration of the polity

In the course of the seventeenth century, leaders of the new order eliminated potential rival systems of governance. They established regular foreign relations and routinized domestic social relationships, not only relationships among samurai but also, more broadly, relationships among all sectors of society.

The task of eliminating rival systems of governance had begun during the political consolidation of the late sixteenth century. The principal rivals of the great barons were groups whose organizing basis included a philosophical ideal of shared religious conviction instead of the samurai ideal of personal feudal loyalty. Two types of such groups were perceived as particularly menacing. One consisted of sects of Buddhism, most notably certain subgroups of Nichiren's

Lotus sect and Ikkō groups of the Jōdo sect. As noted earlier, the great barons such as Nobunaga dealt harshly with militant Buddhist congregations, and from the seventeenth century onward rulers maintained legislation and control procedures aimed specifically at preventing their revival.[5]

The other type of rival group—which sometimes was lumped together with the Lotus subsects[6]—was Christian. Portuguese missionaries had begun arriving in Japan in 1549 and soon won converts. From the outset, Nobunaga, Hideyoshi, Ieyasu, and other barons tolerated Christianity uneasily and took sporadic measures to prevent Christian sectarian groups from acquiring the political momentum of Ikkō congregations. It was not until the seventeenth century, however, that decisive moves were made to eliminate the perceived Christian challenge. When they took place, they occurred as part of a larger policy of regularizing and restricting all foreign relations.

European adventurers and traders had reached Japan along with the missionaries in the final decades of the sixteenth century. At first, powerful barons found advantage in trading with them. But after 1600 or so, as the domestic situation changed, so too did official attitudes toward Europeans. By the 1620s and 1630s the rulers regarded unregulated foreign influence as a threat to the maturing order. Trade seemed to involve a loss of specie, weapons imports were a clear menace, and missionary work appeared to constitute a subversive threat. *Bakufu* leaders, therefore, especially the forceful third shogun, Tokugawa Iemitsu, took steps to eradicate missionary influence, prohibit weapons imports, and regulate all trade. In 1637 a rebellion erupted on the Shimabara peninsula in Kyūshū, and its leaders quickly proclaimed themselves Christian rebels. The revolt was suppressed only with difficulty and severely embarrassed the rulers. The prior

5. On Nichiren see Ishii Ryōsuke, *Tokugawa Kinreikō* (Tokyo: Sōbunsha, 1959), vol. 5, pp. 78–83, and vol. 9, pp. 104–29. On Ikkō see the several injunctions in the first section of regulations translated in Torao Haraguchi et al., trans., *The Status System and Social Organization of Satsuma* (Honolulu: University Press of Hawaii, 1975).

6. Ishii, vol. 5, p. 79.

suspicions of Iemitsu and many others seemed confirmed, and within three years the policy of seclusion (*sakoku*), as it was dubbed much later, was pressed to completion. Almost all foreign contacts were restricted to Nagasaki, which city the *bakufu* governed directly, and only authorized Chinese and Dutch traders were allowed there. Elsewhere, Chinese were allowed to trade only through the Ryūkyū Islands, and Koreans, only through Tsushima Island. Japanese were forbidden to go abroad, and any then living overseas were forbidden to return. An uncompromising domestic police program was pursued resolutely, breaking up Christian communities and forcing into secret worship the several thousand unrepentant faithful.[7]

In half a century the integral bureaucratic order had eliminated rivals and ended nearly all foreign influence in Japan. In the process of doing so it had terminated the whole pattern of Japanese penetration of Asia that had developed during the medieval period. Japanese spatial growth had been arrested and would remain so until the nineteenth century. So far as early-modern Japan was concerned, the lands of other people would remain just that.

Within the boundaries delineated by the policy of seclusion, leaders of the *bakufu* and daimyo domains set about ordering the realm by working out details of the *bakufu*-daimyo relationship and regularizing the condition of samurai in general. The result was an unusually stable structure of interlocking interests. The daimyo became accustomed to attendance requirements of the *sankin kōtai* system, which Iemitsu codified and applied rigorously to all daimyo. In due course the *bakufu* routinely confirmed the succession of each new lord to his predecessor's domain. In essence the *bakufu* had assured daimyo of their privileges, and in return they had accepted Tokugawa primacy. Both *bakufu* and daimyo similarly took steps to secure the well-being of their vassals—in return for loyal obedience—by developing standardized salary ar-

7. On the suppression of Christianity, two solid works are C. R. Boxer, *The Christian Century in Japan, 1549–1650* (Berkeley: University of California Press, 1951), and George Elison, *Deus Destroyed: The Image of Christianity in Early Modern Japan* (Cambridge, Mass.: Harvard University Press, 1973).

rangements and by creating a whole range of civil duties to replace the military functions that were no longer required. The setting up of a stable interlocking interest structure had a price, however. Part of the price was the disenfranchisement of tens of thousands of samurai as armies were demobilized during the early seventeenth century. Facing hardship and dishonor, these *rōnin* ("wave men"), or masterless samurai, became a rowdy social element in the cities. Their unrest reached a high point of violence in the 1640s and 1650s. An anti-Tokugawa plot by an ambitious swordsman, Yui Shōsetsu, was thwarted in 1652, however, and in subsequent years most *rōnin* were slowly absorbed by the expanding general economy and swelling cities. Another part of the price was a loss of mobility for those samurai who remained employed. Low-ranking samurai could perform only menial duties, intermediate men had intermediate administrative and leadership functions, and only higher-status samurai held commanding positions. As one might expect, such loss of mobility gave rise to discontent among low- and intermediate-ranking warriors. A third part of the price was the imposition of limits on the overall size of the *bushi* class. The number of vassals that each lord could retain was clearly indicated in government regulations. And as the seventeenth century advanced, *bakufu* and daimyo became ever more reluctant to provide stipends for new samurai family lines.

The stabilization of the samurai class also involved attempts to separate *bushi* from commoners and to control social movement among the latter. Commoners were sharply distinguished from samurai by the issuance and enforcement of elaborate judicial, sumptuary, and occupational regulations. Among commoners, efforts were made to keep peasants on the soil, to encourage their productivity, to tax them efficiently, and to assure that samurai and not other commoners were the recipients of that tax income. As a result of this last concern, together with the desire to find employment for samurai, during the early seventeenth century merchants and other commoners were gradually separated from government. In their place, bona fide samurai took over various types of warehousing, commissary, construction, fiscal, and civil administrative functions that had been avenues of upward mobility for commoners such as Ōkubo Nagayasu during the sixteenth century.

By the latter part of the seventeenth century the basic character of samurai-commoner relations had become established. The positions of the imperial court, *kuge*, and clerics had by then also become well delineated. In Kyoto, the court passively certified *bakufu* policy, and courtiers handled routine imperial rituals that fulfilled this certifying function. Clerics, whose power had been smashed in the age of pacification, administered their temples and shrines in accordance with regulations issued by the *bakufu* and daimyo and enforced by their officials. These varied survivors of the old Taika-*shōen*-medieval elites were powerless, but in return for their acquiescence the rulers assured them reasonably comfortable hereditary positions. They too were part of the interlocking interest structure of the early modern order.

The regime's success in managing society was not simply a negative triumph of discipline and denial. To a great extent it derived from the existence of an elaborate network of social structure and values that gave place and purpose to most members of society. Part of that structure was governmental bureaucracy, which employed half a million samurai, high and low. The greater part was a plethora of nongovernmental organizations that identified in a positive manner the roles and relationships of the rest of the populace. For example, there developed great merchant houses with complex organizations and authorized realms of activity. Restricted precincts or "licensed quarters" for the demimonde were delineated and maintained. A world of publishing houses came into existence to organize and regulate a new and widely utilized printing technology. Organizations for the accommodation and control of travellers were established. Schools of all sorts, medical facilities, and relief agencies developed, and all found structured places in which to exist and give order to the lives of those involved in them. In the end, the practices and forms of governmental organization came to be highly congruent with the practices and forms of much commoner organization.

Articulation of an ideology of rule

The process of social stabilization was accompanied by development of an ideological rationalization for the new order. In essence the process involved the application to Japan of a Confucian cosmology known as Neo-Confucianism that is generally attributed to the twelfth-century Chinese scholar Chu Hsi.

In Neo-Confucianism the builders of the early modern polity found a universalistic world view that helped them impose on a turbulent and variegated society an unprecedented level of order and regularity. Their Neo-Confucian vision was much more encompassing than the medieval "principle of the fundamental unity of man, nature, and society and of political-ethical, religious, and artistic concerns,"[8] which had been little more than an aesthetic ideal in a social reality of striking disunity. And though Chu Hsi's thought was essentially secular in its concerns, it was as all-embracing as the earlier Buddhist cosmologies of Saichō and Kūkai.[9]

The early-modern order reminds one of the classical period not only because each was based on an integrative universalistic vision but also because early-modern samurai attempted to fill a position analogous to that of the classical aristocrats as a hereditary, diffuse cultural elite in all ways superior to the common folk. The classical *kuge* superiority had been explained in ethical/aesthetic terms of "beauty" or "good people" or in religious terms of karma, whereas that of early-modern *bushi* was explained in secular terms of proper training. At a more basic level, however, the two groups subscribed to a common epistemology. To comprehend reality one did not meditate or have faith or assert ego, as in medieval thought, with the implications of self-directed understanding and the potential for disorder that such conduct entailed. Rather, in Tokugawa as in Heian Japan, one studied prescribed texts and from them came to understand how the

8. See note 31, chapter 3.

9. See, for example, the discussion in Masao Maruyama, *Studies in the Intellectual History of Tokugawa Japan* (Princeton: Princeton University Press, 1974), trans. Mikiso Hane, pp. 19ff.

pieces of reality all fitted together. And insofar as everyone studied the same texts, whether the classical texts of Tendai-Shingon or the early-modern ones of Neo-Confucianism, everyone would have a shared understanding of the proper order of things.

This world view was spelled out in the writings of Tokugawa philosophers. Hayashi Razan (1583–1657), advisor to the first three shogun, taught the Neo-Confucian cosmology of Chu Hsi very effectively. It viewed the rightly ordered society as an expression of universal unchanging principles. As Hayashi put it in one essay,

> Heaven is above and earth is below. This is the order of heaven and earth. If we can understand the meaning of the order existing between heaven and earth, we can also perceive that in everything there is an order separating those who are above and those who are below. When we extend this understanding between heaven and earth, we cannot allow disorder in the relations between the ruler and the subject, and between those who are above and those who are below. The separation into four classes of samurai, farmers, artisans and merchants, like the five relationships [of ruler and subject, father and son, husband and wife, older and younger brother, and friend and friend], is part of the principles of heaven and is the Way which was taught by the Sage (Confucius).[10]

The rightly ordered society was thus hierarchical and organic, and its several parts were articulated harmoniously. It was led by a cultured governing class, sustained by a diligent agrarian class, and serviced by a skilled artisan class and a responsible merchant class. In Tokugawa Japan the samurai were identified as the cultured governing class, and the great bulk of the rest of society was fitted into the other three classes. Their status descended from farmer to artisan to merchant, the last held in least esteem because merchants allegedly produced naught and merely handled transactions.

Samurai were thus to be perceived as one of four main

10. Lu, vol. I, p. 236.

status groups. Underlying this quadripartite division, however, was the more basic division into rulers and ruled, and many scholars subsequently found it sufficient to distinguish between the samurai, who allegedly used their minds, and commoners, who used their muscles.[11]

The newly risen, largely illiterate samurai of the early seventeenth century were in fact poorly equipped to play a *kuge*-like role as cultured rulers. However, Hayashi and others found in Chu Hsi's thought a strategy for overcoming this disability. *The Great Learning* [*Daigaku*; *Ta Hsueh*], the Confucian text most discussed by Chu Hsi, linked learning to political action in this classic statement:

> The extension of knowledge consists in the investigation of things. When things are investigated, knowledge is extended; when knowledge is extended, the will becomes sincere; when the will is sincere, the mind is rectified; when the mind is rectified, personal life is cultivated; when personal life is cultivated, the family will be regulated; when the family is regulated, the state will be in order; and when the state is in order, there will be peace in the world.[12]

"Peace in the world" depended, then, upon "the extension of knowledge," which one achieved by studying widely. That study, however, was not to be random. Quite on the contrary, it was to be firmly grounded in Confucian texts as understood by Chu Hsi. Accordingly Tokugawa proponents of Neo-Confucianism, such as Yamazaki Ansai (1618–82), maintained that *bushi* had the task of studying appropriate texts, cultivating themselves, and then guiding others, thereby bringing tranquility to the realm. His counsel was to "Study widely. Question thoroughly. Deliberate carefully. Analyze clearly. Act conscientiously."[13]

In much the same spirit the samurai scholar Kaibara Ekken (1630–1714), in an essay on the education of children, indicated how Confucian texts were to be used to train samurai

11. See, for example, Maruyama, p. 9.
12. Ibid., p. 25.
13. Tsunoda et al., p. 365.

for life in Tokugawa Japan. The essay spelled out the proper instruction for growing children, as in these fragments:

> [The child's eighth year] is the age when the ancients began studying the book *Little Learning* [*Shogaku; Hsiao Hsueh*]. Beginning at this time, teach the youngsters etiquette befitting their age, and caution them not to commit an act of impoliteness.
>
> [The child's fifteenth year] is the age when the ancients began the study of the *Great Learning*. From this time on, concentrate on the learning of a sense of justice and duty (*giri*). The students must also learn to cultivate their personalities and investigate the way of governing people. This is the way of the *Great Learning*. Those who are born in the high-ranking families have the heavy obligations (*shokubun*) of becoming leaders of the people, . . . If they do not learn the way of governing people, they may injure the many people who are entrusted to their care by the Way of Heaven.[14]

While promoting the study of Confucian thought, these samurai scholars never forgot that the rulers were to be known as *bushi*. They wished to preserve what they saw as virtues of loyalty, simplicity, integrity, forthrightness, and fighting skill imbedded in the indigenous samurai heritage. To preserve those virtues while also inculcating the civil virtues of Confucianism, Hayashi and later proponents of the Tokugawa order argued that samurai were to devote their attention equally to the civil and military arts, or *bun* and *bu* as they were called. Part of military education was training in the use of weapons and part was disciplining of the body and mind to achieve the samurai ideals of self-control, hardiness, courage, and loyalty. Those had been uncomplicated and practical virtues for Kamakura samurai, who provided early modern *bushi* with role models. But during the seventeenth century— when the martial arts ceased to have active utility—they were developed into elaborate moral formulations known as *bushidō*, "the way of the warrior." The most influential statements on "the way of the warrior" were carefully formulated

14. The quotations are excerpted from Lu, vol. 1, pp. 248–50.

principles of conduct developed by Yamaga Sokō (1622–85) and other scholars who were attempting both to rationalize the samurai's hereditary privileges and enable them to handle their governing responsibilities effectively. Thus Yamaga had this to say of the *bushi*:

> Within his heart he keeps to the ways of peace, but without he keeps his weapons ready for use. The three classes of the common people make him their teacher and respect him. By following his teachings, they are enabled to understand what is fundamental and what is secondary.[15]

The samurai was to keep his weapons "ready for use," not because he would in fact be using them but because "eternal vigilance," or preparedness was deemed a virtue in itself. It would help assure a high quality of both samurai and commoner performance.

The medieval samurai ethos, as we earlier noted, involved the celebration of battlefield derring-do and a resolve to die without flinching. In early modern thought, when there no longer were battles to be killed in, even the resolve to die was made an instrumental value to strengthen the *bushi* capacity to function effectively in his lord's service. Thus the author of *Hagakure* [Hidden behind leaves], a major exposition of *bushidō*, asserted in 1716 that by being prepared to die, one eliminated the likelihood of being unable to make difficult decisions or of succumbing to urban decadence. By resolving to die, one would be able to perform his duty "effortlessly":

> If you are ready to discard life at a moment's notice, you and the *bushidō* will become one. In this way throughout your life, you can perform your duties for your master without fail.[16]

Through a proper education in the Confucian texts together with rigorous cultivation of his samurai skills and self-disci-

15. Tsunoda et al., p. 400.
16. The quotation appears in Lu, vol. 1, p. 251.

pline, a *bushi* would prepare himself to handle well his tasks as a member of the ruling elite.

In the Tokugawa Confucian view, society was an integral order composed of dissimilar parts that had dissimilar functions and hence dissimilar educational needs. Not everyone was to rule and therefore, as in the classical age, not everyone need have access to knowledge about governance. Assuming that knowledge was divisible, the rulers tried to restrict philosophical thought to samurai while commoners were encouraged to learn basic virtues and practical skills necessary to their positions in life. Beyond that, they need not study. Yamaga Sokō explained it by analogy.[17] He pointed out that

> Birds and beasts, . . . fish and insects, . . . [not] one of them has any respite from seeking food, and none neglects for a day or an instant in a year its flying, running, or going about [for food]. All things are thus. Among men, the farmers, artisans, and merchants also do the same.

Although they, like samurai, ought to practice the Confucian virtues, Yamaga continued,

> the farmers, artisans, and merchants have no leisure from their occupations, and so they cannot constantly act in accordance with them and fully exemplify the Way.

Hence, as we noted in the earlier quotation from Yamaga, it was the task of the samurai to learn, and to teach the unlettered masses by serving as a model.

Ogyū Sorai (1666–1728), a vigorous proponent of samurai rule, put it this way,

> What possible value can there be for the common people to over-reach their proper station in life and study such books [as the Confucian classics]?[18]

17. Tsunoda et al., pp. 398–99.
18. R. P. Dore, *Education in Tokugawa Japan* (Berkeley: University of Cal-

More darkly, an educator wrote in 1817 of commoners who had studied too much, that

> When they acquire a little skill at letters they tend to become arrogant, they look down on their fellow-men, despise their elders and superiors and question the instruction of the authorities.[19]

By using Neo-Confucian premises and categories, the ruling *bushi* thus articulated a clear philosophical distinction between their own roles and those of commoners, thereby justifying their persistent efforts to dominate the integral bureaucratic order and keep all other interests in their proper place. To this end they grounded valid knowledge in texts the regime could control and maintained limits on the diffusion of such knowledge as would empower others to engage in political action. In a manner of speaking the age of the "sword hunt" had given way to the age of the "preventive book hunt." As elaborated in seventeenth-century Japan, both the theory and practice of integral bureaucracy fitted the many parts of society together as an organic unity subject to control from above. Supposedly it benefited everyone. At least it perpetuated the advantages of those whose ancestors had ended the turmoil of the post-Ōnin century.

It would be misleading, however, to assume that the ideology of integral bureaucracy was merely an instrument of repression imposed upon a sullenly resistant populace. Much as the strength of the early modern structure derived from the congruence of government and nongovernmental institutions, so the strength of *bushi* ideology derived to considerable extent from its congruence with core values of society at large, values that achieved rational expression in widely shared religious systems.

The *bushi* attempt to prevent the spread of unwarranted education was only partially successful because too many

---

ifornia Press, 1965), p. 217. For a fuller exposition of Ogyū's ideas on education, see J. R. McEwan, *The Political Writings of Ogyū Sorai* (Cambridge: Cambridge University Press, 1962), pp. 132ff.

19. Dore, p. 217.

people had access to too many books. Many commoners did in fact gain literacy and learning, and that learning included doctrines that served to sustain the established order by enabling commoners to find worth and fulfillment in their stations in life. For example, Ishida Baigan (1685–1744), who grew up in a merchant household, taught widely a code of self-cultivation, called Shingaku, that linked human worth to performance of one's tasks.[20] In his words,

> To assist the ruler, as retainers, is the Way of the retainer. The trade of the merchants assists the empire. The payment of the price is the stipend (*roku*) of the artisan. Giving the harvest to the farmer is like the stipend of the *samurai*. Without the output of all the classes of the empire, how could it stand? The profit of the merchant too is a stipend permitted by the empire.

Merchants, artisans, and peasants were thus as deserving as samurai. He urged his listeners to "behave prudently,"

> serve your lord with righteousness and serve your parents with love, treat your friends with faithfulness, love men at large and have pity on poor people. Though you have merit, do not be proud. Maintain economy with respect to such things as clothing, furniture and the like and do not seek elegance. Do not neglect the family business, and as for wealth, measure what comes in and be aware of what goes out. Obey the laws and govern the family.

A comparable advocacy of self-discipline and diligence as worthy and fulfilling was evident a century later in Hōtoku, the teachings of Ninomiya Sontoku (1787–1856), a farmer-turned-teacher who is commonly known as "the peasant sage." For Ninomiya it was only through diligence and careful planning that one could repay the debt of gratitude one owed for the elemental privilege of living:

20. The quotations of Ishida and Ninomiya are from Robert N. Bellah, *Tokugawa Religion* (Glencoe, Ill.: The Free Press, 1957), pp. 158, 149, 128, in that order.

> The origin of the body lies in the nurture of the parents. The succession of descendants depends on the painstaking efforts of husband and wife. . . . We must look on the benefits we have received in this way, and make return to heaven, earth and man for them. If we do this we shall be able to accomplish anything we wish. This is a joy to God, and gives our fellow men pleasure in our conduct and confidence in our words.

These were not the precepts of men cringing before the overweening power and arrogance of a ruthless samurai ruling class. Rather, they were the words of people who found in their society sufficient social space and purpose for the common people to whom their words were addressed. The widespread acceptance of this sort of value pattern contributed to the stability and vitality of the early modern order.

Stresses in the polity

The rulers of seventeenth-century Japan had forged a remarkably sophisticated political order. It derived strength from that congruence of elite and commoner structures and values that we have noted. At the same time, however, the order was characterized by patterns of tension and conflict. In part at least, the tension and conflict derived from a profound contradiction built into the very heart of the early-modern order. It was the contradiction between a polity that was from its inception based on a complex economy and intricately linked social order and a theory of state that envisioned society in terms of a single diffuse status hierarchy rooted in a simple agrarian economy. It was a vision reminiscent of Heian society, with the *bushi* trying to fill the old *kuge* role. However, the social foundations for such an order—in terms of economics, demography, social values, and knowledge—no longer existed. The disjunction of theory and reality affected the whole of society, but its consequences were most visible in the relationship of the two groups basic to the integral bureaucratic order, *bushi* and *chōnin*.

The Neo-Confucian dogma of a four-class society, which

furnished a theoretical rationale for the early modern order, had the curious effect of placing samurai and merchants at opposite ends of the socioethical spectrum. It was an outcome foreshadowed in the late-sixteenth-century samurai prejudice against parvenu rivals and the associated custom of treating baronial governance as a samurai phenomenon even when its practices and practitioners were themselves to a significant extent of non-*bushi* origins. It also was an outcome that meshed with the early-seventeenth-century regularization of samurai functions, which removed merchants from government and turned many of their duties over to hereditary samurai. These trends seemed to indicate that the warrior-mercantile linkage central to the rise of integral bureaucracy had been broken. That was not the case, however, because samurai continued to need merchants and merchants were unable to escape samurai and instead worked out a relationship of interdependence with them.

Bushi needed *chōnin* because the fact of governmental dependence on a complex economic base did not end with the coming of peace. On the contrary, it intensified. And the entrepreneurs whose businesses were at the center of commercial activity became the ones on whom the governments of daimyo and shogun relied to meet their growing fiscal needs.

The *chōnin* had good reason to be unhappy with the way *bushi* handled them, denying them high status, hedging them about with myriad restrictions, and eventually denouncing them as greedy egoists. Nevertheless they had to make the best of their situation because they had no way to "beat the system" by escaping or challenging it. With foreign trade strictly controlled and the domains effectively bound by the larger Tokugawa system, merchants could not move from jurisdiction to jurisdiction and exploit vagaries or rivalries in the relationships of rulers. Most striking of all, the cities did not provide a "bourgeois" haven from "feudal" control, because the cities were the very citadels of early-modern rulers.

On the other hand, the cities did provide enough security for merchants so that while they could not escape the samurai, the samurai were not able to eradicate them. The cities, notably Edo, Osaka, and Kyoto, were so large and so full of diverse activity that the rulers never were completely able to impose their own values upon their populations, having to be content with the cooperation that stemmed from congruent values and interests. The cities sustained a massive amount of commercial activity that did not directly involve the rulers, and merchants were able to enrich themselves in that activity. Moreover, the cities became centers of a fugitive bourgeois culture that flourished despite official displeasure. The values of that culture justified *chōnin* in their existence. They enabled generations of merchants to regard themselves, as in the teachings of Ishida Baigan, with the self-respect necessary to use their resources effectively in dealing with samurai, thereby perpetuating the well-being of their families and enterprises.

Preserved by their urban environment but unable to pursue their interests apart from the samurai, merchants even after their separation from government devised ways to cooperate with the rulers and capitalize on their fiscal needs. In so doing, they acquired wealth and security. No longer regarded as members of the polity, leaders of the mercantile community became awkwardly related adjuncts to it because their service remained essential. Through their cooperation with the *bushi* as financiers and technical administrators, they helped perpetuate integral bureaucracy.

The nature of the evolving *bushi-chōnin* interdependence is suggested by Crawcour.[21] During the early seventeenth century the major daimyo established warehouse facilities in Osaka to handle their rice marketing. Forbidden by the *bakufu* to own land in Osaka, writes Crawcour, the daimyo arranged to have their warehouses and associated offices built on the land of Osaka commoners who handled more and more of the daimyo's rice sales and other business. He says of these merchant financiers,

> Through their work for the Shogunate and the *han* [daimyo domains], they became essentially civil retainers or quasi-samurai, with permission to use surnames and wear two swords when on official business.

21. The quotation is from Crawcour, p. 196.

Thus merchants, who in a manner of speaking had been eased out the front door of the samurai establishment earlier in the seventeenth century, had returned to it via the back door, as the operatives of separate establishments whose necessity to the larger order had been recognized in practice even while denied in rhetoric. By the eighteenth century the samurai were more rather than less closely entwined with merchants. But whereas the merchants had formerly been part of the governmental process and a subordinate part at that, in the altered arrangement of the middle Tokugawa period, the merchants had a high level of institutional independence and social separateness. Samurai-merchant interaction was, therefore, much more complex, serving less fully congruent interests, and so under much greater tension.

The frustrating character of *bushi-chōnin* interaction was evident in a change in the tone of intellectual comment on merchants. Yamaga Sokō, who died in 1685, had been able to contrast samurai and merchants with considerable dispassion, seeing both groups as playing their proper roles to mutual advantage. By the eighteenth century, however, many intellectuals were far less charitable in their assessments. Muro Kyūso (1658–1734) contrasted *bushi* and *chōnin* concisely:

> Nothing is more important to the samurai than duty. Second in importance comes life, and then money. . . . To rejoice when one makes a profitable transaction or buys valuable merchandise cheaply is part of the merchant's trade, but it is unpardonable in a samurai.[22]

Ogyū Sorai described the mercenary character of the merchant more fully in the course of explaining the reasons for persistent inflation:

> All the merchants throughout Japan are in communication with one another and arrange among themselves the prices of goods both in Edo and elsewhere.

Price-rigging was, however, only one of the arts of the merchant. He also knew how to corner markets by speculative

22. Tsunoda et al., pp. 437, 439.

purchase and how to drive up prices by creating false scarcities. "Such practices," Ogyū commented, "are the very summit of the merchant's art and something which is altogether beyond the comprehension of the . . . officials of the Bakufu."[23]

The tensions of *bushi* and *chōnin* were also reflected in *bakufu* policy toward the great urban merchants. In 1705 the regime tried to discipline them by intimidation. It denounced the wealthy Yodoya merchant house for ostentation and confiscated all its goods. That gesture merely touched the surface manifestations of the problem, however, and achieved no lasting result. Subsequently the eighth shogun, Tokugawa Yoshimune (1684–1751), who carried out a vigorous policy of fiscal and administrative reform during the 1720s, agreed to license the great merchants. He thus acknowledged their right to monopoly roles even as he tried to regulate them and extract modest license fees from them. At the same time, however, Yoshimune strove to lessen the general use of money in society, to end the use of coins in land tax payments, and to reduce levels of consumption and urban life styles. A half-century later the *bakufu* leader Tanuma Okitsugu (1719–88) tried to improve samurai-merchant relations by adopting a different policy. He encouraged commerce, taxed it more extensively, and increased governmental involvement in productive activities. During the 1790s his successor at Edo, Matsudaira Sadanobu (1758–1829), led the *bakufu* in a vigorous reform movement that aimed to reestablish the practices of Yoshimune's day,[24] but his effort had only limited effect. A half-century later, in 1841, Mizuno Tadakuni (1793–1851) attempted to eliminate the favored position of powerful merchant groups by abolishing their government-sanctioned trading privileges. His action created financial confusion, and his successor in office reversed the policy. In short, despite dramatic shifts in strategy and dynamic pursuit of policy, the tensions

23. McEwan, pp. 45–46.

24. On Tanuma see John Whitney Hall, *Tanuma Okitsugu, 1719–1788* (Cambridge, Mass.: Harvard University Press, 1955), and on Sadanobu see Herman Ooms, *Charismatic Bureaucrat* (Chicago: University of Chicago Press, 1975).

between *bushi* and *chōnin* persisted into the mid-nineteenth century.

The awkward relationship of samurai and merchant was further strained from the eighteenth century by a slowly growing samurai indebtedness. The indebtedness created a series of intra-*bushi* tensions because it was regarded as unethical and politically damaging and because it prompted remedial measures that aided some at the expense of others. Most notably, governments tried to reduce institutional indebtedness by pursuing austerity programs, but the programs often injured vassals by reducing their stipends in one way or another. Also, *bakufu* and daimyo domains tried to generate funds by pursuing fiscal and economic policies that worked to one another's disadvantage. By the late eighteenth and early nineteenth centuries members of samurai society felt a complex set of conflicting antipathies among themselves. Most strikingly, high and low warriors had come to distrust one another in general, and the leaders of the *bakufu* and some great daimyo domains distrusted one another in particular. Samurai as a whole, moreover, felt a general antipathy toward merchants, who, they believed, had become rich at the expense of the samurai class and who, therefore, were blamed for the general difficulties of samurai society. *Chōnin* money remained necessary to the *bushi*, however, and under those circumstances *bushi* morale deteriorated and political efficiency declined.

These trends served to weaken the general effectiveness of government and to foster a widespread but diffuse power vacuum in the area of the links between *bushi* and society in general. Into this vacuum began to move local people of influence and wealth, both rural and urban. In doing so they often acquired marginal *bushi* rank. However, their interests did not because of this really become identified with the interests of the urban rulers in their castle towns even when they sought to ape their betters as evidence of their social success. Their actions, therefore, did not consistently benefit the state. For example, as a minor fief-holding samurai grew impoverished, he would reduce the number of his retainers and turn fief-administration duties over to a local notable,

often a landlord-entrepreneur-usurer type, who was then expected to collect taxes and keep the peace. It was in the notable's own interest, however, to collect only as much tax
income as was necessary to keep the fief-holder pacified,
leaving the rest in the village where he would have access to
it himself.

Tokugawa political history after about 1700 was thus the
story of slowly decaying rule. *Bushi* and *chōnin* remained mutually dependent, but their ability to cooperate was persistently undercut by the tensions that were built into the
structure and values of the integral bureaucratic order. In this
situation, as will be noted again later, a new stratum of society seemed to be rising to power, at least locally, as part of a
larger process of historical change.

HIGHER CULTURE

As we saw in chapter 2, classical arts and letters embodied
the ideals of *kuge* society and helped sustain the aristocratic
order of the day. It was a "higher culture" both in the sense in
which we are using the term—to mean thought, art, and letters as distinct from "culture" in the broader anthropological
sense—and in the sense of "higher" as against "lower" or
plebeian culture. During the medieval period, higher culture
manifested a new body of ideas and values that denied the
validity of aristocratic claims and opened power and opportunity to samurai and beyond them to clerics, merchants, and
other commoners. It was thus less clearly distinguishable
from plebeian culture, especially in the realm of religious
thought and action. In early-modern Japan the gap between
the arts and letters of elite and mass was reduced even more,
despite *bushi* efforts to halt the trend. In the realm of speculative thought the gap was for all practical purposes closed.

This outcome was not what the new rulers sought. As
samurai and would-be samurai of the sixteenth century built
the new order on the wreckage of the medieval polity, they
worked assiduously to conceal their plebeian origins and pro-
claim their historic worth. They celebrated their achieve-

ments in a burst of creative braggadocio known as Momo-yama culture. And they tried to perpetuate their supremacy by specifying the content of acceptable higher culture, urging samurai to master it and restricting it to the samurai elite. They succeeded for a while in establishing a *bushi* cultural purity untainted by vulgar mercantile tastes, but they paid a price in a rapid loss of cultural creativity. After a few exciting decades the "samurai culture" of Tokugawa *bushi* became, in most respects, derivative and retrospective.

Most of the cultural creativity of early-modern Japan was a product of initiatives by townsmen, other commoners, or samurai who consciously rejected the elite tastes of their castle brethren. They gave rise to those new, vigorous, and sophisticated arts and letters that we know as *ukiyo* or "floating world" culture. *Ukiyo* embodied in its literature, art, and drama values that were as brash a celebration of *chōnin* vitality as *bushi* culture was an affirmation of official values. And the disparity between the two not only reflected the samurai-merchant tension in the integral bureaucratic order but also helped sustain it by legitimizing merchant assertiveness and perpetuating official resentment of it.

This flourishing *chōnin* culture reflected a more basic trend, a dramatic spread of literacy and learning. The diffusion of learning went well beyond the limits decreed by the rulers, and one consequence was that in the realm of speculative thought early-modern higher culture cut across status lines and engaged people of varied backgrounds in common dialogue. It gave overt expression to the major concerns of the age, initially articulating and later undermining the philosophical foundations of the regime and the principles upon which it distinguished class from mass. This speculative thought was unprecedented in Japan in its magnitude, variety, and sophistication. Moreover, in sharp contrast to ancient and medieval thought, which had been fundamentally religious, it was primarily secular. It focused above all else on political concerns. But besides wrestling with intractable political issues, Tokugawa thinkers ventured deeply into fields of historiography, literary criticism, religious thought, epistemology, philology, and ethics. In the end they contributed to the human tradition one of its greatest philosophical experiences.

Bushi culture

The upstarts who rose to power and glory during the late sixteenth century gave artistic expression to the self-assertiveness that earlier was exemplified in medieval war tales and subsequently in Hideyoshi's attempts to conquer China. Mighty daimyo built great castles with soaring walls, towering keeps, and elegant residences and gardens. They hired the best craftsmen they could find to design, build, and decorate them. The great castles were aesthetic masterpieces, of necessity rooted in the principle that form follows function. The principles of general design and the styles of stonework, framing, roofing, lighting, and ventilation were all based on careful military analysis.

As areas were secured and peace gradually came to the country, castle-holders grew wealthy and used their wealth to decorate and glorify. The finest artists of the day painted great screens in bold design, using rich colors and expanses of gold leaf. Great lords lavished resources on display, celebration, and pageantry, and on the collecting of such art treasures as painting, pottery, and the makers thereof. This bold, brash Momoyama style, so called after a great castle that Hideyoshi built near Kyoto, was a forthright expression of the elegant, arrogant taste of the new rulers. It dominated the century after 1550, continuing in modified form into the early decades of the Tokugawa peace. Elements of that taste are still evident in the sprawling Himeji castle west of Osaka, the elegant Katsura villa near Kyoto, and the lushly decorated Nijō castle within Kyoto. The most awesome surviving examples of the later modified Momoyama style are the Nikkō mausolea, built as memorial shrines to early Tokugawa leaders. They consist of a series of gates and buildings done in a highly ornate architectural style, brightly painted in the Chinese manner, and set amidst towering cryptomeria trees in the mountains north of present-day Tokyo.

Momoyama art was saved from outright vulgarity by the new rulers' desire to prove their worth by mastering the cultured sensibilities of Kyoto. That desire combined with their penchant for triumphant excess to produce a burst of bold and brilliant creativity. Ceramics was an area of exceptional vigor. Pottery techniques learned from Korea and China during the decades of continental trade and during Hideyoshi's invasion attempts were adapted to Japan. They gave rise to a wide range of splendid ceramic styles, most notably bowls for use in the tea ceremony. Painting also flourished. Hired to decorate castles, temples, and mansions, artists of the Kanō and other schools painted screens and scrolls of great organizational and chromatic splendour. During the seventeenth century this creative impulse was sustained by such master artists as Tawaraya Sōtatsu (?–1643) and Ogata Kōrin (1658–1716). Their screens and scrolls have an overall discipline, a sophistication of design, and a boldness of color that is as appealing to the modern eye as it was to their patrons.

Besides surrounding themselves with tasteful artifacts, the new rulers attempted to put distance between themselves and the general run of people and, in many cases, between themselves and their own origins, by emulating the conduct of medieval Kyoto sophisticates. They promoted the study of poetry, calligraphy, and painting. They cultivated the tea ceremony, patronized the Nō drama, and encouraged scholars and artisans to pursue old traditions. The effort was essentially uncreative. It did, however, preserve archaic cultural forms and provided a yardstick by which to measure a person's refinement. Early modern *bushi* were expected to become masters of one or more of the gentle arts: calligraphy, the tea ceremony, Nō, poetry-writing, the *nanga* (southern) style of water-color painting, or approved forms of music. In due course these arts became part of the attainments of all polished samurai.

Chōnin culture

By imposing clear limits on the range of acceptable taste, the early-modern rulers choked off *bushi* creativity. By the mid-seventeenth century samurai culture had lost its vitality. Arts and letters did not, however, become moribund, because the process of stifling samurai originality had simply driven creative energies into new channels. As samurai culture lost its freshness, artists and writers increasingly found that they could not abide by the restrictive aesthetic canons of the rulers. Turning elsewhere for artistic fulfillment, they found an eager market among commoners and an agreeable subject matter in their lives and dreams. In doing so they also discovered a new class of patrons, the wealthy townsmen.

The rulers of seventeenth-century Japan unwittingly created that new class of patrons when they, in effect, evicted their merchant collaborators from polite society by defining them as a low-status group utterly divorced from samurai and by removing them from a sanctioned role in the process of governance. The merchant elite was driven from high society, but its members were not denied the leisure, literacy, and income necessary to develop polished tastes and cultural attainments. Denied, for example, opportunity to view the Nō with daimyo or exchange poems with high-placed persons, merchant aesthetes turned elsewhere to satisfy their tastes, and they found gratification in the cultural production of *ukiyo* writers, artists, and dramatists.

Much as the newly risen *bushi* had engaged in the bombast of Momoyama, so the newly risen townsman welcomed and thereby fostered a bold, boastful *chōnin* culture, loud, proud, and self-assured. And much as the Momoyama samurai tempered his braggadocio with medieval restraint, so the merchant disciplined his expensive taste. However, whereas the samurai did so in the course of emulating the sensibilities of medieval Kyoto, the merchant seems to have done so more as a way to escape the critical gaze and punitive censure of puritanical rulers. Nonetheless, *chōnin* culture, the culture of the *ukiyo* or "floating world," acquired in time a richness in which pride was tempered by a sense of transience, brash lasciviousness by a sense of vulnerability, and joy by a sense of emptiness.

The interaction of creative minds and merchant aesthetes thus fostered the development of a sophisticated higher culture that involved new forms of writing, pictorial arts, and drama. The master of floating-world fiction (*ukiyo-zōshi*) was Ihara Saikaku (1642–93), whose zesty characters epitomized Tokugawa city life. With irony, farce, and compassion he described the demimonde, the daily neighborhood, and the dilemmas of their entanglement. In one of his short stories, for example, he caught the humor and pathos of the poor townsman's plight. In this story a small group of people, gathered in a Jōdo Shin temple at year's end, are exchanging confessions. One man tells his story:

> "If I'd stayed at home tonight, the bill collectors would have been bothering the life out of me. There's not a soul in the world who'd lend me as much as ten coppers. I wanted to drink some saké tonight and I was cold. I thought of one reckless scheme after another, but still I couldn't find any good way to get through New Year's. But then I hit on a really foul scheme. I knew that crowds of people would be gathering at the Shinshu temples tonight to hear the sermons about Heitaro, and so I decided that I'd steal a few pairs of straw or leather sandals and sell them to buy myself some saké. But I found that all the temples—not only this one—were deserted tonight, and so it's been hard for me to pluck out the Buddha's eye." The man finished his story in tears.[25]

The works of Saikaku and other writers were lavishly illustrated with wood-block prints known as *ukiyo-e* or "floating-world art." Wood-block art evolved during the seventeenth and eighteenth centuries from skillful monochromes to complex polychromes. Hishikawa Moronobu (1618–94) was a founder of the art and Suzuki Harunobu (1725–70) one of its greatest practitioners. Working at times with Saikaku, Moronobu made the demimonde the focus of *ukiyo-e*. Harunobu, like many *ukiyo* artists, was noted for his skill in portraying beautiful young women of both the demimonde and the bourgeoisie in sensuous poses and languorous settings. The rulers disapproved, but the prints kept appearing.

Women of the licensed quarters, their lives, and their tragedies were at the heart of much floating-world literature

25. Ihara Saikaku, *The Life of an Amorous Woman and Other Writings*, trans. Ivan Morris (New York: New Directions Publishing Co., 1963), pp. 261–62.

and art. In those quarters women offered entertainment that ranged from the most highly aesthetic discourse to the most commonplace prostitution. The elaborate social stratification of the outside world was mirrored in the quarter's range of talent and accompanying courtesan ranks. For the greatest merchants—and the finest samurai lords, who entered the quarter incognito—there were high-ranking and highly cultured courtesans, and for all lower levels of wealth and polish the licensed quarters furnished appropriately lower levels of feminine pomp and propriety.

It was the kabuki drama that most tellingly portrayed the pride and pathos of the denizens of the entertainment districts. The human affections that inevitably arose from time to time between courtesan and client furnished a rich source of material for those writing kabuki librettos. The best-known librettist was Chikamatsu Monzaemon (1653–1725), who wrote plays for both kabuki and the enormously popular puppet theatre (*bunraku*). Chikamatsu entertained his audiences with many stories of star-crossed lovers, sometimes resolving their ethical dilemmas through love-suicides. His plays gave voice to the tensions in the lives of his audience. For example, in this passage from *Nebiki no kadomatsu* [The uprooted pine], we find the drunken merchant Hikosuke openly parading his arrogance and frustration.[26] He is berating the madam of a house of prostitution in this way:

> Yes, you can call her my lady Azuma, the great courtesan, all you please, but when you come down to it, she's just a high-priced whore—right? No, you can't deny it. Well, on top of that, she sells herself to Yojibei of Yamazaki. Why doesn't she sell herself to me, Hikosuke the tobacco merchant? I've never asked her to come down on her price, no, not a penny, not a fraction of a penny. Who does she think I am? . . . Doesn't she realize what a rich man I am? . . . I spent a fortune on Takahashi from Shimabara in Kyoto, and got her to send me a lock of her hair. . . . But to have Yojibei get the bet-

26. The quotations appear in Donald Keene, trans., *Major Plays of Chikamatsu* (New York: Columbia University Press, 1961), pp. 322–23, 332–33.

ter of me and be refused three, no four times by Azuma
of the Wisteria House—that doesn't leave my pride a
leg to stand on. Not half a leg.

Later, Hikosuke manages to frame Yojibei, the love-struck
son of the wealthy merchant, Jōkan. The father of Yojibei's
wife is an ex-samurai who accuses Jōkan of the most cruel
greediness for refusing to save Yojibei from execution by paying Hikosuke's blackmail. Heart-sick, Jōkan defends himself
in this way:

> A samurai's child is reared by samurai parents and be-
> comes a samurai himself because they teach him the
> warrior's code. A merchant's child is reared by merchant
> parents and becomes a merchant because they teach
> him the ways of commerce. . . . This trouble would
> never have arisen if only Yojibei had realized that mon-
> ey is so precious a treasure that it can even buy human
> lives. I am well aware that however much I begrudge
> spending my money, however much I hoard it, all that
> will be left me when I am dead is a single hempen
> shroud. But until I die I am bound to respect my gold
> and silver like the gods or Buddha himself—that is the
> way prescribed by Heaven for merchants. . . . Money is
> not the only thing I prize. I am loath to part even with
> dust and ashes. How could I not be reluctant to lose the
> life of my only son?

It is difficult to say who suffered more—Jōkan, whose life exemplified strict adherence to the ethics taught by Ishida
Baigan, or Hikosuke, whose life epitomized crass abuse of
those ethics.

Equally successful were Chikamatsu's dramatic, thun-
derous stories of samurai heroism. Their plots, like some Nō
plots, often were taken from the legendary days of Taira and
Minamoto. Whereas the Nō was stately and stylized, however, kabuki was big, bright, and showy. The grand sets,
large casts, vigorous dialogue, lively movement, and loud
music stood in sharp contrast to the sedately cadenced Nō.
Yet the two shared some story themes. And like the Nō the
kabuki often used the moment of "no action," an abruptly

frozen tableau culminating a series of developments, as the dramatic highlight, the emotional pinnacle.

One element contributing to the electricity and tension of kabuki was its musical accompaniment. There were more choral voices and orchestral instruments than in Nō. Moreover, the samisen, a long-necked lute recently developed from Okinawan and Chinese prototypes, was used as the principal component of the orchestra. Its loud twanging could evoke a wide range of sensibilities, but most effectively those of compelling urgency, terrifying expectation, and crushing finality.

Samurai sneaked into the licensed quarters, and into kabuki shows. They read Saikaku surreptitiously. And their eyes lingered over the wood-block prints that accompanied every text. Not a few of the writers and artists, including Chikamatsu himself, were men of samurai origin who had chosen to pursue other careers, often surrendering their samurai status in order to gain the necessary occupational liberty. This was happening in the seventeenth century when the integral bureaucratic order was most effective in restricting learning to the samurai class. Doubtless the familial origins and consequent childhood training of these ex-samurai helped enrich the emerging *chōnin* culture and infuse it with elements of *bushi* taste.

Enriched as it was by "deviant" samurai, the vital *chōnin* culture flourished within the integral bureaucratic order of early modern Japan. That order and the contradictions it embodied created tensions between samurai and merchants that imposed restraint and doubt on both, because each needed the other despite the partial incongruence of their values and interests. One can regard society-wide patterns of emotional discipline, denial, and release as extensions of this central tension. And one can see the tension expressed aesthetically in two disciplined art forms that sanctioned and gave voice to the most acute feelings of joy, fear, sorrow, regret, rancor, and humor. One was haiku poetry; the other, music of the *shakuhachi*.

The poet Matsuo Bashō (1644–94) is credited with perfecting from a tradition of humorous linked verse (*haikai*-style *renga*) the concise, seventeen-syllable haiku. The brevity and discipline of medieval Kamakura and Kyoto, the delicacy of classical Heian, and the crisp vitality of Momoyama and *ukiyo* were all compressed into the best of these telegraphic creations. Let us savor a few.[27]

> Snow melts,
>
> and the village is overflowing—
>
> with children.
>
> *(Issa)*

> All the rains of June:
>
> and one evening, secretly,
>
> through the pines, the moon.
>
> *(Ryōta)*

> "Now many years ago . . ."
>
> tales of earthquakes being told
>
> round the brazier's glow.
>
> *(Kyoroku)*

> The piercing chill I feel:
>
> my dead wife's comb, in our bedroom,
>
> under my heel. . . .
>
> *(Buson)*

The other equally compelling epitome of the early-modern age was music of the *shakuhachi*. A large bamboo flute played by itinerant monks, samurai, and professional musicians, it could convey the most haunting evocations of misted mountains, battles lost, villagers returning at dusk, warriors

27. Harold G. Henderson, *An Introduction to Haiku* (New York: Doubleday Anchor Books, 1958), pp. 138, 118, 65, and 113, respectively.

locked in combat, and mothers singing babes to sleep. From birth to death, people in all walks of life could hear their joys, their sorrows, their anticipations, and their outcomes all conveyed in the deep, resonant tones of the *shakuhachi*, tones that could be as urgent or languorous, as harsh or mellow, as pellucid or murky as the musician wished. Just as *gagaku* music can still evoke the world of Lady Murasaki, so the *shakuhachi* can recall that of Bashō, a civilization reborn, a world reknown.

The spread of literacy and learning

The emergence and flourishing of both *bushi* and *chōnin* arts and letters were part of a more basic trend of expanding literacy and learning. Despite the regime's attempt to treat knowledge as divisible, literacy and learning in Tokugawa Japan were not preserved as expressions of elite status. When one recalls the spread of popular Buddhism and the widespread appeal of notions of autonomous knowledge in medieval Japan, the diffusion of learning in the Tokugawa period does not seem surprising. However, when one bears in mind both the strenuous effort and striking success of early modern samurai in reimposing order on society and segregating the new elite from the masses, such a spread of literacy commands our attention.

It would be misleading to suppose that the newly risen warriors wished to reimpose total illiteracy on society. They did not. On the contrary, while study and commentary on the nature of society and on the ways in which people could purport to know its nature were to be prerogatives of the samurai class, the rulers actively promoted among the general populace "practical" and "moral" knowledge of the sort taught by Ishida Baigan. Many commoners also valued such practical learning. As generations passed, they acquired a general mastery of basic principles of moral conduct and such practical literary arts as elementary reading and mathematics. In the course of doing so, moreover, and despite *bushi* displeasure, they also developed an ever-greater knowledge of philosophical thought. The economic vitality of Tokugawa society and the burgeoning cities of the age created opportunities for commoners to learn much more than their rulers deemed appropriate. And once people had mastered the basic mechanics of reading, the thoughtful among them could not be held back.

Literacy was usually acquired by children at school. Most daimyo domains maintained schools for the offspring of their samurai. There they not only learned the mechanics of reading and writing but also studied philosophical texts and commentaries and mastered to some degree the other civil and military arts of the samurai. Some commoners were allowed to attend domanial academies, especially late in the Edo period. Generally, however, commoner children were taught by professional or amateur teachers in local schools operated by temples, merchants, wealthy farmers, local notables, or the teachers themselves. Mostly these schools taught basic literary skills and practical subjects, but as the decades passed, more and more commoners studied philosophical texts of all sorts, whether at school or at home.

Doubtless the rulers' strictures against commoner education slowed the spread of higher learning. In any case, however, even the restricted practical and moral education that was authorized constituted an extraordinary spread of literacy. It is very possible that by the mid-nineteenth century some 40 percent of men and 10 to 15 percent of women in Japan were able to read and write basic Japanese, making Japan's society one of the world's most literate.[28] Moreover, it was a functional literacy. It equipped people to read and understand practical writings, to keep family records and accounts, to comprehend official announcements, and to enjoy recreational reading of a simple sort.

To be literate, however, one must have something to read. Commoners could not read that which they could not afford to buy or otherwise obtain. A key factor in the spread of literacy was the development in seventeenth-century Japan of an economical means of mass communication.

The art and literature of earlier ages had been set down by brush. Screens, scrolls, and manuscripts were laboriously drawn and written a stroke at a time, one copy at a time. Dur-

28. Dore, pp. 317–22, examines school attendance at the end of the Tokugawa period.

ing the first century and a half of the early-modern age, however, printing developed into a major vehicle for disseminating the written word, and publishing firms developed to operate the new technology. Printing with moveable type was practiced briefly in the late sixteenth century, but it soon gave way to block printing. This shift in printing systems probably occurred because the latter was technically simpler and functionally more flexible. Because early-modern printers were selling to a public that ranged from the erudite to the illiterate, they had to be able to print materials of wide variety, ranging from exegeses on Confucian tracts to primers for the most elementary learner. They therefore had to publish some works using Chinese characters (*kanji*) without notation, some utilizing pronunciation guides (*furigana*), some written solely in the Japanese syllabary (*kana*), some accompanied by explanatory pictures, and some that were simply picture books. Block printing permitted this variety of textual treatments with an ease that moveable type did not. Because of its versatility it became a key element in all the forms of *ukiyo* culture. Floating-world fiction and art were both block printed, as were the librettos, advertising handbills, posters, and programs of kabuki drama. It seems likely, therefore, that the choice of block printing over moveable type not only reflected the educational levels and needs of the populace but also facilitated the rapid spread of literacy, learning, and higher cultural interests throughout society.

The pattern of early-modern thought

The intricate and changing relationship of early-modern samurai and townsmen was evident in the field of philosophical speculation. During the early seventeenth century, when samurai were most successful in putting distance between themselves and merchants, almost all the active intellectuals were samurai. By the century's end, however, as merchants reasserted their influence in affairs, they—and other commoners—also began to appear as important commentators, teachers, and scholars.

The growing diversity of the intellectual community's

social background was paralleled by growing diversity of thought. The most influential thought of the early seventeenth century was the Neo-Confucian political thought examined earlier. Rather as Nara Buddhists had eclectically studied diverse Buddhist teachings, however, early-modern scholars initially studied not only Chu Hsi's writings but also the other major traditions of Confucian thought, Buddhism, Christianity, and the monuments of Japan's own heritage, such as the *Kojiki*, the *Tale of Genji*, and works of medieval scholarship. By the end of the 1700s these strands of thought were being sorted out, Christianity was tabooed, and the Neo-Confucian thought favored by Tokugawa authorities was being challenged by vigorous proponents of other lines of Confucian thought. As the eighteenth century progressed, intellectual diversification intensified. Japan experienced an extraordinary proliferation of thought that derived inspiration from various Chinese, Japanese, and even Western intellectual traditions. By the nineteenth century, as will be noted later, this body of thought had acquired a subversive quality. It challenged basic tenets of the established order and suggested reasons and ways to reform or even transform it.

One factor that gave rise to the outpouring of seventeenth-century *bushi* thought was the minimal duty required of so many samurai, which gave them ample time for study. Another was the pervasive, government-encouraged conviction that a person ought to be busy at something useful and uplifting and that learning was just such a busyness. A third factor, which in a sense resulted from the other two, was the spread of literacy to the whole samurai class during the seventeenth century.

To explain why *bushi* thought was so heavily political, one probably must point to the age and the political order that took shape. The samurai who rose to power in the late sixteenth century were concerned above all with justifying their privileges and sustaining their positions. Political questions, therefore, were the most pressing ones in their lives. They had to rationalize their success, and the Neo-Confucianism of Chu Hsi provided a means of doing so. As the integral bureaucratic order took shape, however, it became evident that there was a fundamental disjunction between theory and reality. The theory of a simple hierarchical society run by a cultured ruling elite did not correspond sufficiently to the fact of a complex economy and intricately linked social order dominated by an underemployed samurai class that had compelling need to get along with people of entrepreneurial ability. Thoughtful samurai, and eventually other observers, were tormented by the disjunction of established theory and evident reality and wrestled with the problem. Some tried to make reality conform to theory, others tried to shape ideas to reality. In the course of doing so they digested much more than the teachings of Chu Hsi, and they produced a body of political writings that was striking in its diversity and perceptiveness.

Having set sail upon the waters of Confucian thought, samurai intellectuals of the seventeenth century ranged well beyond political questions. Concerning the nature of reality they worked out statements the subtlety of which can only be hinted at in this brief study. Kaibara Ekken, for example, rooted his principles of human conduct in a basic perception of man's infrangible ties to the universe, and observed that

> All men may be said to owe their birth to their parents, but a further inquiry into their origins reveals that men come into being because of nature's law of life. . . . [If] we go to the root of the matter, we find that we sustain ourselves using the things produced by nature for food, dress, housing, and implements. Thus, not only do all men at the outset come into being because of nature's law of life, but from birth till the end of life they are kept in existence by the support of heaven and earth. . . . It will be seen therefore that man's duty is not only to do his best to serve his parents, which is a matter of course, but also to serve nature throughout his life in order to repay his immense debt.[29]

Nakae Tōju (1608–48) confronted the elemental question of man's nature and found moral sense basic to all people. He asserted that

29. Tsunoda et al., p. 376.

There is no distinction among men, be they sages or ordinary persons, so far as their Heaven-bestowed nature is concerned. They are all gifted with the divine light that tells good from bad. All men hate injustice and are ashamed of evil because they are born with this intuitive knowledge. It is only from the self-watchfulness of the one and the self-deceit of the other that the vast distinction arises between the superior man and the inferior man. If, however, the inferior man realizes where he has erred and becomes watchful over himself, correcting his mistakes and turning to the good, he may then become a superior man.[30]

In this passage Nakae reveals not only how thinkers pressed their inquiries to fundamentals but also how from the very outset early modern thought sustained the medieval notion of self-determination or intuitive insight.

The medieval perception that understanding arose within oneself constituted an epistemology fundamentally at odds with the Neo-Confucian view that correct knowledge and sound understanding were derived from the study of approved texts. That perception continued to flourish in Sōtō Zen monasteries. It appeared in secular philosophy in the Ōyōmei (Wang Yang-ming in the Chinese pronunciation) school of Confucianism. Chu Hsi's thought called for the "investigation of things," meaning the study of the external world, as the basis for an understanding that must precede action. By contrast, Ōyōmei intuitionism, in H. D. Harootunian's words, favored

the authority of speculation over against moral precedent in guiding behavior; interiority was prior to exteriority, public behavior followed private impulse. This kind of intuitionism . . . held that men always know how to act correctly, without recourse to investigation, and that learning can only confirm this self-knowledge.[31]

30. Ibid., p. 382.

31. H. D. Harootunian, *Toward Restoration* (Berkeley: University of California Press, 1970), p. 139.

Nakae, who studied Ōyōmei deeply, evinced this perception in his concept of the "divine light that tells good from bad."

The corpus of Confucian thought, as absorbed and recast by *bushi* thinkers of the seventeenth century, thus embodied definable grounds of knowledge. It also contained explicit statements about the character of being, the relationships of the parts of existence, the role of humans, and principles of proper conduct. Parts of the corpus, notably Neo-Confucianism, served to legitimize the integral bureaucratic order that Momoyama culture celebrated. However, other parts, notably Ōyōmei, provided foundation for sophisticated counterideologies that could legitimize strategies for change should an observer conclude that social conditions no longer were tolerable.

During the early eighteenth century, Tokugawa thought branched out, acquiring great diversity and even more vitality. This diversity and vitality may be considered a result of the combination of successes and failures characterizing seventeenth-century cultural policy. The successful encouragement of both elite and commoner learning, the regime's preference for Chu Hsi's "investigation of things," and the value attached to an integrated explanatory strategy all promoted intellectual inquiry. The failure of the seventeenth-century policy of treating knowledge as divisible, the inadequacies of Chu Hsi's teachings as guide to political strategy, its vulnerability to logical criticism, and the persistence of the medieval intuitionist approach to understanding all worked to drive intellectual inquiry beyond the boundaries of practice and content sanctioned by Neo-Confucianism.

The rulers' inability to reserve some learning for samurai, while other learning was authorized for commoners, was evident in the changing social character of those thinkers whose ideas commanded attention. Most of the famous intellectuals of the seventeenth century, such as Yamazaki, Kaibara, Nakae, and Yamaga, were *bushi*. There were few exceptions, one being Itō Jinsai (1627–1705), the son of a Kyoto merchant who studied ancient Confucian texts and was an early critic of Chu Hsi's thought.[32] From the eighteenth cen-

32. On Itō Jinsai, see Joseph J. Spae, *Itō Jinsai* (Peking: Catholic University of Peking, 1948).

tury on, however, more and more of the major creative figures were of commoner origin or, occasionally, samurai who surrendered their titles. Among them were Ogyū Sorai, son of a daimyo's physician, and Ishida Baigan, whose teachings were noted earlier. There was the Shintō priest Kamo Mabuchi (1697–1769), and his student the Shintō scholar, Motoori Norinaga (1730–1801), who was the son of a merchant. There were the "rationalist" scholars Tominaga Nakamoto (1715–46), son of an Osaka merchant who had founded a school for Confucian studies, and Miura Baien (1723–89), the son of a village physician. Most of these thinkers also symbolized the challenge to the Neo-Confucian order, in the sense that they went far beyond the prescribed body of authoritative texts and questioned essential aspects of the Neo-Confucian philosophical vision.

Among Confucian scholars the seminal thinker in this story of intellectual exploration was Ogyū Sorai. We have already noted his distaste for commoner excess and his particular dislike of merchants.[33] Ogyū charged that Hayashi Razan and others had erred in relying upon the writings of Chu Hsi and other scholars of the Sung dynasty. He considered it axiomatic that

> the world changes, carrying words [or language] with it. Words change, carrying the Way with them. This is the main reason why the Way is not clear.[34]

This philological premise then led him to argue that one could properly understand Confucius's explanation of the Way and hence properly understand governance only by scrutinizing the original writings of Confucius's own day (*kogaku*; ancient studies). On the basis of his reading of these texts, he denied that the Tokugawa order deserved to exist, as Neo-Confucian theory seemed to imply, merely because it was there as the social manifestation of the larger Way of the universe. He con-

33. In identifying Ogyū Sorai as the seminal thinker here, I am following the powerful argument developed by Maruyama in his study of Ogyū's thought and legacy cited in note 9, above.

34. Maruyama, p. 76.

tended, instead, that its worth constantly had to be demonstrated by rulers ruling competently.[35]

As Ogyū described the political process, a regime was established by a great founder, a farsighted sage who would establish institutions, "in such a way that these will give rise to the smallest number of disruptive influences." As generations pass, Ogyū went on, less able men come to power and bad practices arise.

> As a state grows more "extravagant" the degrees of status become more sharply defined than was the case at the time of its foundation. This is not done in conformity with the institutions of the Sage who founded the dynasty but is the work of men of much inferior capacity acting in accordance with the changes in the manners and customs of the times.

These men of inferior capacity are in power because of the malign and unnatural practice of treating government office as hereditary. It is natural, he argued, that "old things should pass away and new things be brought into existence." Aware that men of talent constantly appeared among "the lower classes," by which he meant lower ranks of the samurai class, Ogyū said,

> The Sages . . . instituted a system of "rewards and punishments," encouraging and promoting to office men of ability from the lower classes, and removing men of ability from the upper classes as the mind of Heaven willed it, either by their dying without direct descendants, or as a result of their committing some offence.

If this is not done, incompetents come to dominate affairs. An age of disorder then sets in, and "men of ability" from below overthrow the regime, thus setting the stage for a new dynastic cycle. In Ogyū's view the Tokugawa order had reached a parlous state by the eighteenth century, with the rulers profligate, the samurai class impoverished, lesser peoples

---

35. The following quotations are taken from McEwan, pp. 30, 32, 77, 78, 59, and 63, in that order.

out of control, merchants piling one unwarranted profit upon another, and the enervating ways of urban luxury destroying the moral fiber of society. To cope with these malign trends, Ogyu recommended some major policy changes. He argued that daimyo who failed to govern effectively could properly be stripped of their titles and privileges. He advocated changes in the *sankin kōtai* system of daimyo attendance upon the shogun so as to return samurai to the countryside. He reasoned that

> If the members of the military class were resident in the country, they would incur no expense in providing themselves with food, clothing and shelter, and for this reason their financial condition would be much improved.

Such a policy would also restore the vitality of the samurai, strengthen their control over the people, and reestablish peasant respect for their samurai betters. The samurai could then collect rice directly from the peasants and thus reduce city supplies and drive up the cost of food in Edo. That would have the salutary effect of forcing commoners "to eat coarse grains," thus distinguishing the food of the rulers from that of the ruled, "which is also in accordance with the ancient Way."

Clearly Ogyū, in his struggle to resolve the contradiction between political theory and social reality, wished to bend the latter a great deal. To do so he was prepared to call upon the rulers to take forceful actions because only by doing so could they cope with their problems. And only by coping could they justify and save their regime. It certainly was not Ogyū's intention to undermine the regime. However, by arguing that performance, and not existence per se, justified it, he undercut the sanctity of the established order and paved the way for others to propose much more radical solutions to the problems of integral bureaucracy.

Ogyū's thought was important because it directly influenced many later intellectuals, and it also illustrates how logicians could challenge Neo-Confucian dogma. The challenge to Chu Hsi's thought was also apparent in the works of two other scholars. Tominaga Nakamoto shared Ogyū's disbelief in an unchanging way with its corollary ideal of historical stasis. And like him Tominaga used linguistic analysis to support his position. Where Ogyū's analysis, however, was Confucian in character, Tominaga's used Buddhist categories. Miura Baien also questioned Neo-Confucianism. Whereas Chu Hsi scholars tended to treat the existence of the symbiotic opposites, *yin* and *yang*, as givens, for example, Miura sought to understand them by asking "why that which belongs to *yang* is hot and why that which belongs to *yin* is cold." [36] For Miura the "investigation of things" meant empirical study grounded in critical thought. Like Tominaga, his was a universe in motion. It was a logical universe, but it was in constant flux, in contrast to the fixed Way of Chu Hsi. And it was composed of entwined contradictions and syntheses, not integral parts that properly articulated in harmonious stability.

Challenges to Chu Hsi's thought were also raised by students of the Japanese tradition. The medieval revival of Shintō and the apotheosis of imperial rule by writers such as Kitabatake Chikafusa reappeared in historical consciousness during the Tokugawa period and contributed to a reordering of political priorities. During the seventeenth century, scholars tried to fit the Japanese legacy into a Confucian framework. But during the eighteenth, as they grew dissatisfied with the established intellectual order, thinkers began to reassert the autonomous worth of the native heritage.

Motoori Norinaga was a seminal figure in the development of this "national learning" (*kokugaku*), successfully articulating a cosmology grounded in the Japanese tradition. He grew up in a merchant family that practiced a popularized form of Jōdo Shin Buddhism involving worship of family ancestors and various Shintō and Buddhist divinities, notably the Sun Goddess Amaterasu and Amida. After leaving his family, he began to practice medicine, teach Japanese literature, and study eclectically, giving close attention to the Confucian writings of Ogyū Sorai. Being himself far from power and finding Ogyū persuasive in treating the Way as basically

36. Tsunoda et al., p. 490. Italics added.

a political matter, Motoori turned his interest to questions of human values. He regarded "human feelings," sensibilities such as love, rather than rationalism as espoused by Neo-Confucian thought, as basic to behavior. He maintained that the cultivation of sensibilities, as demonstrated in the *Tale of Genji*, was the distinguishing mark of Japanese civilization. Rather like such proponents of Ōyōmei thought as Nakae Tōju, he believed that the "natural man" knows good from bad. Unlike them, however, he attributed this capacity to the benevolence of the ancient Shintō divinity, Musubi no kami, whose mysterious powers gave rise to all things:[37]

> "All human beings, having been born through the spirit of Musubi no kami, are naturally endowed with the knowledge and capability of what they ought to do."

Indeed, "All living things in the world, even birds and insects, are, owing to Musubi no kami, aware of and able to do what they should do."

The Shintō divinity Musubi no kami was thus a critical formative figure in Motoori's cosmology. However, his careful philological study of Shintō led Motoori to conclude that *kami* included

> the deities of heaven and earth that appear in the ancient texts and also the spirits enshrined in the shrines; furthermore, among all kinds of beings—including not only human beings but also such objects as birds, beasts, trees, grass, seas, mountains, and so forth—any being whatsoever which possesses some eminent quality out of the ordinary, and is awe-inspiring, is called *kami*.

Thus *kami* included not only the creator deities of ancient days, most notably Amaterasu, but also many awe-inspiring beings or sites that exist in the world of man. Because the former had established themselves in Japan rather than else-

---

37. Motoori is quoted from Shigeru Matsumoto, *Motoori Norinaga, 1730–1801* (Cambridge, Mass.: Harvard University Press, 1970), pp. 101, 101, 84 (italics added), 63–64, 77, 139–40, in that order.

where and founded the imperial lineage there, Japan was a special land, its special quality being attributable to its divine origins.

In primordial Japan that special quality had prevailed. Through the spirit of Musubi no kami, rulers and people had practiced natural virtue:

> In ancient times, both the lord and the people [of our country] dedicated themselves to natural Shintō, in accordance with which they were moral without personal cultivation and the land was at peace without government. Propriety and righteousness existed naturally; there was no need to depend upon the [Confucian] Way of the Sages. Later, however, in medieval times, customs gradually changed and the people became deceitful; disloyal subjects disordered the land and corrupted morals. Then it became necessary to rule the land and to maintain morals by borrowing the Way of the Sages from an alien country.

Motoori found this ancient age of natural virtue embodied in the *Kojiki*, which, he wrote,

> accurately records what was orally transmitted from antiquity, without any artificial addition. Hence, the spirit, deeds, and words which the *Kojiki* records are all representative of the reality of ancient times. This is because this book [unlike the Chinese-language *Nihongi*] was written in such a way as to preserve the ancient [Japanese] language.

The more Motoori studied the *Kojiki*, the more hostile he became toward Chinese influence in Japan. He saw in it a corrupting rationalism that thwarted the human capacity to develop one's natural feelings and hence one's capacity to have faith in the myriad *kami* and the tranquillity of life. As a result, he observed, rulers found themselves forced to impose the "rigid Way" of China upon Japan to keep the peace.

Motoori's perception that through the centuries the ancient virtue of Japan had become corrupted led him to conclude that the integral bureaucratic order of the day was necessary and appropriate but that it was also accountable to Amaterasu for the way it governed the descendants of the *kami*. Its continued well-being depended upon the quality of its rule. He asserted, for example, that Ieyasu's success sprang from the fact that he

> gradually restored the imperial household, which had been in decline, and further had deep respect for it, and thus pacified successively the samurai and the common people.

Motoori's reading of the central role of the imperial institution thus juxtaposed it against the Tokugawa rulers insofar as its virtue derived from its origins in the *kami* and was inherent, whereas their virtue required constant demonstration through effective governance. This understanding did not lead him, in the manner of Go-Daigo, to advocate a return to the structure of antiquity. Rather, he urged compassionate administration by the established rulers, both shogun and daimyo, with reverence for emperor, court, and Shintō shrines and mercy toward commoners, "the people of Amaterasu," as he called them. Like Ogyū, he ended up holding the regime accountable. Its only justification for existence was its ability to govern well.

By the mid-eighteenth century, Tokugawa thought had moved beyond the articulation of a Neo-Confucian position advantageous to the rulers and had come to embody various perceptions based on both Chinese and Japanese precedents. Insofar as the early modern *bushi* had attempted to forge through use of Chu Hsi's thought an integrated philosophical order akin to that of the classical *kuge*'s Tendai-Shingon, they had failed. Instead they, their unwelcome *chōnin* collaborators, and articulate scholars from other strata of society had given rise, as had their medieval predecessors, to lines of thought that did not mesh nicely. From the latter part of the eighteenth century, as will be noted later, the implications of this intellectual pattern began to become apparent. As doctrinal lines hardened, antiestablishment positions became more pronounced, and scholars began attempting to formulate new integrative statements to replace the defunct Neo-Confucian vision.

SOCIAL CHANGE: TOWARD COMPLETION OF A METAMORPHOSIS

During the medieval period, as suggested in the last chapter, Japan began a metamorphosis that narrowed the gap between classical patrician and pleb and endowed society with important characteristics of nationhood. The metamorphosis continued during the Tokugawa period, and by the nineteenth century had moved far toward completion. In some aspects it involved continuities between the medieval and early modern ages. In others it involved major discontinuities. One discontinuity was the shift from a very weak feudal polity to a very strong bureaucratic one. Another was the reversal in long-term continental relations from an expanding involvement in Asia to a severe limiting of that involvement. Another was a shift from a predominantly Buddhist and religious cultural orientation to a predominantly Confucian and secular one.

In other ways the process involved continuities, perhaps most notably in the accelerated spread of literacy and learning. That literacy and learning was crucial to the flourishing of *chōnin* culture, as has been noted. And in a more fundamental way it was basic to the whole age, just as elite literacy had been of basic importance to classical Japan. For example, the capacity of samurai to govern by routinized civil administration depended upon their general ability to manage bureaucratic forms and their success in formulating and comprehending a sophisticated ideology of rule. Moreover, the general public's capacity to develop and sustain their own complex organizations and manage their own affairs depended upon literate skills.

The metamorphosis of Japan continued or accelerated in other ways that can usefully be subsumed under the labels urbanization, commercialization, and rural change.

Urbanization

From the founding of Nara onward, the form and experience of Japanese cities were tied to the character and vicissitudes of the larger political order. Nara and subsequently Heian were imperial capitals that waxed and waned with aristocratic bureaucracy. The cities and towns of medieval Japan flourished and faded with the varied religious, military, and commercial groups who dominated them. In early-modern Japan, castle towns emerged as the primary urban form. Like the integral bureaucratic order in which they existed, and whose fortunes they shared, they were dominated by *bushi* and *chōnin*. And like that larger order they embraced the multiple activities of society: political, economic, religious, and cultural. Despite their multifunctional character, however, castle towns were basically political creatures, and specific political processes underlay their development. One could even argue that the urbanization of early modern Japan was a bizarre and unintended byproduct of the country-wide application of two simple political practices of late-sixteenth-century samurai leaders. One was the practice of holding hostages to assure the good behavior of one's allies; the other, the practice of requiring one's vassals to reside at one's castle.

The gathering of vassals at one's castle gave rise to most of the towns of Tokugawa Japan. After peace came to the land, those vassals-in-residence became a permanent urban consumer class. They were joined by equally large numbers of commoners, who provided goods and services of myriad sorts. In consequence of this clustering of people about the castles, early-modern Japan contained some two hundred fifty castle towns. Most ranged in population from about three to twenty thousand souls. Several, however, were larger: Kanazawa and Nagoya, each with more than one hundred thousand; Kagoshima, Hiroshima, Okayama, and Sendai with some sixty-five thousand or more; Tokushima, Fukui, and Akita with about forty thousand each; and thirteen castle towns in the twenty to thirty thousand range. In most of these towns about half the residents were of samurai status and half nonsamurai.

In a similar manner the hostage system lay at the heart of the great cities. Edo was the greatest of them, its eighteenth-century population of over a million also consisting of roughly equal parts samurai and nonsamurai. Most of the former were there in conjunction with the *sankin kōtai* hostage system, and the latter, by and large, were service, processing, and purveyor groups whose income traced ultimately to the tax monies that samurai spent in the city. Osaka became a great city of four hundred thousand primarily because it was a great entrepôt for *sankin-kōtai*-related transactions of the western daimyo. Kyoto's population of some four hundred thousand was to a great extent sustained by the presence of *kuge* and *bushi* who received and spent their tax income in the city. They were in the city to maintain the linkage between *bakufu* power and imperial authority, living there in a state of de facto captivity as hostages to the established order.

During the sixteenth and seventeenth centuries, castle towns grew and flourished as a consequence of these political practices. Some developed out of medieval port, transit, and temple towns, others arose on newly selected sites. A number of the old towns also flourished in their own right: Sakai with over fifty thousand people; about eight port towns with ten to twenty thousand people, and a handful of temple towns of over five thousand souls. More than two hundred new transit towns dotted the highways along which *sankin kōtai* retinues moved, and about ten of them had populations in excess of five thousand. Some new commercial towns, such as the silk-processing town of Kiryū and the metal-working town of Takaoka, also developed in conjunction with new patterns of production and distribution. In time many castle towns themselves developed a whole range of internal economic relationships and ties to the hinterland that were independent of governmental finances.

The extent of this urban growth was impressive. Most medieval towns had fewer than five thousand inhabitants, a score or so were in the five to thirty thousand range, only a half-dozen or so were in the thirty to sixty thousand range, and Kyoto was the one major metropolis. Tokugawa Japan, by contrast, had three great metropolitan centers, at least ten regional cities of forty to one hundred twenty thousand, one hundred fifty or more towns of five thousand or more inhabitants, and an even larger number of smaller towns. By the eighteenth century, upwards of 15 percent of the Japanese public, some 4 million people, lived in towns, chiefly in the castle towns.[38] It was a vastly greater absolute number and a much greater proportion of the total public than ever before, and it lived in a far greater number of towns than had ever before existed in Japan.

As the Neo-Confucian tenet that peasants were the true foundation of the economy acquired ideological validity, *bushi* rulers became alarmed at the movement of people into cities. This alarm, so evident in the writings of Ogyū Sorai, led to action after about 1700, when taxable rural production ceased its rapid growth. Fearful that the swelling urban population would impoverish society and wreck the regime, rulers tried to stop the urbanizing trend. They attempted by edict and action to force people back to the soil. And their efforts seemed to bear some fruit in that the rapid pace of urbanization slowed dramatically after the early 1700s.

It seems more likely, however, that the stabilization of castle-town populations was primarily a byproduct of the stabilization of tax income that could be spent in the cities. With no greater tax income pouring into them, the cities lost a major means of supporting a larger populace at the ongoing level of living. The magnet of opportunity lost much of its pull. Then the stabilization was reinforced by the spread of commercial activity to the hinterland because that shifted work and investment opportunities away from the city and reduced proportionately the economic advantages of urban migration. Population movement did not cease, but its patterns became more varied, with some people moving, for example, from castle towns out to rural districts or from rural areas to small commercial centers. The process probably in-

38. These population figures derive from Yazaki, pp. 123ff. For a sociological study of Tokugawa urbanism, see Gilbert Rozman, *Urban Networks in Ch'ing China and Tokugawa Japan* (Princeton: Princeton University Press, 1973).

creased rather than decreased the total urban populace of Japan, but it had the net effect of eroding the economic primacy of the older, larger cities such as Osaka. In the process it led to urban unemployment, severe price fluctuations, hardship, and sporadic outbursts of rioting.

In the end, then, the early modern order had fostered urbanization, but it had also placed outer limits on the growth potential of large towns. Such urbanization as still continued during the nineteenth century did so in response to new commercial patterns that were developing in ways destructive of the seventeenth-century settlement. Like stresses in the polity and new trends in higher culture, it seemed symptomatic of more general changes in the making.

Commercialization

A number of economic trends that had become evident during the medieval period accelerated during the early modern age. In sum they accounted for the commercialization of society.

The most visible part of commercialization occurred during the seventeenth century and involved city people most directly. One major aspect of the process was the development of wealthy merchant houses to which allusion was made previously. By the early eighteenth century, great merchant houses such as Yodoya, Kōnoike, and Mitsui and organized groups of wholesale distributors (*ton'ya*) had come to manage elaborate mercantile empires and legal monopolies. These involved such activities as transporting, storing, wholesaling, retailing, banking, and brokering.

Most of these urban mercantile barons reached their pinnacle during the early 1700s. Thereafter their positions tended to stabilize. One reason for the stabilization was that they were urban, and given the character of Tokugawa cities, the end of urban growth meant an end to most opportunities for economic expansion in the city. Moreover, as samurai acquired the ideological conviction that commerce was harmful, governments enacted more severe, although sporadic, measures to curb and intimidate the merchant elite. These measures prompted wealthy merchants to conceal their wealth, to use it conservatively, and to avoid risky ventures that might prove so lucrative as to invite official plunder. This very conservatism left to others the profits of eighteenth- and nineteenth-century rural economic development, and the shift of commercial growth to the hinterland gradually undercut the monopoly positions of great city merchant houses. By the time they recognized the danger, they were unable to reverse the trend, even when they secured governmental support. To cite two examples, by the nineteenth century cotton processors in Osaka were unable to stop competitors in the hinterland from taking away their business.[39] And silk merchants in Edo were unable to control the sales activity of producers in Kiryū and other rural centers.[40]

The stabilizing of great-merchant activity thus did not signal the end of economic development but rather a change in its scale, location, and participants. The use of money developed rather similarly. Its use spread first in the cities and later in the hinterland. By the latter part of the Tokugawa period all parts of society were familiar with it. Samurai, urban laborers and servants, peasants, and even rural laborers all used money. No part of society was fully monetized, but none could get along without some cash. As the decades passed, money and products that were assigned cash value on the basis of market worth became ever more basic to the daily lives of everyone. Thus peasants always paid part of their taxes in kind. By the eighteenth century, however, about a third of the *bakufu*'s agricultural tax levy was legally payable in money, and an even larger proportion actually was paid in that way. An ever-larger proportion of the regime's total income was from nonfarm sources, usually commercial and mostly paid in money. By the mid-nineteenth century, money taxes constituted the great bulk of *bakufu* income.[41]

39. William Hauser, *Economic Institutional Change in Tokugawa Japan* (Cambridge, Mass.: Harvard University Press, 1974), examines the Osaka cotton trade.

40. Yazaki, p. 266. Yazaki sees this growing merchant power vis-à-vis the samurai as evidence of feudal disintegration in the face of popular opposition to oppression.

41. Totman, pp. 80–83. Harold Bolitho, *Treasures Among Men* (New Haven: Yale University Press, 1974), pp. 58ff., discusses commercialism in daimyo domains.

Despite its pervasiveness, the monetary system was not fully rationalized. From the outset the Tokugawa *bakufu* claimed a monopoly right to mint coin of the realm. However, its gold, silver, and copper mints issued a large number of coins, and their purchasing power differed from issue to issue. The daimyo were permitted to issue paper notes for local use, and in time there came to be many types of coins and notes in circulation, their value being inconstant and varying from place to place. On the other hand, the monetary system was uncommonly sophisticated insofar as the legal value of most coins of daily use was determined in the manner of modern currencies not by their metallic content (as were contemporary European coins) but by their assigned face value.

In this nationwide market system, rice was the single most important commodity. At the same time an immense variety of other products was also transported from nationally known production areas to markets throughout the land. These included diverse textiles in all stages of processing, an extraordinary variety of sea products, myriad other foodstuffs, and a wide range of manufactured goods.[42]

The organizational elaborateness of commerce, the complex and pervasive monetary system, and the nationwide patterns of trade that characterized early-modern Japan added up to a highly integrated national economic system. One may envisage it as a bipolar magnetic field linked to the fields of lesser magnetic poles. The great centers of Osaka and Edo were the two main poles, with continuous transfers of people, produce, and monetary instruments binding the two closely together. From these two poles there radiated outward to all the castle towns smaller streams of people, produce, and financial instruments. And from all those castle towns in turn there extended into the hinterland lesser transactional threads involving tax income, supervisory personnel, employed people, and a proportionately smaller flow of commodities and monetary instruments.

As the Tokugawa period advanced, these patterns of linkage were supplemented and sometimes supplanted by other irregular transactional linkages. The latter bypassed

42. Tsuchiya, pp. 182–84, lists goods extensively.

castle towns, linked separate rural areas, or joined rural areas and noncastle towns directly to the great cities. It was in this "irregular" commerce, whose particularistic nature made it difficult for *bushi* and *chōnin* to regulate and exploit, that rural entrepreneurs found their greatest opportunity to flourish and to acquire the capabilities for social development.

Rural change

Viewed in broadest terms, early-modern rural change was part of the long-run trend that was gradually closing the ancient gap between classical pleb and patrician and giving rise to Japanese nationhood. In doing so it was foreshadowing the emergence of a new post-Tokugawa epoch. The spread of Buddhism and other aspects of medieval change, and subsequently the diffusion of literacy and the emergence of a zestful *chōnin* higher culture narrowed greatly the gap between class and mass in urban areas. Rural change extended the trend into the hinterland. It had the eventual effect of creating a rural populace that was ever more economically self-conscious, more self-directed, and more capable of managing its affairs even in defiance—albeit judicious defiance—of the rulers.

To oversimplify a complex process, early-modern urban growth and change seem to have had profound rural ramifications. The growth created a labor shortage that gave the poor and discontented alternatives to the village status quo. They could leave the village, and the emergence of that choice undercut established village relationships, which had been strongly hereditary, hierarchical, and kin-based. Improvements in agricultural technology and the expansion of crop land permitted increased production, thereby creating new opportunities for material gain within the village. Then the spread of commercial activity to the hinterland added yet other opportunities for gain.[43] Concurrently, levels of literacy and learning in the village were rising. The cumulative effect of all this was to enhance greatly the possibility that the in-

43. Thomas C. Smith, *The Agrarian Origins of Modern Japan* (Stanford: Stanford University Press, 1959), remains the definitive monograph on Tokugawa village change.

dustrious, the adventurous, and the lucky would flourish. Conversely, of course, the whole process created opportunities for the careless or unlucky to fritter away a patrimony or slip into the most abject and exploitable poverty.

The entrepreneurial possibilities were recognized by villagers of the day. To quote a didactic account from an agrarian treatise of the Tokugawa period,[44]

> A certain person in Usui District in Jōshū [Kōzuke Province] lost his father when young and served his mother faithfully. The family was poor and . . . passed their days in want. Having exhausted all means of caring for his mother, the young man determined that nothing brought a greater profit to farmers than sericulture. He therefore studied the secrets of raising worms, . . . planted mulberry bushes on a part of his land . . . [and] listened carefully to successful sericulturists in his village and nearby as they discussed the pros and cons of the various methods of raising silkworms. He began raising worms himself, working at the task night and day, and in five or six years his profits increased. He bought up arable fields and forest land and became one of the wealthiest men in the vicinity of Takasaki. This was the "virtue" [*toku*, a word that also means "profit"] of filial piety.

The other side of the coin was not ignored. An awareness of the risks of indolence, error, or accident doubtless underlay Ninomiya Sontoku's emphasis on frugality, diligence, and careful planning. As another writer put it,

> Since this is an era of increasing prices, if a man does not get the maximum yield from his crops, he will be unable to perpetuate his family [*ie*] and to support his wife and children. Let him pray to the gods that his children will surpass others . . . and thereby get on in life. For if they do not—if they let his hopes come to nothing and by indolence ruin the family—how great will his crime then be.

44. Thomas C. Smith, *Nakahara* (Stanford: Stanford University Press, 1977), pp. 116–17. The quotations are complete in Smith.

By the nineteenth century the rural Japanese population contained large numbers of landless laborers and poor tenant farmers, vast numbers of farmers with small holdings of their own, and a considerable number of landlords. Many of the landlords used their capital to operate various small commercial activities, such as oil-making, sake-brewing, shipping, money-lending, and textile or handicraft production. Perhaps a quarter of this populace was literate, and some were well-read, cosmopolitan, and informed concerning urban and national affairs. Almost all rural people were familiar with money. They had some knowledge of one or another higher religion, most commonly a Buddhist sect. And they knew well the basic rules and regulations of the polity as a whole.

These processes of social change did not touch all parts of Japan equally. The greatest degree of change was experienced by those rural folk living near the highways, towns, and cities, who were most accessible to the urban world and its rulers. It was they who were most exposed to effective tax collection, corvée recruitment, and conscription on the one hand, and economic, educational, and political opportunity on the other. Their situation blurred the distinction between rural and urban. In a sense, it made nineteenth-century Japan a metropolitan network that was slowly expanding and encroaching upon those hinterland enclaves that still existed farther back in the mountains and along the coastlines away from the arteries of commerce and administration.[45] Those integrative structural and cultural elements of nationhood that first appeared in the medieval age had grown and spread, preparing the island populace for yet a new historic epoch.

The processes of urbanization, commercialization, and rural change were linked to the other aspects of change in early modern Japan—to the formation and evolution of the

45. A strikingly different picture is presented in Dan F. Henderson, *Village "Contracts" in Tokugawa Japan* (Seattle: University of Washington Press, 1975), where the isolation and immobility of the Tokugawa village is stressed. The contrast illustrates well how a scholar's frame of reference shapes the argument. Whereas I am juxtaposing Tokugawa to earlier Japanese society, Professor Henderson is juxtaposing Tokugawa to modern industrial society.

polity, the spread of literacy, and the cultural advancement of samurai and townsmen. All this was reflected in the chronology of development. The seventeenth century was the great age of the new polity, the age when it showed its greatest vitality and effectiveness. It was also the age in which the samurai class acquired general literacy and learning. It was the heyday of *bushi* higher culture: the latter part of Momoyama and the first grand flowering of Japanese Confucian thought. It was the great age of *chōnin* culture and, one suspects, the decisive era in the diffusion of literacy among urban commoners. Not surprisingly it was also the great age of urbanization. And, significantly no doubt, it was the great age of growth in agricultural productivity, tax receipts, the use of money, and the devising and diffusion of complex commercial techniques.

In sum, the seventeenth century was the heyday of the samurai, who dominated the new integral bureaucratic order, and of the merchants, whose collaboration was essential to that order. By the eighteenth century, the *bushi-chōnin* relationship was becoming strained. Structurally and functionally it was based on institutional relationships that were characterized by conflict as well as symbiosis. And public commentators, such as Ogyū Sorai, tended commonly to emphasize the conflictive element with almost total disregard for the symbiotic.

During the seventeenth century, social change had been most evident in the cities, but during the eighteenth and nineteenth, it became more apparent in the hinterland. Gains in literacy continued to be made, but it was now the rural populace that was acquiring the secrets and capabilities of the written word. Commercialization continued, but it was now more significant in the hinterland than the city. It was operating on a smaller scale but much more broadly than before. One could argue that urbanization continued, too, but that it did so in the countryside—and at the expense of the large towns and cities. There in the hinterland small-scale producers, distributors, and retailers gradually appeared, turning peasant villages into small towns, in functional terms even if not in the sense of growing numbers of households.

These trends meant also the appearance of wealthy rural families who used their monetary, social, and educational resources to pursue learning well beyond the limits decreed by the regime. By the nineteenth century, rural Japan contained a considerable population of socially and politically conscious gentry farmers and entrepreneurs whose presence the rulers could not ignore. "Patricians and plebs," words that served us well for describing ancient Japan, had become inappropriate to Japan of the early modern age.

THE DECAY OF AN AGE

By the middle of the eighteenth century the samurai and merchants who managed the integral bureaucratic order had ceased to be the most creative forces in Japan. They seemed to be losing control of society in terms of ideas, economic primacy, and political initiatives. New social forces and new intellectual priorities were emerging, and they presaged a new age. It was not clear from those signs what the eventual character of the new age would be. But they did reveal that the early modern order was decaying. The process was most visible in the changing pattern of rural disorder, in the content of arts and letters, and in political thought.

Rural disorder

The processes of rural change described above tended to dissolve the glue of local custom and communal solidarity. Local frustrations, ambitions, resentments, and rivalries fueled unrest. Hardships caused by crop failure, price instability, or excessive taxation led to protests and riots, especially during successive years of famine in the 1780s and again in the 1830s.

Several long-term trends were evident in the patterns of peasant unrest. Most obvious was an increase in the number and magnitude of outbursts. Whereas disturbances of all kinds —from the simple presentation of a petition to massive risings involving thousands of people—had occurred on average only once or twice a year in seventeenth-century

Japan, after 1750 they averaged more than six a year.[46] Accompanying this increase in activity was a change in the type of protest. In the seventeenth century, peasant dissent had most often involved the presentation to officials of petitions, usually legal, seeking tax relief or other forms of fiscal redress from the government. By the eighteenth century, mass protest demonstrations were more prevalent, and as the decades passed they gave way to sprees of property destruction. Linked to this evolving style of protest was change in the group configuration of action. Seventeenth-century villagers had acted as community groups whose petitioning was led by village leaders. By the eighteenth century, ordinary farmers were mobilizing the demonstrations, in disregard of, or even in opposition to, the advice of elders. And by the late 1700s the violent demonstrations and destructiveness often were directed not at the government at all but at elders and other wealthy villagers.[47]

This escalating peasant activism also reflects the impact of the dissemination of learning. During the early Edo period, peasant village leaders had evidently been able to present village sentiments most satisfactorily. In their petitions, they skillfully used against the rulers the very rhetoric about benevolent governance and the responsibility of the rulers that apologists for the regime had employed from the time of Hayashi Razan. As education spread, more villagers learned both how to write petitions and how to construct arguments that would give maximum legitimacy to their complaints or demands.[48] Consequently, even though village leaders' interests increasingly came into conflict with those of lesser mem-

46. Hugh Borton, "Peasant Uprisings in Japan of the Tokugawa Period," in *Transactions of the Asiatic Society of Japan*, Second Series, 16, May 1938, p. 39.

47. Stephen Vlastos, "Tokugawa Peasant Movements in Fukushima: Conflict and Changing Patterns of Peasant Mobilization" (Ph.D. dissertation, University of California, Berkeley, 1977), chap. 1. See also Irwin Scheiner, "Benevolent Lords and Honorable Peasants: Rebellion and Peasant Consciousness in Tokugawa Japan," in Tetsuo Najita and Irwin Scheiner, ed., *Japanese Thought in the Tokugawa Period, 1600–1868* (Chicago: University of Chicago Press, 1978), pp. 39–62.

48. Anne Walthall, "The Ethics of Protest by Commoners in Late Eighteenth Century Japan," in *Select Papers from the Center for Far Eastern Studies*, University of Chicago, no. 2, 1977–78, pp. 5–39.

bers of the village, there emerged, from among the latter, spokesmen who could provide the necessary leadership to carry on organized activism in pursuit of their aims.

This growth of rural turbulence reminds one of the spread of political action in the late medieval period insofar as it was evidence that commoners were prepared to defy established authorities to promote their own interests. In another way, as well, late Tokugawa rural activity seemed to reflect that medieval experience. We earlier noted how Ikkō congregations had formed and become active politically, only to be crushed by successful *bushi* of the sixteenth century. In the latter half of the Tokugawa period, as established patterns of village leadership decayed, more spontaneous forms of communal cooperation began to appear. Sometimes they were millennial in nature, calling for universalistic reform and righteousness (*yonaoshi* or "world renewal"). Occasionally they were inspired by ideals and legends of godlike folk heroes (*myōjin*). The movements provided a basis for cooperation by members of a village or even supravillage areas. It was an ideal of congregational activism that seemed to embody much of the revolutionary potential of the earlier Ikkō movements.

Moreover, some of the activism acquired a fundamentally antiestablishmentarian character. Earlier protest activity had been characterized by denunciations of particular officials or administrative arrangements. By the nineteenth century these had given way to attacks on the local elite and sometimes to bitter denunciations of whole daimyo lineages, of the rulers as a body, or even of the social order in its entirety. Its flaws, some argued, could be overcome only by radical transformation of reality.[49]

New directions in arts and letters

Rural disillusionment with the established order was paralleled by the intelligentsia's disillusionment with established arts and letters. By 1650, *bushi* culture had, apart from phi-

---

49. See Scheiner in Najita and Scheiner and also Irwin Scheiner, "The Mindful Peasant: Sketches for a Study of Rebellion," in *The Journal of Asian Studies* 32: 4 (August 1973), pp. 579–91.

Poetry Composition Matches and Lion Dances at the Great Shrine of Isobe

losophy, lost most of its creativity and become a museum of elegant, completed attainments. The summertime of *ukiyo* came at century's end, the Genroku period, so called for a calendrical period embracing the years around 1700. During the eighteenth century, print-makers elaborated their art by improving the use of color and printing more complex pictures. Kabuki librettists and *ukiyo* writers polished, expanded, and manipulated themes already established. And people high

伊
いそへふしんら
雜
大
神
宮

The shrine was built in the 1630s and affiliated with the Ise Shrine. The annual festival was held on June 26.

and low dashed off haiku in an endless stream. But all the industry could not conceal an inner emptiness. That special combination of *bushi* and *chōnin* vitality that had given rise to Momoyama and Genroku had lost its creative powers. Nowhere was the frustrating state of samurai-townsman relations more poignantly evident than in the life and works of the prolific nineteenth-century author, Takizawa Bakin (1767–1848).

Bakin was born into a marginal samurai family that subsequently was reduced to penury by his father's death. He surrendered his *bushi* status and became a professional author hoping thereby to overcome his family's poverty, obtain samurai status for his son, and thus restore the family fortunes. Bakin became an immensely prolific and popular writer. His finest works were heroic celebrations of samurai virtue that proclaimed to the universe the steadfastness of his own commitment to the ideals celebrated by Yamaga Sokō and other thinkers of the seventeenth century. By way of giving those virtues vitality, however, Bakin felt compelled to fill his works with romantic chinoiserie, supernatural incidents, and superhuman achievements. The merit of samurai society thus seemed to be found in a world quite beyond the reach of ordinary *bushi*. In Bakin's life, as well, samurai society proved beyond reach. Despite his own economic success and professional fame, his son died ill and unsung and his family was never restored to samurai rank.[50]

Even as Bakin symbolized the futility and archaism of one social vision, however, he also was a vital participant in a new cultural era in the making. Artists of the *chōnin* tradition, for example, began pursuing new, tentative lines of creativity. The late-eighteenth-century artist Shiba Kōkan (1738–1818) found inspiration in Western motifs and techniques.[51] The nineteenth-century print artists Katsushika Hokusai (1760–1849) and Andō Hiroshige (1797–1858), facing more government restrictions on lascivious and satirical art, turned away from the licensed quarters to portray scenes of travel, towns, highways, and rural vistas.

A similar aesthetic quest was evident in literature. Authors such as Ueda Akinari (1734–1809) turned to older traditions of Japan and China and wrote stories of mystery and the supernatural as means of examining the complexities of personality and experience. Even Bakin, that pillar of established virtue, was successful largely because of the skill with which he exploited the popular elements of mystery and drama. Many authors poured their energies into a dilettan-

50. Leon M. Zolbrod, *Takizawa Bakin* (New York: Twayne Publishers, 1967).

51. Calvin French, *Shiba Kokan* (New York: Weatherhill, 1974).

tish absorption with the licensed quarters, writing to entertain but investing their characters' situations with none of the significance that Saikaku had found in them. Others, such as Jippensha Ikku (1765–1831), wrote comic travel farces, sending their plebeian characters through one silly and irreverent adventure after another. Other authors, discovering the large audience of literate women, wrote romantic works (*ninjōbon*) that sympathetically followed their heroines, often geisha, through the tribulations of love and duty.[52] These authors' and artists' choice and treatment of subject seemed to suggest that old truths were dead and old ideals unsatisfying. They were a cultural acknowledgement that the great cities of early-modern Japan were in decline, that the vitality and creative forces of society lay elsewhere.

New trends in political thought

Disillusionment with established truth and the resulting search for something new and more satisfying was especially apparent in the realm of philosophical speculation and political thought. Building on the legacy of seventeenth- and early eighteenth-century scholarship, intellectuals mined the wisdom of Confucianism. They reexamined the Japanese tradition and forged new statements about the imperial legacy, about Shintō, and about the world significance of the empire's historical experience. They searched out information about Europe from Dutch traders at Nagasaki and developed a modest corpus of wisdom about the West. By the late eighteenth and early nineteenth centuries they were beginning to draw together insights derived from these several bodies of thought in attempts to reconceptualize the nature of their times and troubles and point out the way of the future.

These tendencies were evident in the writing of Hirata Atsutane (1776–1843), a disciple of Motoori Norinaga. Hirata studied eclectically, reading in varieties of Confucianism, Buddhism, Western learning (*rangaku*), and Japanese studies (*kokugaku*). Powerfully influenced by Motoori, Hirata became a harsh antagonist of Chinese studies and a shrill partisan of

52. Donald Keene, *World Within Walls* (New York: Holt, Rinehart and Winston, 1976), pp. 371ff.

Shintō superiority. As had Nichiren, he detested rival doctrines. He considered them destructive of Japan and asserted that his own teachings were the correct ones, superior to all others.[53] He insisted that Confucian studies was an undemanding discipline and that Buddhist scholarship was much more sophisticated:

> Buddhist learning is thus broader in scope than Confucian, but Japanese learning is even more embracing. All the various types of learning, including Confucianism and Buddhism, are joined in Japanese learning, just as the many rivers flow into the sea, where their waters are joined.

Like Nichiren, Hirata sought to impose his interpretation on society. And he aspired, in the spirit of Kūkai, to show how all other doctrines were lesser ones that led to his all-encompassing message. In the end, however, he, like Nichiren, only added to the diversity of nineteenth-century thought. He did bring into sharper focus Motoori's view of creator deities, which he found validated in the ideas of creator gods present in other religious traditions. Hirata argued that evidence in the *Kojiki* proved that the god Takamimusubi

> must be credited with the creation of Heaven and earth, that he is a god of incomparable power, and that he without doubt resides in Heaven and reigns over the world. Despite the pellucidly clear nature of these truths, scholars whose minds have become damaged by Chinese and Indian learning (as well as people who in their ignorance display impious disbelief) do not understand that the very fact of their own birth is immediately attributable to the creative power of this god. . . . In many other countries it is believed that the seed of man and all other things owe their existence to the powers of this god. As proof of this we may cite different foreign traditions. In the ancient Chinese legends. . . . In the ancient Indian legends. . . . Far to the west of India

53. Hirata is quoted from Tsunoda et al., pp. 543, 545–46.

there are numerous other countries, and in each of them [too] there are traditions of a god of Heaven who created the heavens and earth, man and all things. This [about lands west of India] may be known from reading Dutch books.

Hirata's use of information from Dutch books to support his argument reflected the impact that renewed access to Western learning had upon intellectuals from the late 1700s. The way in which the content of this learning could threaten the Neo-Confucian order is suggested by the experience of the physician, Sugita Genpaku (1733–1817). Western learning, which was known as "Dutch learning" (*rangaku*) because it was usually obtained through Dutchmen trading at Nagasaki, attracted more and more scholars from about the 1770s on. Medicine was perhaps the most exciting part of the new wisdom. The profound impact it could have on perceptive scholars was demonstrated by the experience of Sugita, who wrote his reminiscences in 1815 at the age of eighty-two.[54] In them he described the immense excitement with which in 1771 he had discovered the accuracy of a Dutch anatomical text and the sense of accomplishment he had experienced when he and his friends successfully translated it into Japanese. He learned the accuracy of the text by comparing it with dissected viscera. At the time, he wrote, even the shogun's doctors

had beheld dissections seven or eight times before, but always what they saw [was] different from what had been taught in the past thousand years, and their puzzle had never been solved.

But on that magic day, the puzzle of a thousand years was solved. Realizing how wrong the Chinese texts on which he had relied had been, he commented,

We [doctors] felt ashamed of ourselves for having come this far in our lives without being aware of our own

54. Genpaku is quoted from Genpaku Sugita, *Dawn of Western Science in Japan* (Tokyo: Hokuseido Press, 1969), pp. 31, 31–32, 37, 70 in that order.

ignorance. How presumptuous on our part to have served our lordships and pretended to carry [out] our duties as official doctors when we were totally without knowledge of the true make of our bodies which should be the foundation of the art of healing!

Later as he and his colleagues struggled with the task of translating the book of anatomy into Japanese, he observed,

I was struck with admiration by the great difference between the knowledge of the West and that of the East. And I was inspired to come to the determination that I must learn and clarify the new revelation for applying it to actual healing and also for making it the seed of further discoveries among the general physicians of Japan.

As a result of his efforts and those of his colleagues, the new learning came to be centered in Edo and began to be called Dutch learning (*rangaku*). Thus began "the flourishing learning" of his day.

With the path thus opened, the physicians in the coming years, a hundred or a thousand years, will acquire the true art of healing for saving human lives.

Sugita may well have exaggerated, in hindsight, the significance of his own contribution. However, his experience with the Dutch text had served to negate the validity of his former body of professional knowledge, Chinese medicine. And it had led him to the striking conclusion that Western learning as a whole was superior to that which had undergirded the established order. That new viewpoint may not, in fact, have been objectively superior to his old one, but it nevertheless constituted a radical change in outlook. As a result, his life became a mission directed to the great task of introducing to his countrymen a body of learning that presumably would benefit them forever more.

The politically radicalizing impact of new knowledge was evident in the writings of Honda Toshiaki (1744–1821), one of the most well-read and thoughtful of Tokugawa Dutch scholars. Honda advocated at length a vigorous governmental policy of economic development and foreign expansion.[55] He urged government management of the shipping industry, buttressing his argument with the assertion that impoverished Japanese were turning to banditry and that in Europe

> It is considered to be the appointed duty of a king to save his people from hunger and cold by shipping and trading. This is the reason there are no bandits in Europe. A similar approach would be especially applicable to Japan, which is a maritime nation.

He then went on to describe an elaborate policy of colonization in adjacent lands, warning that if it were not pursued, Japan would fall prey to an expanding Russia.

New information, such as that derived from *rangaku*, could thus serve to break down the credibility of established truth. Equally destructive was the intuitionist claim that right conduct could be known without reference to Neo-Confucian dogma. We saw how Nakae Tōju promoted the intuitionist epistemology of Ōyōmei during the seventeenth century. Ōyōmei thought continued to attract support during the next two centuries, most notably in the person of Ōshio Heihachirō (1793–1837).[56] Ōshio, *bakufu* police officer (*yoriki*) in Osaka, asserted that

> The fundamental spirit of the ordinary man . . . is no different from that of the sage, . . . [that of] the wretched man identical with the aristocrat.

He considered it intolerable, therefore, that the rulers were not moved by the suffering he saw during the famines of the 1830s. On the ground that "men are fundamentally one with heaven, their essences one with moral truth," he called upon virtuous people to right the wrongs of society. In 1837 he launched an ill-fated rebellion to achieve that end.

55. Donald Keene, *The Japanese Discovery of Europe, 1720–1830* (Stanford: Stanford University Press, 1969). The quotation is from p. 179.

56. The quotations of Ōshio are taken from Tetsuo Najita, "Ōshio Heihachirō (1793–1837)," in Albert M. Craig and Donald H. Shively, *Personality in Japanese History* (Berkeley: University of California Press, 1971), pp. 165, 161, 171 in that order.

Ōshio thus turned the Ōyōmei principle of intuitive knowledge to political action. In his denunciation of the Tokugawa regime, moreover, Ōshio called for an "imperial restoration" that would have the effect of "restoring the moral government of Emperor Jimmu," the mythical first emperor of Japan. In his reference to the emperor, Ōshio was touching that element of late Tokugawa ideology, *kokugaku*, that was, as we have seen, central to Hirata Atsutane's position.

In the arguments of Ōshio and Hirata one sees how insights and information from Ōyōmei, *kokugaku*, and *rangaku* could be combined to form new arguments about the proper character of polity and society. Hirata's and Motoori's view of history as a process of creation and change also meshed with Ogyū Sorai's perception of the sage who creates political systems. Both views repudiated the Neo-Confucian one of a timeless order made manifest in the existing integral bureaucratic system.

Ogyū's advocacy of active government and his insistence that its merit could be measured by its performance was shared by Kaiho Seiryō (1755–1817). Whereas Ogyū's analysis had led him to advocate a "natural" economy, however, Kaiho was led to reject the basic idea of such an economy, invoking evidence derived from Dutch learning to help make his case.[57] He considered it ridiculous that "the aristocracy and military class in Japan should disdain profit," or at least claim to disdain profit. The houses of shogun and daimyo functioned as businesses, he argued, "lending" their domains to the people and living off the "interest"—meaning taxes. Government officials, too, were profit-seekers, "who sell their talents to the ruler and live on the wages he pays," thus being comparable to common porters,

> who obtain wages for their labor on the roads, in order to get something to drink or a bite to eat. They all live in the same way. . . . The warrior laughs when told that the King of Holland engages in commerce. But he himself buys and sells commodities; it is a law of the uni-

57. See Tsunoda et al., pp. 500–2, for Kaiho's argument.

verse that one must sell in order to buy, and hardly a thing to be laughed at.

The conviction that rulers could and should construct effective systems and change ineffective ones was clearly expressed by Satō Nobuhiro (1769–1850). In his advocacy of radical change he invoked the *kokugaku* vision of a pristine primordial age and of creators who shaped the realm.[58] Satō was well versed in western studies and Confucian learning as well as in national studies. He advised daimyo to develop local industries and establish trading monopolies, advocating such policies not as ad hoc actions but as parts of a basic reordering of society.[59] As he saw it, in the existing order

> the ruling class concerns itself exclusively with the administration of government and national defense, giving no attention to the production of goods from land or sea, and placing the burden of production for the entire country on the other three groups: the farmers, craftsmen, and the merchants. . . . Each trade is left largely uncontrolled, and thus is unable to develop any skill and ingenuity. Profits dwindle from year to year, and some people have to turn over their businesses to others losing house and home as well. The number of homeless destitutes gradually increases, and leads in the end to the decline of the nation itself.

To reverse this trend, Satō advocated the formation of an elaborately structured corporate state. He proposed that

> The country's industries should be divided into eight groups, namely: plant-cultivation, forestry, mining, manufacturing, trading, unskilled occupations, shipping, and fishing. The people, once classified into these eight groups, would then be assigned to one occupation and attend diligently to his own occupation. The law should strictly prohibit anyone from trying his hand at another occupation. . . . [The] six Ministries will care

58. Maruyama, pp. 292–93.
59. Satō's comments are taken from Tsunoda et al., pp. 572–73.

for the groups of people assigned to them, inducing them to study their occupations and making them devote their attention constantly and exclusively to the performance of their occupations without faltering or becoming negligent, and to the fullest extent of their energies. In this way, as the months and the years pass, each industry will acquire proficiency and perfect itself, providing steadily increased benefits for the greater wealth and prosperity of the state.

In these several arguments one can see elements of a new political order taking shape. Parts, such as the character and role of the imperial institution, were only vaguely suggested, even when seen as central features of the larger society. Other parts were more visible. It is clear from the writings of Honda, Kaiho, and Satō that the three regarded the polity as being based on a combination of administrative, entrepreneurial, and military skills. They were proposing to have a single ruling elite use those skills to manage all activities, thus ending the clumsy alliance of *bushi* and *chōnin* classes that had characterized the mature Tokugawa order. If pursued successfully, policies such as they advocated would eventually reintegrate mercantile and *bushi* activities, minus wealthy independent merchants, in a manner akin to that of the late sixteenth century. A number of daimyo domains did implement a few such mercantilist policies, especially during the 1840s. The most successful of them found the undertakings of considerable value in solving their fiscal problems.

By the middle of the nineteenth century, then, it was obvious that the integral bureaucratic order as it had evolved during the seventeenth century was no longer functioning effectively. However, it was not at all certain whether the ruling elite or some major segment thereof would be able to devise an effectively modified system or whether members of the newly rising segment of society would be able to exploit the disarray of the decaying order and thrust themselves into a new power position.

In this late Tokugawa intellectual process, in which new thought repudiated the Neo-Confucian vision and articulated alternative schemes, one can see similarities to the pattern of medieval thought. There, too, an old universalistic vision (Shingon-Tendai) was repudiated, various new explanatory strategies emerged (such as Zen and Amidism), and unsuccessful attempts were made (notably in Nichiren and Yuiitsu Shintō) to forge new interpretive statements that would subsume all lines of thought in one larger whole. In the later Tokugawa case the larger whole did not emerge until late in the nineteenth century. However, it was apparent even before the coming of Perry that the seventeenth-century intellectual order was in ruin and a new world was being sought. Perhaps the key to that new world lay buried in the historic tradition. Perhaps it lay in far civilizations. Or perhaps it lay in the hinterland, among those rural people who had in the course of time mastered the secrets of literacy, of commerce, and of governance, and who had, as a corollary, begun forming a new rural commoner elite with the tastes, talents, and ambitions necessary to create a new age and a new cultural epoch.

GROWTH AND REGULATION

At the beginning of this study, the luxuriant verdure of Japan was noted. Now, near its end, it is appropriate to remark again upon the improbability of that verdure. How can Japan be so luminously green? It is, after all, a land of precipitous mountains whose soil fertility is constantly leached away by torrential rains and melting snow. Should one not expect its lowlands to be inundated repeatedly by roaring, flooding rivers bearing stones, gravel, mud, and debris? Should not that process wreck the small area of productive soil and force tillers to press farther up the hillsides, denuding ever more land, and ruining ever more fertile plains? Surely this geological potential was all the more likely to be realized because of the sustained population growth of historical Japan: perhaps two or three million in the sixth century, growing to nearly five million by the eleventh, some eighteen million by ca. 1600, and some thirty-two million by 1870. Why is Japan, as a result of this experience, not a barren, eroded, exhausted land supporting a miserably impoverished populace of subsistence farmers and urban slum dwellers?

The question is not easy to answer because it has never really been investigated, for the reason that historians, like others, have tended to take their environmental context for granted, assuming that there were no serious historic questions relating to it. Instead they have limited their concern to "social" questions, meaning questions dealing with human relations, not human-environment relations.

Now, however, near the end of the twentieth century, we are belatedly discovering that we cannot take this good green biosphere for granted. We know that such is the case because of the way humankind has dealt—and still is dealing—with that biosphere. Because on the face of things it seems reasonable to assume that the combination of geological and historical factors could easily have turned Japan into an ecological disaster zone, it seems worth asking why such a result did not come about. Given the dearth of historical attention to the problem, however, the thoughts on the matter that follow are of the most tentative and speculative sort.

The environmental legacy

Before humans settled in the islands there was, of course, no environmental problem. Until the introduction of Yayoi culture in about the third century B.C., the island surface was nearly undisturbed by human activity. The ubiquitous *sasa* and other indigenous vegetation had proven entirely capable of mastering the island chain's youthful and hostile geological foundation. However, in subsequent millennia more and more of that primeval forest and ground cover was torn from the land. In its place, tillers had to devise artificial means of preserving the ecological order or see their handiwork ruin their future.

In all likelihood, tillage was from the start accompanied by environmental misfortunes of local consequence as flooding streams, landslides, volcanic eruptions, and other natural disasters struck the unlucky or careless. The problem first becomes visible historically, however, in records of the classical age. The imperial government repeatedly undertook to repair broken river banks, construct levees, and maintain canals, and admonished landholders to keep their waterways in good repair. The government, which claimed ownership of most forest lands in the Taika era, issued prohibitions against excessive and unauthorized tree harvesting. However, the frequency of their reiteration suggests the futility of such bans. The government's forest regulations doubtless were designed to preserve economic capital directly, but in part their objective was to prevent abuse of watersheds on which downstream agriculture (and government income) depended.[60]

By the late classical age, government intervention in ecological matters had ceased. Later the Kamakura *bakufu* pursued some riparian works, but during most of the medieval period environmental matters commanded little high-level attention. Forest lands passed from government to private possession, and considerable deforestation and destruction of wooded uplands occurred. Not until the daimyo of the late sixteenth century began to organize their regional domains did forest and riverine management again become a significant political activity.[61] Despite the evidence of medieval ecological abuse, however, the continuing growth of population and the medieval economic metamorphosis suggest that the environmental foundation of Japanese civilization remained in generally good health. Indeed, the long-term increase in agricultural output—with yields roughly doubling from the early-classical to the late-medieval age[62]—suggests that soil fertility was being maintained even as more land was being brought under cultivation.

The opening of Japan to tillage and the accompanying growth of population had an inevitable impact on wildlife. In classical Japan, deer antlers and the hides of deer, bear, and wild boar had been items of commerce in Heian. Those animals still existed in Japan in the late sixteenth century, but the

60. Tsuchiya, pp. 71, 77.
61. Ibid., p. 126.
62. Ibid., pp. 67, 119.

products had disappeared from the marketplace, perhaps because of a decline in the numbers of each species.[63] Doubtless
many other species of flora and fauna also suffered, but the
land itself did not deteriorate commensurately. Thanks perhaps to the stabilizing effect of paddy tillage, which spread
and slowed water flow, the denuding of land did not ruin it
during the millennia from Jōmon to late medieval times. Perhaps, too, prior to the early-modern period the population in
most of Japan did not press excessively upon the land because of the long-term improvement in agronomics and the
availability of virgin land in the expanding realm. These
rather than governmental efforts were probably the major
factors that enabled Japanese society to enjoy, without severe
damage to the environment, that long period of unrestrained
growth that continued until the seventeenth century.

During the seventeenth and eighteenth centuries, the
situation changed. Territorial expansion ceased. The last large
regions of easily tillable land were opened to cultivation.
Concurrently the population experienced a great surge of
growth, increasing from some 18 million in ca. 1600 to about
26 million in ca. 1720. Forms of village communalism disinte-
grated, giving way to more ruthless patterns of competitive
economics. The growth of castle towns and of the population
as a whole created immense demand for lumber and fire-
wood. At the same time, the rulers found themselves pressed
for income, and they sought to extract ever more from the
soil. All the forces of society seemed to be conjoining in ways
that could only ravage the land in desperate shortsighted attempts to extract a bit more food and fodder from the hectares
available.

Yet that did not happen. On the contrary, the people of
Tokugawa Japan came to terms with the limitations of their
land and developed its positive capabilities to an extent
nearly unknown elsewhere. As a result, that long story of
growth and achievement that characterized the classical and
medieval epochs continued during the Tokugawa period. By
the nineteenth century, Japan was a huge and densely popu-

63. Ibid., pp. 87–89, 168ff. Michael Cooper, trans., *This Island of Japon*
(Tokyo: Kodansha International, 1973), p. 58, mentions animals in Japan in
the late sixteenth century.

lated society, enjoying a level of living that compared favorably with nearly any other that one might find at the time, even in areas far more blessed in terms of geography and population density.

That outcome requires explanation. Certainly it was not foreordained. After all, there is plenty of evidence that Japanese of the Tokugawa era repeatedly taxed the environment beyond its limits. Even in the early years of the Tokugawa period, for example, construction consumed so much lumber that one observer reported,

> the country is already running short of it and many mountains which were formerly covered with timber are now as bare as if there had never been a tree growing there.[64]

Hills were denuded and floods and landslides resulted. Excessive demand on the land—often manifested in onerous taxes—was at the base of many peasant riots and cases of hardship. And the local and regional famines that ravaged parts of the country at one time or another, especially during the 1780s and 1830s, may have been evidence that population had grown dense enough so that major climatic and biological cycles were affecting human well-being more harshly than ever before.

The farmers themselves were not always models of agrarian prudence, especially during times of hardship. The problem was recognized even among Confucian scholars. One of these was Kumazawa Banzan (1619–91), a samurai student of Ōyōmei and proponent of compassionate government, who prepared a long essay on affairs, organizing it in interlocutory style, as in the following example.

> *Question*: In many provinces efforts have been made to control the mountain streams, but the mountains become more and more bare, [rain water promptly flows off], and the torrents keep getting shallower. What should be done?
> *Answer*: Do what you may to control the torrents, as

---

64. Cooper, p. 57.

long as many of the people cannot keep on hand food enough for three days nor buy wood to cook what they have, they would go to the mountains and cut stolen wood today even though they knew they would lose their heads for it tomorrow. And if the village headman and elders happen to get wind of it, there is nothing for them to do but look the other way.[65]

Besides denuding hills, tillers would open land too close to rivers, and they—and the tax collector—would suffer for it. A *bakufu* ordinance of the year 1800 reminded the public that regulations on the opening of land to tillage were issued during the 1720s and 1770s, but that river areas had nevertheless been opened to use and much flood damage had resulted. It asserted that thenceforth the tilling of floodplains or even the cutting of natural growth there was to be strictly forbidden.[66]

Despite such instances of abuse of the environment, however, the basic health of the land was preserved, or where badly impaired, gradually restored. Why? And how? Perhaps the question "why" can best be answered by suggesting that the early-modern settlement placed power solidly in the hands of people who habitually saw their interests being best served by the pursuit of policies that were, as a corollary to their main purpose, ecologically beneficial. At higher levels the ruling elite were convinced that their well-being depended upon a flourishing agriculture. Accordingly, as the ordinance of 1800 illustrates, despite their hunger for more and more tax income, they devoted much effort to assuring that village production was maximized over the long run even at the sacrifice of short-term profit. At lower levels the dominant elements in city, town, and village stood to lose more than they would gain by exploiting the land excessively. They were therefore disposed to favor those regulations and husbandry practices that were beneficial in the longer term. In striking contrast to our own age, then, the

65. Galen M. Fisher, tr., "Dai Gaku Wakumon By Kumazawa Banzan," in *Transactions of the Asiatic Society of Japan*, Second Series, 16, May 1938, p. 306.

66. Ishii, vol. 7, pp. 117–18.

perceived interests of the dominant forces of Tokugawa society usually worked to preserve rather than to plunder the environment, or at least those portions of the environment of immediate material value to humankind.

As these comments have implied, the "how" of environmental preservation involved the enduring application of concrete measures of deliberate regulation and self-regulation. Early-modern Japan therefore came to embody two seemingly irreconcilable characteristics. One was great growth, the other, strict regulation and self-regulation. The regulation was to a considerable extent intended to prevent much of the growth, but it seems to have had the less drastic but equally favorable result of channeling and shaping the growth so that it was, by and large, benign, occurring without ruining the land and its civilization.

Early-modern growth

We have already noted several aspects of early-modern growth: in the size, capability, sophistication, and organizational complexity of the ruling elite; in the variety and scope of arts, letters, and thought; in the number, size, and elaboration of cities and their relationship to the hinterland; in the conceptual and organizational complexity of the economy; and in the secular capabilities of both the urban and hinterland populations.

Beyond these many dimensions of social growth were more basic expansionary trends. One was the increase in overall production. The phenomenal growth of commercial activity created a vast number of new occupational opportunities. It improved manpower efficiency, facilitated fuller use of natural resources, and thereby added to total production. Mining expanded enormously. In the classical and medieval ages, large quantities of copper had been mined, as well as some gold, silver, iron, lead, and a few other minerals. During the late sixteenth century, mining activity intensified sharply as daimyo struggled to maximize their resources. Mines were opened throughout the country. Then during the early-modern era the *bakufu* and many daimyo extracted from the earth large quantities of gold, silver, copper, iron, lead, tin, and coal. The techniques of mining changed little, and the sharp increase in output during the sixteenth and seventeenth centuries was due to more intensive operation and to the discovery and opening of more mines.[67]

The increase in overall production is more fully traceable to increased agricultural production, which nearly doubled during the two and a half centuries before 1850. That doubling was caused mostly by the familiar factors of expanded arable land—largely developed prior to the eighteenth century—and increased production per hectare through crop diversification and improved agronomics. More specifically, irrigation was expanded by the popularization of treadmills to lift water from wells and reservoirs. Moreover, fertilizer use increased. The great cities generated vast quantities of night soil that were carried to the fields, processed, and applied, and more fish and food-processing by-products were added to the list of fertilizer materials. Rice threshing was streamlined by the utilization of stationary combs (*senba koki*) in place of flails. Their use increased a thresher's productivity and reduced wastage. Rice processing was improved by the widespread adoption of water-powered mortars. Crop diversification proceeded apace, encouraged by the growth of urban centers and a monetized economy. Not only were existing varieties of crops grown more widely, but new crops were introduced from the Asian continent and by European visitors. These included "waxtrees, sugar-cane, sweet potatoes, potatoes, tobacco, rape, Indian corn, pumpkins, French beans, ground-nuts, carrots, and spinach."[68] Silk production increased several times over, and the quality of domestic silk products improved. Indeed, the improvement was sufficient to end the importation of Chinese luxury silk that had persisted since the Yamato age.

These several threads of horticultural development were drawn together in an emerging body of scientific agronomic writings. The government itself published advisory tracts

67. Tsuchiya, pp. 82, 131, 172–74.

68. Ibid., p. 155. On Tokugawa economic matters, see also Hanley and Yamamura.

and agricultural regulations, and from the late seventeenth century on, private individuals also began to write and distribute works on agronomy. These works, known collectively as *jikatasho*, ranged over such technical matters as seed selecting, planting, irrigating, fertilizing, and harvesting. They discussed marketing considerations and often dwelt at length on the principles and philosophy of farm management, family life, and peasant-career attitudes and values. *Jikatasho* were widely read and contributed to the spread of better farming practices and the consequent increase in production.[69] The work ethic that informed these writings and that fostered agrarian productivity was promoted with enthusiasm. As one contemporary writer put it,

> From the age of 8 boys should gather grass for the animals, pick up horse dung from the road, make rope, and help with other light work. When they work well, they should be praised and given a coin. When coins accumulate to a sufficient sum, the children should be allowed to buy something they want. Also, when they are given clothes they should be told it is a reward for work. Thus their childish hearts will develop the spirit of industry and perseverance. If they are given suitable work in this way when young and taught farming skills as they get older, by age 14 or 15 they will be industrious and meticulous farmers.[70]

Accompanying the growth in production was an increase in population, as was noted earlier. It is important to bear in mind, however, that much of the increase in population occurred during the seventeenth century, and that from the 1720s to the 1840s it seems to have slowed appreciably. Continuing gains in productivity consequently became gains in well-being, at least for the more successful sectors of society. Nineteenth-century Japan, therefore, was on balance one of the largest, most densely populated and most well-to-do societies in the world of its day.

69. Smith, *Agrarian Origins*, pp. 87ff., discusses agronomic literature. See also Thomas C. Smith, "Ōkura Nagatsune and the Technologists," in Craig and Shively, pp. 127–54.

70. Smith, *Nakahara*, p. 109.

Early-modern regulation

The pervasive pattern of growth described above was matched by equally pervasive patterns of regulation and self-regulation.

The government's dedication to management was expressed through a plethora of regulations and hortatory admonitions that were issued and reissued time and time again by *bakufu*, daimyo, and lesser urban and rural administrators. In the most fundamental act of regulation, the extent of the realm itself was fixed by the policy of seclusion. Furthermore, the size of the elite was regulated by enforcement of rules governing hereditary status. Other regulations sought to limit urban growth. A much more extensive set of regulations was intended to maintain urban order and security. Complex firefighting organizations, sanitary regulations, limitations on size and construction of buildings, and extensive judicial and police organizations existed for all large towns and cities. Sumptuary laws and laws governing family relations, legal residence, and travel were applied to both rural and urban peoples.

Besides these regulations designed to control human relations, others were issued with the aim of increasing productivity and government income. Comparable to the ordinances prohibiting tillage close to streams were others dealing with forests and hillsides, tree harvesting, and replanting. And there were ordinances regulating water use, seed allocation, and granary storage. The leaders of one village, for example, drew up a list of fifty-three rules to guide members of their village. The rules, which reflected government instructions, included these clauses:

41. The farmers must attend to their business diligently. The best seed must be selected and great care taken as to the time of sowing and planting. That they should look well after the fields and the water-supply is to be expected. . . .
42. Where land is left uncultivated for a long time because of an overflow, etc., and some one afterwards brings it under cultivation, this must be reported. If

not, the [village officials] will be held responsible.
43. Where mountain land, swamp land, or floodplain is brought under cultivation, it must be done in winter, so as to save time.
44. All drains must be looked after carefully.
45. During a freshet [village officials] with the farmers must turn out and prevent the dikes from breaking. Minor repairs of roads and bridges must be immediately attended to, but matters of great expense may be reported to the [district administrator].[71]

The motive behind all such rules and regulations seems straightforward enough: to keep the peace and sustain tax income, thereby securing the material base of the regime and giving expression to its sense of governing responsibility. The ordinances did not spring from a "postmodern" awareness of the environment as a concern per se. Nor did they flow from a Shintō reverence for natural beauty or a Buddhist sensitivity to the "ecological rights" of all sentient beings. Whatever the origins of this approach to environmental issues, however, the outcome can reasonably be labeled an ecological success.

Two examples of that success come to mind. Still apparent today is the Japanese accomplishment in preserving forested lands—that verdure that impresses all travelers. Both the angular lines of forest harvesting and the rows of hand-planted young trees clinging to precipitous slopes indicate the humanly managed character of this seemingly wild scenery. No longer apparent is the greatest mark of Tokugawa urban triumph: the fresh clean waters of Edo city and bay. Tokyo bay today is one of the foulest bodies of water in the world, its vileness sustained by the filth flowing through the canals and rivers of the whole metropolitan district. Until late in the nineteenth century, however, it was one of the cleanest bays in the world. The greatest city on earth pressed along its western shore, and yet in the rivers and canals of that city flourished seafood of all sorts, including edible seaweed whose quality made it a national delicacy. Spared the debilitating effects of uncontrolled rubbish and liquid-waste-

---

71. John H. Wigmore, "Notes on Land Tenure and Local Institutions in Old Japan," in *Transactions of the Asiatic Society of Japan*, 19: 1 (1891), p. 184.

Fish Market at the East Side of Nihonbashi (Bridge of Japan)

disposal systems, the refuse of over a million people and their industries enhanced rather than sabotaged the life-supporting capacity of the metropolitan area. Waste wood and paper products became fuel. The resulting ashes, along with night soil and food byproducts, became fertilizer. Metal products were reused. Scrap tile, stone, and ceramics became land fill.

The urban arrangements of Tokugawa Japan were in some ways as beneficial to city residents as to the surrounding environment. Besides the sanitary regulations, building

codes, and fire and police organizations, even the flimsy, fire-
prone wooden buildings that filled every Tokugawa city contributed to their benignity. The near-absence of stone structures reduced appreciably the capacity of cities to support rat
populations that could carry bubonic plague and certain
other epidemic diseases. The replacement every few decades
of decaying buildings and, more dramatically, the periodic
conflagrations that ravaged the cities had the compensatory
benefit of cleaning up whole neighborhoods, destroying dis-
ease vectors and their habitats. Even the care with which fire-

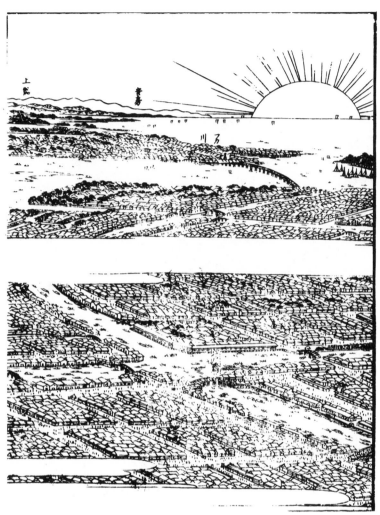

The Bay Seen from City Streets in Southeastern Edo

fearing residents kept their areas clear of debris helped to this end.

The body of Tokugawa-era regulations and the favorable ecological consequences of their enforcement suggest very strongly that early-modern Japanese had a keen awareness of the personal advantages of a constructively ordered world. After all, the regulations were effective only insofar as the general public at least tacitly approved them. The ineffectiveness of many sumptuary regulations, for example, is

surely implicit in the frequency of their reiteration. By contrast, the general effectiveness of riparian regulations, despite the constant pressure on them, is suggested by the general stability of riverine topography.

This is to argue, then, that purposeful self-regulation more than governmental edicts lay at the heart of Tokugawa ecological success. More people stood to gain in valued ways by adhering to the main tenets of early-modern environmental rules than stood to gain by disregarding them. This positive public support for self-regulation was evident in the house laws that guided nearly every family enterprise. Like *jikatasho* and official government pronouncements, those house laws universally admonished family members to cherish their patrimony, work hard, avoid foolishness, and bequeath a flourishing business to their descendants.

Purposeful self-regulation was central to one other striking phenomenon of Tokugawa Japan: the large-scale trends of population growth. How can the sharp slowdown in the rate of population growth after the early eighteenth century be explained? Demographic studies suggest that it cannot be attributed to an increased mortality or reduced fecundity caused by famine. There is no evidence, either, of any widespread practice of sexual abstention or contraception. The factors of marriage regulation, abortion, and infanticide all seem significant,[72] and in a new study T. C. Smith suggests that the key factor was infanticide. Although the rulers inveighed against infanticide as amoral and uneconomic, it appears to have been resorted to frequently as a means of regulating family size.[73] A factor of uncertain importance was the practice of abortion. Like infanticide, abortion was condemned by society's leaders, but the practice was utilized, especially in towns where skilled practitioners could be found.[74] Thus Ihara Saikaku in his *ukiyo-zōshi*, *The Life of an Amorous Woman* [*Kōshoku ichidai onna*] put these words into the mouth of his old courtesan.

> One night, as I lay gazing into the past through the window of my heart, calling to mind my various wanton doings, I seemed to see a procession of some ninety-five different childlike figures, each child wearing a hat in the form of a lotus leaf and each one stained with blood from his waist down. . . . Then I perceived to my grief that these were the children whom I had conceived out of wedlock and disposed of by abortion.[75]

72. See especially Hanley and Yamamura, pp. 226–66.

73. Smith, *Nakahara*, examines this matter with great care.

74. Ibid., p. 63.

75. Ihara Saikaku, *The Life of an Amorous Woman*, p. 194.

The story was widely read, and this incident may have reflected a particular regret known to many. It seems entirely possible, moreover, that with the spread of learning into the hinterland went techniques of abortion as a means of family control. On the other hand, as Smith notes, in comparison with abortion,

> Infanticide is sex-selective, less dangerous to the mother, simpler in technical requirements, and actually more efficient in controlling fertility owing to the much longer period of sterility associated with a full-term pregnancy.[76]

Whatever the technique of family control, however, it was a matter of choice exercised for private reasons and in defiance of the rulers' wishes. And though the motives were immediate and the choice doubtless a matter of the least evil among unwanted alternatives, cumulatively those choices contributed to the overall ecological success of Tokugawa society.

In the end we are left with one last historical irony. In this exploratory exercise in ecological history it has been suggested that Japan's long centuries of unrestricted growth had given way in the early-modern era to centuries in which patterns of conscious restraint accompanied patterns of growth. A widespread acceptance of regulation together with the ordinances that helped implement that regulation assured that population pressure and competitive economics would not combine to destroy the roots of Japanese civilization. As a result, the massive growth of early-modern Japan was turned into a blessing rather than a curse, and nineteenth-century Japan was well prepared to enter a new historic epoch. We have maintained, however, that the basic motivations resulting in that outcome were the rulers' desire to perpetuate their advantages and give expression to their Confucian vision of a good society and the commoners' desire to secure their own interests as best they could, given the range of choices available to them. Although the Tokugawa configuration of options and intentions resulted in an ecological success, per-

76. Smith, *Nakahara*, p. 151.

haps it did so at the price of undermining the very order that had given rise to the success in the first place by fostering discontents which fueled those antiestablishment movements of thought, politics, and economics that have been described. In the post-Perry dénouement, Japan joined other societies in that larger process of exploding population, resource wastage, and environmental pollution that has forced us all to give thought to ecological questions in ways our forebears never had to do.

CONCLUSION

Let us attempt to pull together the several themes that run through this study.

The beauty and affluence of contemporary Japan were made possible, we suggested, by favorable historical developments that offset geological disadvantages and seemingly malign historical trends. Specifically we contended that the potentially disastrous effects of long-term population growth and intensifying pressure upon the land were more than offset by development in the early-modern era of a series of regulatory arrangements whose basic social and ecological value were so widely recognized as to make them publicly acceptable and effectively enforceable. In this context one can speak of early-modern Japan as a fundamentally new age, with a long "premodern" era of nearly unregulated and actively encouraged growth giving way to a "modern" era in which a complex balance was struck between growth and regulation.

We also remarked that one striking characteristic of classical Japan, the great gulf between the cultured classes of Heian and the rude masses of the hinterland, was largely closed during the medieval and early-modern periods. We suggested that intellectual, economic, political, and military trends all contributed to that process, and that it led to the emergence of a central characteristic of nationhood: a population having a high level of shared culture and experience.

The history of Japan, as described here, constituted a series of discernible epochs. Each epoch—Jōmon, Yayoi, Yamato, classical, medieval, and early modern—had an internal coherence and a distinctive character. We attempted to capture the distinctive political essence of each of the three epochs after Yamato in our labels aristocratic bureaucracy, political fluidity, and integral bureaucracy. We then sought to show how core elements of higher culture and social organization and relations were congruent parts of the three.

At the same time we pointed out that each epoch contained processes of long-term growth that led to crisis, change, and supersession. The crisis of the Yamato state led to the Taika reform and the grandeur of classical Japan. The crisis of aristocratic bureaucracy led to the emergence of *bushi* rule and an exciting age of social change. The crisis of late-medieval Japan led to the forging of integral bureaucracy and the splendor of early-modern Japan.

The terminal crises of classical and medieval Japan involved the rise to historic prominence of new sectors of the general public, an elite samurai element in the first case, more-plebeian samurai and their merchant collaborators in the second. Following that pattern, we suggested that in eighteenth to nineteenth-century Japan one could perceive the beginnings of a similar trend as a landlord-entrepreneur sector of the rural populace began to exercise an unprecedented degree of influence in affairs that perhaps foreshadowed the rise of yet a new and larger segment of the populace to a preeminent historic role.

We also argued, however, that within the classical and medieval epochs a "mid-phase" reconsolidation of the elite occurred, finding it in the formation of the *shōen* system and later the Ashikaga polity. In line with that pattern we suggested that the social evolution of nineteenth-century Japan appeared to be ambiguous: the *bushi-chōnin* system might have been collapsing in the face of a challenge from below, but it might have been in process of realigning and revitalizing itself.[77]

Before this ambiguity could be dispelled, unprecedented foreign complications arose, and the diplomatic crisis

---

77. The question of whether it is better to see late Tokugawa history in terms of a reconsolidating *bushi-chōnin* system or the rise of a new sector of society is akin to the most intense historiographical debate in twentieth-century Japan, the debate of the Marxist scholars of the *kōza* and *rōnō* schools

of the 1850s and 1860s precipitated a political reform of great magnitude, known as the Meiji Restoration. One might maintain that the foreign intrusion disrupted the historical trends of earlier decades and thrust Japan into an entirely new line of development. However, one might contend with equal persuasiveness that the foreign crisis only accelerated existing trends. One might say, for example, that it provided those landlord-entrepreneurs an opportunity to ally themselves with alienated samurai to overthrow the established order and forge a new system, a bourgeois order more responsive to their own interests. Alternatively, one might argue that it forced the established samurai to make the reforms necessary to secure their advantages—indeed that it made it easier for them to do so—and that they did so, perhaps by compromising with those landlord types. They thereby secured for nearly another century the favored positions of descendants of a major segment of the early-modern elite. Then, however, in great part because of the arrangements they had devised to perpetuate their interests, by the middle of the twentieth century their revitalized position had given way, much as that of the late-Heian and late-medieval elites had. And out of the wreckage of disorder and war a new sector of society emerged supreme after 1945, the sector, perhaps, that derived from those early-nineteenth-century landlords and that is thought of today as a white-collar class.

In the final analysis, the enchantment of Japan before Perry is not the enchantment of the exotic, the primitive, or the simple. Rather, it is the enchantment of the complex, the ambiguous, and the instructive. It makes us think. But it leaves us uncertain, eager to understand better, and convinced that understanding is important.

---

concerning the nature of the Meiji Restoration: was it a bourgeois revolution or a mixed feudal-bourgeois authoritarian realignment? The debate is described briefly by James W. Morley in James W. Morley, ed., *Dilemmas of Growth in Prewar Japan* (Princeton, N.J.: Princeton University Press, 1971), pp. 18–20.

GLOSSARY

Azuma kagami	*Mirror of the East*
bakufu	"tent government"; shogunate
bikuni	nun
biwa	lute
bu	military arts
bun	civil arts
bunraku	puppet theatre
bushi	samurai; warrior; military man
bushidō	"the way of the warrior"
chōnin	townsman; merchant
Daigaku	*Ta Hsueh; Great Learning*
daikan	district administrator
daimyō	feudal lord
Dainichi-kyō	*Mahávairocana; Great Illuminator* sutra
Eiga monogatari	*Tales of Glory*
fudai	hereditary retainer

Fudoki	*Topographical Records;* fragmentary local records
furigana	pronunciation guides for Chinese characters
fusuma	sliding door
gagaku	court music
gekokujō	"those below toppling those above"
Genji monogatari	*The Tale of Genji*
Gikeiki	*Annals of Yoshitsune*
giri	duty
gokenin	"houseman"; vassal of the shogun
gunki monogatari	war tale
Hagakure	*Hidden Behind Leaves*
haikai-style renga	humorous linked verse
haiku	seventeen-syllable verse
han	daimyo domain
haniwa	clay figurine
Heiji monogatari	*The Tale of the Heiji Incident*
Heike monogatari	*Tales of the Heike*
hichiriki	double-reed woodwind
hijiri	holy man
Hokke-kyō	*Saddharmapundarika; Lotus* sutra
hō-ō	retired emperor
ie	family; patrilineage
jikatasho	writings on agronomy
Jinnō shōtōki	*Records of the True Imperial Succession*
jiriki	"self-power"
jitō	land steward; supervisor of estate

Jōdo	Pure Land; "western paradise"; Amidism
Jōdo Shin	True Pure Land
Jōei shikimoku	law code of the Jōei period
kabuki	theatre of the Tokugawa period
kami	the awe-inspiring or godlike
kamikaze	"divine wind"
kamon	relative; kinsman
kana	Japanese syllabary
kanji	Chinese characters
Kannon	Avalokiteshvara; "Goddess of Mercy"
kanpaku	regent to an adult emperor
Kegon sutra	*Avatamsaka*; *Flower Wreath* Sutra
kogaku	ancient studies
Kojiki	*Records of Ancient Matters*
Kokinshū	*Collection of Ancient and Modern Poetry*
kokufu	capital town of a province
kokugaku	national learning; Japanese studies
Kōshoku ichidai onna	*The Life of an Amorous Woman*
koto	harp or dulcimer-type instrument
kuge	noble house; aristocrat; courtier
kumi	neighborhood organization
kwampaku	*see* kanpaku
Makura no sōshi	*The Pillow Book*
mandokoro	family office
Man'yōshū	*Collection of Myriad Leaves*
mappō	the "degenerate age" of the "latter law"
Muryōju-kyō	*Greater Sukhavati-vyuha*; *Sutra of Infinite Life*
myōjin	benevolent deity; godlike folk hero

namu Amida butsu	"praise to Amida Buddha"; an invocation
nanga	"southern painting"
Nebiki no kadomatsu	*The Uprooted Pine*
Nembutsu	*see* nenbutsu
nenbutsu	namu Amida butsu; an appeal to the grace of Amida buddha
Nihongi	*Chronicles of Japan*
ninjōbon	romantic works
Nō	medieval theatre
o-fumi	"pastoral letters"
Ōjōyōshū	*Essentials of Rebirth*
Ōkagami	*Great Mirror*
Ōninki	*The Chronicle of Ōnin*
rangaku	Dutch (European) learning
ri	principle
roku	stipend
rōnin	"wave men" or masterless samurai
sakoku	seclusion
samisen	long-necked lute
sankin kōtai	"alternate attendance"
sasa	miniature-bamboo ground cover
seiitaishōgun	"barbarian-subduing generalissimo"; shogun
senba koki	stationary comb for threshing
sesshō	regent to a child emperor
shakuhachi	large bamboo flute
shamisen	*see* samisen
shiki	officially sanctioned estate rights
shikken	regent to a Kamakura shogun
shō	small hand-held, seventeen-reed musical instrument
shōbō	the period of the true law
shōen	aristocratic estate

Shogaku	*Hsiao Hsueh; Little Learning*
shogun	*see* seiitaishōgun
shokubun	vocation or heavy obligation
shugo	provincial-level commander of
	military forces; constable
sumi-e	ink-line painting
Taiheiki	*The Chronicle of Grand Pacification*
tariki	"other-power"
tatami	sedge mat
tokkuri	sake serving bottle
toku	virtue or profit
tokonoma	alcove
ton'ya	wholesale distributor
Towazugatari	*The Confessions of Lady Nijō*
tozama	"outside lord"
daimyō	
Tsurezuregusa	*Essays in Idleness*
uji	aristocratic familial group
uji no	head of the (Fujiwara) family
chōja	
uji no kami	hereditary chief
ukiyo	"floating world"
ukiyo-e	"floating-world" art
ukiyo-zōshi	"floating-world" fiction
wagon	type of cittern; Japanese harp
Yamato-e	"Japanese painting"
Yamato-goto	type of cittern; Japanese harp
yin/yang	symbiotic opposites
yoki hito	"good person" or "person of quality"
yonaoshi	"world-renewal" movement
yoriki	bakufu police officer
za	guild
zazen	meditation
zōbō	the period of the simulated doctrine

Bibliographical Note

In the belief that English-language scholarship on Japan should now be able to provide an adequate base for the preparation of at least a short interpretive essay such as this, I have attempted to limit my references to works in English. Citations in the footnotes will identify many, but certainly not all, of the valuable books on premodern Japan that are available in English. Readers wishing to go more deeply into Japanese history will find Mikiso Hane, *Japan: A Historical Survey* (New York: Scribner, 1972) helpful. The work is a sound textbook, and it contains an excellent bibliography that will lead readers to more specialized volumes. A more recent and very readable introduction to the history of modern Japan is Peter Duus, *The Rise of Modern Japan* (Boston: Houghton Mifflin, 1976).

The student wishing to delve further in English-language sources will find several helpful bibliographical guides. The most useful is Bernard Silberman, *Japan and Korea: A Critical Bibliography* (Tucson, Ariz.: University of Arizona Press, 1962). Its major drawback is that it is outdated and provides no guidance to the rich body of scholarship that has appeared since 1961. There exists no comparably selective and organized bibliography for the more recent scholarship. Accordingly one must turn to the sections dealing with Japan before 1850 in the exhaustive bibliographies published by the

Association for Asian Studies. The *Cumulative Bibliography of Asian Studies, 1941–1965* (Boston: G. K. Hall and Co., 1969) lists in four volumes the books and articles published in Western languages during those years. The subsequent *Cumulative Bibliography of Asian Studies, 1966–1970* (Boston: G. K. Hall and Co., 1973), in three volumes, lists works published during the latter period. Until successor compilations in the series appear, students will find the annual *Bibliography of Asian Studies* (Ann Arbor, Mich.: Association for Asian Studies) the best source for locating books and articles published after 1970. To locate books published in the last year or two, it is useful to scan the book-review sections of scholarly journals such as the *Journal of Asian Studies*, the *Journal of Japanese Studies*, and *Monumenta Nipponica*, which also contain articles dealing with Japan. Students wishing to make an exhaustive search of Western-language materials published prior to 1940 may do so by consulting the Wenkstern-Nachod-Praesent-Pritchard bibliographical series that is listed on page 2 of the Silberman bibliography.

Index

Designer: S. Don Fujimoto
Compositor: G & S Typesetters
Printer: Vail-Ballou Press
Binder: Vail-Ballou Press
Text: Linotron 202 Palatino
Display: Linotron 202 Optima